AF843143

The Theories and Developments of Crowdfunding

Anton Miglo · Victor Miglo

The Theories and Developments of Crowdfunding

Combining Theory with Practical Insight and Examples

palgrave
macmillan

Anton Miglo
Wilfrid Laurier University
Waterloo, ON, Canada

Victor Miglo
CEM Benchmarking
Toronto, ON, Canada

ISBN 978-3-032-10723-7 ISBN 978-3-032-10724-4 (eBook)
https://doi.org/10.1007/978-3-032-10724-4

© The Editor(s) (if applicable) and The Author(s), under exclusive license to Springer Nature Switzerland AG 2026

This work is subject to copyright. All rights are solely and exclusively licensed by the Publisher, whether the whole or part of the material is concerned, specifically the rights of translation, reprinting, reuse of illustrations, recitation, broadcasting, reproduction on microfilms or in any other physical way, and transmission or information storage and retrieval, electronic adaptation, computer software, or by similar or dissimilar methodology now known or hereafter developed.
The use of general descriptive names, registered names, trademarks, service marks, etc. in this publication does not imply, even in the absence of a specific statement, that such names are exempt from the relevant protective laws and regulations and therefore free for general use.
The publisher, the authors and the editors are safe to assume that the advice and information in this book are believed to be true and accurate at the date of publication. Neither the publisher nor the authors or the editors give a warranty, expressed or implied, with respect to the material contained herein or for any errors or omissions that may have been made. The publisher remains neutral with regard to jurisdictional claims in published maps and institutional affiliations.

This Palgrave Macmillan imprint is published by the registered company Springer Nature Switzerland AG
The registered company address is: Gewerbestrasse 11, 6330 Cham, Switzerland

If disposing of this product, please recycle the paper.

To our friends Andrej and Reuben.

Preface

The book covers the major ideas of crowdfunding such as learning market demand ("crowd wisdom"), online signalling, network benefits and the role of behavioural finance in crowdfunding. Entrepreneurs and investors still appear to lack an understanding of the nuances of crowdfunding. There are a large number of crowdfunding campaigns that fail and a large number of firms that do not deliver promised rewards after successful campaigns, including cases of fraud. This illustrates the depth of asymmetric information and moral hazard problems in crowdfunding that are covered in the book. The book also covers the most recent developments and ideas related to the many important and interesting topics in the area of crowdfunding including the historical aspects of crowdfunding development e.g. the JOBS act of 2012, the major steps in the development of the different types of crowdfunding, the different types of crowdfunding platforms, the connections between crowdfunding and security design, the comparison of crowdfunding with other fintech related strategies of financing like token issues, the links between crowdfunding and spot sales strategies and crowdfunding regulation and bankruptcy.

The primary intended audience of the book includes advanced undergraduate and graduate economics, finance, business and entrepreneurship students. The book will also be of interest to professionals including entrepreneurs, managers and people interested in developing their knowledge of fintech and crowdfunding. Although the book includes quantitative portions, it is mostly written in a comprehensive fashion and introduces complicated concepts in an approachable fashion. It combines theoretical results with examples, exercises and applications. At the end of each chapter we provide 4 types of practice questions that help develop different skills for every reader: "multiple choice", "true–false", "problems" and "mix".

Further, note that crowdfunding and token issues theories continue to gain recognition at universities and in the real world. Some universities offer entire programmes on crowdfunding. Many universities and business schools offer crowdfunding or crowdfunding related courses as a part of their finance, business and economics programmes or as part of their newly created fintech programmes. For example, in recent years Anton taught courses on crowdfunding and token issues at the University of Glasgow, which is a top 100 ranked university in the world.[1]

The main focus of the book is on the microeconomic foundations of crowdfunding and token issuance theory. Some sections are based on traditional cost-benefit analyses, but most include the analysis of different market imperfections, primarily asymmetric information, moral hazard problems and behavioural finance. Knowledge of game theory and contract theory prior to reading this book is beneficial, but we tried to present the material in the most accessible way possible, with lots of examples for readers of all levels. The book attempts to explain the basic concepts of crowdfunding and token issues as well as more advanced topics in a consistent fashion. The first part is focused on providing an introduction to the terminology and major theories of crowdfunding. The majority of the basic ideas in crowdfunding complement each other quite logically although significant disagreement between researchers still exists about which theory is more important in practice. Part 2 discusses topics such as crowdfunding regulation, pecking order and crowdfunding,

1 See e.g. https://www.usnews.com/education/best-global-universities/university-of-glasgow-500110.

crowdfunding and new forms of financing related to fintech and crowdfunding like token issues, and examples of optimal crowdfunding analyses for some companies. Many advanced theories of crowdfunding discussed in part 2 are still growing areas of research. At the same time, the objective of the book is not to cover as many topics of crowdfunding as possible but rather to review the major theoretical concepts and provide basic tools to understand the complicated area of crowdfunding. For additional readings in the field of crowdfunding, we recommend "*Crowdfunding: Fundamental Cases, Facts, and Insights*" (Ed. Cumming, D. and Johan, S.A. (2020)), "*Advances in Crowdfunding*" (Ed. Shneor, R. 2020) and Lenart-Gansiniec, Regina, and Jin Chen, eds. (2021). *Crowdfunding in the Public Sector: Theory and Best Practices*. These works have a more applied approach to crowdfunding, including empirical research and econometrics, and cover a lot of interesting topics related to crowdfunding. The latter provides an excellent review of the literature related to the role of crowdfunding for public and non-profit firms.

One of the most important theoretical and practical problems in crowdfunding is the choice of the optimal crowdfunding type. This problem is similar to the problem of the optimal capital structure for large firms.[2] In 1958, Nobel Prize winners Franco Modigliani and Merton Miller argued that when markets are perfect (e.g. investors and entrepreneurs possess the same amount of information) capital structure is irrelevant. Many/most capital structure discoveries in the last 60–70 years have been mostly related to the analysis of the impact of different market imperfections including moral hazard problems, asymmetric information and behavioural finance. Studying crowdfunding under imperfect market conditions is important because the reality is that the world is imperfect and imperfections like asymmetric information play important roles in crowdfunding.

We would like to also mention that crowdfunding (in particular reward-based crowdfunding) is a completely new way of raising funds and is different from traditional debt and equity. It is often called one of the top business innovations of the twenty-first century and also in our view represents quite a revolutionary development in the area of capital structure and raising funds since for centuries it has mainly been about the optimal choice between debt and equity (Table 1).

[2] About capital structure theories see e.g. Miglo (2025).

Table 1 Top 4 technology innovations of 2012 (based on MIT ranking)[3]

Rank	*Technology*
1	Crowdfunding
2	Facebook's timeline
3	High-speed materials discovery
4	3-D transistors

This book was inspired by our extensive practical, teaching and research experience in crowdfunding in the last 15 years. Between the two of us, we have worked at a firm that organizes donation-based crowdfunding campaigns, and we have taught courses related to crowdfunding at different universities in Europe and North America including courses directly related to capital structure such as Fundamentals of Crowdfunding, Crowdfunding and Token Issues, Financing Strategies and Corporate Governance and Entrepreneurial Finance. Further we have had some joint research projects on crowdfunding including publishing a joint paper (one of the first theoretical papers on crowdfunding) in a top journal Small Business Economics back in 2018. Prior to that Anton spent more than 20 years working theoretically in the area of capital structure including working in a department dealing with issuing securities. This book was also inspired by Anton's experiences managing fintech programmes where crowdfunding and token issues were a part of the curriculum. This book also discusses the new inspirations recent fintech developments have brought to the world of entrepreneurial finance by creating new ways for firms to raise funds including similarities and differences between crowdfunding and token issues.

Finally, note that the number of jobs and businesses requiring knowledge and skills in the area of crowdfunding is quickly growing. A large number of crowdfunding platforms require specialists in the area. Entrepreneurs who intend to use crowdfunding also need some knowledge and skill. Many financial, private equity and venture capital firms that offer portfolio services to investors that include a variety of different

[3] Source: https://www.engineering.org.cn/sscae/EN/10.15302/J-SSCAE-2017.05.015; Table 6

investment opportunities often also need specialists with a knowledge of crowdfunding.

Anton Miglo
Wilfrid Laurier University
Waterloo, ON, Canada

Victor Miglo
CEM Benchmarking
Toronto, ON, Canada

References

Cumming, D., & Johan, S. A. (2020). *Crowdfunding: Fundamental cases, facts, and insights*. Academic Press, an imprint of Elsevier.

Lenart-Gansiniec, R., & Chen, J. (Eds.). (2021). *Crowdfunding in the public sector: Theory and best practices*. Springer.

Miglo, A. (2025). *Capital structure in the modern world* (2nd ed.). Palgrave Macmillan.

Shneor, R. (2020). *Advances in crowdfunding*. Springer International Publishing.

Acknowledgements A. Miglo has benefited a lot from the conversations with Paul Belleflamme, Jamie Zender, Gilles Chemla, Thomas Hellmann, David de Meza, Thomas Chemmanur and Armin Schwienbacher regarding many ideas that are part of this book. Also, many thanks to Anna Menichini with whom he had a good number of conversations that were also very helpful and inspiring especially conversation they had regarding crowdfunding. Also note that Dr. Menichini wrote a review of one of A. Miglo's books that was published in the Journal of Economics. We would also like to thank Tula Weis, the editor from Springer/Macmillan who provided very high-quality support throughout the initial stages of the application, approval and work on the book. Also, many thanks to the anonymous referees and Supraja Yegnaraman (technical editor).

Competing Interests The authors have no competing interests to declare that are relevant to the content of this manuscript.

Contents

Part II Different Topics

List of Figures

List of Tables

PART I

Basic Ideas of Crowdfunding

This section covers such topics as the types of crowdfunding, the main "players" involved in the crowdfunding process including project initiators, funders/backers and crowdfunding platforms, as well as the basic principles and ideas behind the usage of crowdfunding. It includes such ideas as learning "crowd wisdom", signalling, moral hazard problems, network benefits and behavioural aspects.

CHAPTER 1

Introduction

1.1 Crowdfunding Overview

In our experience, conversations about crowdfunding (especially regarding reward-based crowdfunding[1]) often begin with a comparison to advanced sales. However, even though there are some elements of advanced sales in crowdfunding, the primary function of crowdfunding is to provide help with funding for start-up entrepreneurs. In many entrepreneurial surveys, funding is recognized as the most important problem for start-up entrepreneurs.[2] What is the origin of the word crowdfunding?! The first part is "crowd" or a large number of people, and the second part is "funding", which in finance is used interchangeably with a word you are probably more familiar with: financing. In finance, there are two big areas: investments and financing. Investments are how firms use their funds: what assets they acquire and what projects

[1] We will discuss different types of crowdfunding later in this chapter.

[2] See e.g. https://www.startupcan.ca/wp-content/uploads/2021/04/SC_2020_Entrepreneur_Census_Report.pdf.

Supplementary Information The online version contains supplementary material available at https://doi.org/10.1007/978-3-032-10724-4_1.

© The Author(s), under exclusive license to Springer Nature Switzerland AG 2026

A. Miglo and V. Miglo, *The Theories and Developments of Crowdfunding*, https://doi.org/10.1007/978-3-032-10724-4_1

they undertake. For these activities and decisions we use the term investments. Financing is how firms raise their funds. This gives you some ideas about the origin of the word crowdfunding: raising funds from a large number of people. The innovative element here is that it contrasts traditional financing ideas where often firms raise funds from a few large investors like commercial banks. The main idea of crowdfunding is to raise funds from a large number of so-called "small" investors. There are of course advantages and disadvantages to this idea. For example, a large investor usually intends to monitor/control your business while small investors like to discuss your business with other investors which may result in good feedback. These differences with traditional financing make crowdfunding an interest topic of study. One of the main objectives of this book is to discuss what crowdfunding can bring to firms, especially entrepreneurial firms like small- and medium-sized businesses, when compared to traditional funding strategies and traditional financing.

Some researchers argue that crowdfunding, in its most basic sense (raising funds from a large number of small investors) has been used for a long time. For example, it was used by (book) writers in the eighteenth–nineteenth century (see e.g. Simons, 2016) as well as in the construction of the Statue of Liberty in New York, USA.[3] In its modern form, crowdfunding is "*an open call, essentially through the Internet, for the provision of financial resources either in form of donation or in exchange for some form of reward and/or voting rights in order to support initiatives for specific purposes*" (Lambert & Schwienbacher, 2010, p. 4).[4] One of the key words here is internet. Indeed, because of the internet, crowdfunding has become a part of what is called fintech, which is a new wave of technological innovation in finance penetrating many areas of the finance industry including traditional areas such as payments, investments and financing. It is on one hand based on the latest technological developments and on the other its philosophy is based on the concept of "no-middle–men" (for example, traditional financial intermediaries like commercial banks) so it has the potential to become a much more efficient

[3] BBC online (2013).

[4] Moritz and Block (2016), Alegre and Moleskis (2016), Cumming and Johan (2017), Kuppuswamy and Bayus (2018), Cumming and Hornuf (2018), Estrin et al. (2018), Cumming et al. (2020) and Mochkabadi and Volkmann (2020) provide good reviews of the literature.

way of conducting financial transactions (Das, 2019). Under the traditional approach, investors bring funds to a financial intermediary (FI), e.g. a commercial bank, who then accumulates these funds and makes investment or credit decisions (Fig. 1.1). Under the new approach, the FI plays a different role: investors and firms deal directly with each other and the role of the FI is to facilitate these transactions by making them more efficient or secure for example.

We have discussed the historical background of crowdfunding and the new wave of interest in the phenomenon which was raised as a result of significant difficulties experienced by innovative and entrepreneurial firms in raising funds using traditional methods[5] and technical developments including the internet, online technologies and fintech. Crowdfunding belongs to a new type of financial services that connects suppliers of capital and its users directly, which is similar to other areas of fintech that do not rely on traditional financial intermediaries.[6]

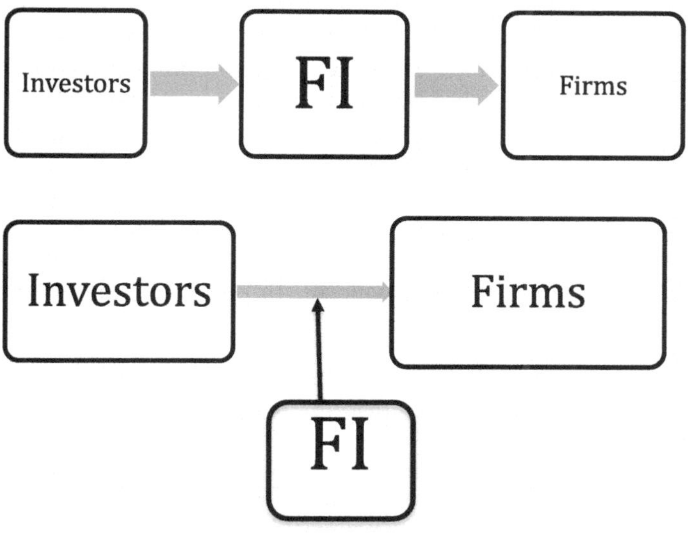

Fig. 1.1 The role of Financial Intermediaries (FI)

[5] For a review of theories of financing for entrepreneurial firms see e.g. Miglo (2022).

[6] For example, fintech offers a similar approach in other areas of finance such as payments using cryptocurrencies. To prove that a transaction took place one does not need

As previously mentioned, crowdfunding is sometimes credited as one of the top inventions of the twenty-first century. The global crowdfunding market size was about $1.67 billion in 2023 and is expected to reach $7.82 Billion by 2032.[7] In addition to the previously mentioned advantages of crowdfunding compared to traditional ways of financing, note the ability to quickly reach a large number of potential investors, opportunities to directly exchange information with crowdfunding participants and receive market feedback ("crowd wisdom"), and a minimal level of required bureaucracy (Miglo, 2021).

There are 4 main types of crowdfunding: reward-based crowdfunding (used by Kickstarter and Indiegogo, the leading platforms in the area), equity-based crowdfunding, debt-based crowdfunding and donation-based crowdfunding.[8] In the case of reward-based crowdfunding, a non-financial reward is expected by the investor. Rewards can vary from something simple such as a thank-you postcard or a T-shirt with a firm logo to a production version of the crowdfunded product. Equity-based crowdfunding is a financing method for entrepreneurial firms where investments by a large number of investors/backers/funders are made online in exchange for firm equity. One of the differences with traditional equity financing is that equity investments in crowdfunding do not have an active secondary market although some crowdfunding platforms have been recently working on improving this aspect.[9] Under debt-based crowdfunding (also called P2P: peer-to-peer lending) the debtor is supposed to return the money to a group of creditors (or crowdloan providers) at a specified time. In return for financing a project with a loan, each creditor receives interest payments. In contrast to traditional debt

a banking account as with traditional finance but should rather rely on Blockchain principles. For more details see e.g. https://hbr.org/2017/03/the-promise-of-blockchain-is-a-world-without-middlemen.

[7] https://www.skyquestt.com/report/crowdfunding-market#:~:text=Crowdfunding%20Market%20size%20was%20valued,period%20(2025%2D2032).

[8] For more discussions related to different concepts of crowdfunding and terminology used see e.g. Brüntje and Gajda (2016), Kraus et al. (2016) and Assenmacher (2017). Also see crowdfunding blogs such as https://www.beauhurst.com/research/following-the-crowd/.

[9] Republic Europe (former Seedrs)—one if the two largest equity-based crowdfunding platforms- is known for working its secondary market offering to all private businesses. See e.g. https://www.seedrs.com/learn/blog/the-seedrs-secondary-market-now-open-to-all-investors.

financing where the debtor usually faces one creditor such as, for example, a commercial bank, in the case of debt-based crowdfunding, there are multiple creditors and this may create different dynamics in the case of financial distress.[10] Under donation-based crowdfunding donors or backers provide funds to a recipient via an online platform. The investors support the recipient's objective or mission, but they are not expected to receive any financial or other types of specified rewards. Literature on donation-based crowdfunding is not as numerous as it is for other types of crowdfunding, but it is growing (see e.g. Cason & Zubrickas, 2019).

The main parts of the crowdfunding process are presented in Fig. 1.2.

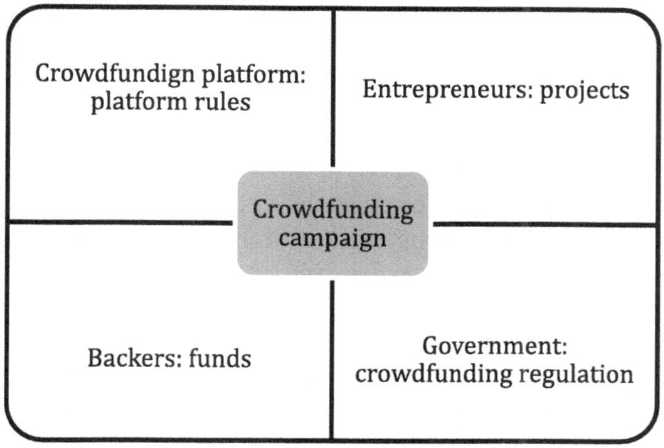

Fig. 1.2 The main parts of crowdfunding process: platform, entrepreneurs, funders and regulators

The term "crowdfunding platform" can refer either to the organization or to the website that brings together companies seeking investments and investors with funds to invest.[11] Crowdfunding platforms that offer services for reward-based crowdfunding usually offer two types of campaigns: "All-Or-Nothing" (AON) and "Keep-It-All"

[10] For an analysis on the economics of debt-based crowdfunding see e.g. Milne and Parboteeah (2016).

[11] Examples of popular crowdfunding platforms include among others, Kickstarter, Indiegogo, Crowdcube, Seedrs etc.

(KIA). In the former, the campaign initiator does not keep any of the funds if the funding target is not reached. In the latter, the campaign initiator can keep the entire collected amount, irrespective of whether the targeted goal is achieved or not. Belleflamme et al. (2015) provide a good analysis on the economics of crowdfunding platforms. In particular, they argue crowdfunding platforms face the challenge to make relevant information easily available while at the same time to encourage information gathering. The largest crowdfunding platform Kickstarter offers services in reward-based crowdfunding by using the AON method. Indiegogo, the second-largest platform, also deals with reward-based crowdfunding but was traditionally known for using the KIA method. In recent years, Indiegogo developed several innovative projects including offering a method choice to entrepreneurs and partnerships with firms like Amazon that provide special services for firms conducting crowdfunding campaigns (Amazon Launchpad).[12] Note also that the rates of success have been traditionally higher on Kickstarter (see e.g. Cumming et al., 2020). Dushnitsky et al. (2016) analyze the distribution of crowdfunding platforms across different countries in Europe. They found for example that the development of crowdfunding platforms depends on country culture, including internet culture, entrepreneurial culture and the level of entrepreneurial activities (that reflects entrepreneurial spirit of crowdfunding). They also found that the development of debt-based (lending) crowdfunding platforms depends on the level of competition in the finance and banking industries, which highlights direct and indirect links between crowdfunding and traditional ways of financing and how they compete with each other.

When developing crowdfunding campaigns for their projects, entrepreneurs usually prepare a video (often called a video pitch or crowdfunding pitch), a short slogan and/or project description, a menu of prices and rewards (in the case of reward-based crowdfunding), select the type of campaign (AON or KIA), and if AON is selected they should also select the level of threshold/target etc. An example of a campaign that selected reward-based crowdfunding is Oculus Rift. They developed a virtual-reality (VR) headset for gamers. The CEO Palmer Luckey mentioned: "Kickstarter is the most visible crowdfunding platform out there, and it was clear that crowdfunding was a good match for the

[12] See e.g. https://www.woodshed.agency/blog/use-amazon-launchpad-after-your-successful-crowdfunding-campaign. Also see Miglo (2020).

Rift. We knew that there was a passionate crowd of VR enthusiasts out there and that people want to take gaming to the next level, particularly developers. Kickstarter offered a great way to tap into that audience. The project was originally much smaller, but the massive amount of support we got let us scale way up".[13] An example of a campaign with equity-based crowdfunding is POD-point, an innovative firm that develops charging equipment/charging points for electric vehicles (EV). It is a very innovative risk-taking firm. The founder Eric Fairbairn mentioned that Crowdcube (an equity-based crowdfunding platform) provides an opportunity to invest in something that's fundamental to the UK's entrepreneurial endeavours (Hurst, 2016). "We were attracted to equity crowdfunding as an innovative way to fund POD Point's growth that also allowed us to invite the electric vehicle community to become part of our journey. Like us, EV drivers are passionate about seeing the mass adoption of zero emissions transport in the UK and globally", said James McKemmy, head of insights team at POD Point. "We thought it would be appealing and reflective of the wider community if those passionate about EV were able to help accelerate the growth of the charging infrastructure by investing in POD Point – and they seemed to agree", The business chose equity over reward-based crowdfunding because it wanted to give the EV community a chance to own a stake and benefit from its growth (Booty, 2017).

The regulation of crowdfunding formally on a significant scale probably started with the 2012 JOBS act in the United States that helped firms to raise different types of financing using online platforms without necessarily registering a prospectus with the Security Exchange Commission (SEC).[14] This was followed by similar regulations in the UK, Canada and other countries. Some recent research also shows that the success of crowdfunding is positively correlated with the degree of regulation development in the country (see e.g. Rau, 2019). Many interesting practical questions regarding crowdfunding regulation are still being debated in theory and practice. For example, what happens (should happen) in the case of bankruptcy if the firm has both outstanding debt claims and

[13] https://www.popularmechanics.com/culture/gaming/a8990/10-questions-for-oculus-rift-ceo-palmer-luckey-15502842/.

[14] See e.g. https://econsultancy.com/the-crowdfund-act-everything-you-need-to-know/.

unfinished crowdfunding projects. In this case, who would/should have priority etc.[15]

1.2 Crowdfunding and Finance

Crowdfunding is a form of financing. Traditional financing strategy or capital structure choice is considered one of the most important topics among practitioners and theorists (see e.g. Graham & Harvey, 2001 or Miglo (2025)). As we will learn in this book, several features of traditional capital structure theory have a lot of applications in crowdfunding. This includes for example the role of market imperfections. Modigliani and Miller (1958) argue that capital structure is irrelevant when markets are perfect i.e. investors and firms have the same amount of information (including about the firms' prospects), there are no moral hazard problems i.e. investors and firms can sign contracts that can describe and perfectly enforce every possible action firms can take, and there are no taxes or bankruptcy costs. This sounds quite unrealistic. As a result most of capital structure theory in the last 60–70 years has been based on analyzing the impact of different kinds of market imperfections on firms' capital structure/financing decisions. In most cases the same idea would apply for crowdfunding so we expect the readers by the end of this book to clearly understand the difference between perfect and imperfect markets and their role in explaining many phenomena about crowdfunding. Another interesting and important feature of traditional capital structure theory is that unlike other areas of finance there is no dominant theory. There are a few theories that seem to be competing with each other. The same applies to crowdfunding. We will see that there are several approaches for modelling and understanding crowdfunding. Some of them seem to be emerging as leading theories based on their consistency with empirical evidence. Yet the area is still very far from recognizing so-called winners in this theoretical competition between different theories not least because the area to some extent still lacks empirical evidence when compared to traditional finance. Finally, as was mentioned for example in Miglo (2025), the capital structure area of research has been producing a significant number of Nobel prize winners

[15] For more discussion see e.g. Tamburro (2018).

which is another sign of the topic's importance so hopefully crowdfunding follows in its footsteps.

Next notice that crowdfunding can also be considered part of a separate branch of finance namely entrepreneurial finance. This is logical since it is a branch of finance that is more applicable to innovative firms, to small businesses and to medium-sized businesses. Entrepreneurial finance is not usually a part of traditional finance courses, for example corporate finance courses, taught at business schools around the world. Entrepreneurial finance courses include such areas as the estimation of start-up financing needs, preparing detailed monthly financial plans, break-even analysis, detailed cash flow projections etc. Monthly planning is important because it is related to the problem of start-up firm survival, which is crucial. Also, entrepreneurial finance deals with financial cycles or stages of financial development for entrepreneurial firms. It is not only important for entrepreneurial firms to understand some big theoretical ideas, but it is also crucial for them to be able to create detailed monthly financial plans for the first couple of years, as well as annual plans for a number of years. Further, it is important for entrepreneurial firms to analyze different financing strategies, perhaps anticipate multiple rounds of financing because one round may not be sufficient to support their development, to be able to negotiate conditions with providers of capital under objectively hard conditions like lack of objective information about the firm etc. These are typical topics covered in entrepreneurial finance courses and they have started to become applicable to crowdfunding in the last 10 years or so. As mentioned before, banks are less comfortable lending to start-up or risky firms than to large established firms. The lack of credit history and the absence of valuable assets that can be used as collateral for example create problems for entrepreneurial firms when raising funds using traditional bank loans.

As mentioned previously many aspects and problems in the area of crowdfunding are related to capital structure management in traditional (corporate) finance. Let us take a closer look at this. The capital structure problem is generally the choice between debt and equity. What's the difference between debt and equity? Debt does not usually include an ownership interest. Creditors do not have voting rights. Interest on debt that the company pays to debtholders is considered a cost of doing business and usually can be used to reduce the amount of corporate income taxes firms need to pay. Creditors have legal recourse if interest or principal payments are missed and that can lead to financial distress and bankruptcy. On the other hand, equity claims usually represent ownership interests for common or ordinary shareholders. The shareholders also participate in the strategic decision-making of the firm. For example, they vote at shareholders' meetings and often get seats on the Board of Directors. Dividends are not considered as a cost of doing business and do not help reduce the income tax for the firm. Dividends also are not a liability of a firm and stockholders have no legal recourse. Unpaid dividends cannot force a firm into bankruptcy; so an all-equity firm cannot go bankrupt.

Modigliani and Miller proposition (1958), which remains the most cited paper in the finance literature, shows that in a perfect market, the financing choice is irrelevant. It does not matter how you slice your pizza, whether into 15 slices or 8, the nutritional value of it does not change. Similarly, in a perfect market the capital structure does establishes the rules for how a firm's revenues are distributed among claimholders, but the value of the firm does not change regardless of how you divide it among different claimholders. So regardless of how you slice your pie/earnings, to whom the firm's earnings go at the end does not matter. And so in this sense, a firm's financing strategy is irrelevant. But this is not exactly what happens in practice as many capital structure researchers argue (see e.g. Baker & Martin, 2011). We know for example that firms in some industries systematically select some typical capital structures and financing strategies which is not consistent with the capital structure irrelevance idea. A large portion of capital structure research has been built on analyzing optimal capital structure under different market imperfections.

Can we apply the Modigliani and Miller capital structure irrelevance proposition to crowdfunding? Firstly, can the same reasoning be applied if in addition to debt and equity, a firm may use reward-based crowdfunding to raise funds? The answer is usually yes, (see an example in Chapter 6). Secondly, if market imperfections are important to the discussion of crowdfunding, what kind of imperfections are important for small/entrepreneurial firms who are mostly interested in using crowdfunding? There are many interesting theories of optimal financing that can be applied to both large corporations and small firms. They are based on market imperfections like taxes, bankruptcy costs, asymmetric information and moral hazard. In the last 15–20 years there has been a growing interest in the capital structure of start-up and small companies (Hall, 2009; Mach, 2014; Wilson, 2015). Traditionally, it was assumed that most financing comes from entrepreneurs' friends and relatives and other sources of financing was not important. Recently, it was argued that entrepreneurial firms use a variety of different sources of financing (see e.g. Miglo, 2022).[16]

Imperfect information and moral hazard problems have emerged as important issues in crowdfunding. On one hand investors do not have complete information about firms conducting crowdfunding and their projects (see e.g. Ahlers et al., 2015; Belleflamme et al., 2014; Chakrabotry & Swinney, 2020; Hildebrand et al., 2017; Miglo & Miglo, 2019; Vismara, 2016). On the other hand, there exists a risk of potential funds expropriation/misuse, and a system that can perfectly monitor and control how start-up entrepreneurial firms conduct crowdfunding campaigns is difficult to implement (see e.g. Babich et al., 2021; Belavina et al., 2020; Chemla & Tinn, 2019; Cumming et al., 2023; Moores, 2015; Schwienbacher, 2018; Strausz, 2017). The degree of campaign failure is very high in crowdfunding. Many of these failures are related to the inability to provide sufficient information about a project's qualities and to problems with convincing potential funders to invest in the project. Many other projects fail because of their inability to develop the production of products/services using funds collected during the campaign or their inability to deliver the product on time (see e.g. Jensen & Özkil, 2018; Mollick, 2014). The problem of asymmetric information and moral hazard and their role in crowdfunding will be discussed in detail throughout the book (especially in Chapters 3 and 4).

Some research explains the network benefits of crowdfunding. The crowdfunding process is by nature very different from traditional ways of raising funds. Among these differences note the mutual exchange of information that occurs with crowdfunding: the "social value" feeling from joining a large group of people driven by similar interests, and opportunities to solve coordination problems between large number of participants etc. (see e.g., Belleflamme et al., 2014; Charbit & Desmoulins, 2017; Davies, 2014, 2015; Hudik & Chovanculiak, 2018; Hummel, 2016; Stiver et al., 2014; Van Montfort et al., 2021; Wenzlaff, 2020). Network benefits will be discussed in Chapter 5.

[16] See also The Capital Structure Decisions of New Firms, Kauffman Foundation. (2009). http://www.kauffman.org/what-we-do/research/kauffman-firm-survey-series/the-capital-structure-decisions-of-new-firms.

1.3 Crowdfunding, Firm Production and Marketing

The previous section argued that crowdfunding is closely related to finance and that many crowdfunding-related decisions have a lot in common with one of the central problems in finance: the firm capital structure choice. This section argues that crowdfunding is also closely related to firm production and marketing strategies and activities.

The connection between firm financing strategies and production strategies is not new. Debt financing literature considers these links (Bolton & Scharfstein, 1990; Brander & Lewis, 1986; Williams, 1995; and for a recent review see Li & Wang, 2019)[17] and argues that debt financing strongly affect the firm production decisions. For example, Brander and Lewis (1986) argue that product markets and financial markets have important connections. They consider a model in which financial and output decisions follow in sequence and show that limited liability may commit a leveraged firm to a more aggressive output stance. Applying a similar idea to crowdfunding one can expect a lot of similarities between traditional debt and debt-based crowdfunding and respectively connections between debt-based crowdfunding and firm production decisions.

With reward-based crowdfunding a further step can be made. Following from the definition of crowdfunding discussed earlier, under reward-based crowdfunding the firm promises to deliver rewards to backers in the form of future products and services. Reward-based crowdfunding is an innovative method of financing where investors/backers of a firm also receive the firm's product/services, which is equivalent to product pre-sales (Belleflamme et al., 2014), which in turn directly affects the firm expected production scale. This links crowdfunding and production decisions very closely since in order to fulfil its promises the firm will have to produce the products/services that were promised to backers during the crowdfunding campaign. This affects the firm's decisions related to its production scale.

Crowdfunding is also related to firm pricing strategies since the magnitude and quantity of the promised rewards is related to the backers' contributions during the campaign. It means a higher investment for

[17] A recent example is Platt (2020) that studies interactions between product strategy and corporate bonds spreads.

backers usually means a better reward. Further, some papers argue that crowdfunding is often used as a substitute for sales (Brown et al., 2017).

There are several interesting lines of research related to advanced pricing. For example, one line analyzes the advantages of advanced sales in the presence of consumer heterogeneity regarding discount rates (see e.g. Schaaf & Skiera, 2014) and another line analyzes advanced sales in the presence of asymmetric information about firm qualities (see e.g. Bagwell & Riordan, 1991; de Meza & Reito, 2020; Prescott, 1975). Both lines find that advanced sales can be used as an optimal strategy and that firms use advanced sales as a signal of quality. Crowdfunding to some extent has both aspects. Potential backers can differ in their discount rates/time preferences which may affect their decision to participate in a crowdfunding campaign (or wait until the product appears on the spot market). Crowdfunding is also usually used by start-up firms in environments with a high degree of asymmetric information about firm quality.

Combining these two observations would suggest that crowdfunding can be considered a tool to demonstrate/signal a firm's quality. We will discuss signalling opportunities using crowdfunding further in Chapters 3 and 6, among others. On the other hand, many entrepreneurs use crowdfunding as a funding source for investments/development of projects/products. Lower the investment costs that should be covered by funds received via crowdfunding closer is a reward-based crowdfunding campaign to traditional advanced sales and vice versa. Combined with previous observations this suggests that the amount of investment may play an important role in moderating the connections between a firm's quality and its choice between spot sales and advanced sales/ crowdfunding pre-orders. Another difference between typical pre-sale forms like forward sales and crowdfunding is crowdfunding decisions are publicly observed since campaigns are done on public websites. Note that there exists literature that argues that disclosure of forward sale contracts is desirable (see, among others, Allaz, 1992; Hughes & Kao, 1997). In Chapter 7 we will discuss the entrepreneur's choice between crowdfunding and spot sales.

1.4 Crowdfunding and Fintech

Crowdfunding is a part of fintech. FinTech refers to various financial technologies used to automate process in the financial sector. It is a new area that carries significant importance in the development of the finance industry. There are several fundamental ideas here that began 15–20 years ago and continue to this day. Fintech is still in its early stages and in the next 20–30 years we will see many further developments. Fintech has already changed the landscape of the finance industry, and many experts believe that it will change significantly more so in the coming years.

Crowdfunding is a part of this development since it uses online technologies (see e.g. Alt et al., 2018; Das, 2019; Horvat & Bobek, 2020). More specifically, crowdfunding is a part of the capital-raising activities of fintech (see e.g. Thakor, 2019). It has a lot of common features ideas with other elements of this area for example token issues. Token issues is a quickly growing area of interest among practitioners and theorists (see e.g. Ahlstrom et al., 2018; Masiak et al., 2020). The number of theoretical papers[18] is quickly growing and the structure of these research areas and their main directions are not quite established yet.

Innovative companies can issue different types of tokens. These include ICOs (initial coin offerings), STOs (security token offerings), IEOs (initial exchange offerings) and NFTs (non-fungible tokens).[19] Under ICO, a firm pre-sells utility tokens which give their holders the right to purchase a company's product/service when it becomes available. Under STO, a firm raises capital by selling tokenized traditional securities (security tokens) e.g. equity where tokenholders obtain rights to a firm's profits. Security tokens are often regulated (Ante & Fiedler, 2020). Under IEO, a firm raises funds by selling tokens with the help of an organized exchange that is usually a cryptocurrency exchange like Binance (see e.g. Myalo, 2019). The exchange is involved in promoting the tokens (ICO & IEO report, 2020). Unlike traditional cryptoassets, NFTs typically cannot be traded on an interchangeable basis since they are unique

[18] For a review of literature on tokens issues see, for example, Howell et al. (2020), Bao and Roubaud (2022) and Chalmers et al. (2022).

[19] Tönnissen et al. (2020) and Bachmann et al. (2021) provide a description of different business-models/ideas related to firms that use tokens.

and non-divisible. They are often used in trading, for example, pieces of arts.[20]

Many ideas behind token issues are similar to those of crowdfunding. For example, the idea of learning market demand is used in reward-based crowdfunding as well as in utility token issues. We will discuss these issues in more detail in Chapter 9.

1.5 Crowdfunding Analysis: The Beginnings...

This section considers a hypothetical start-up firm that is about to make its first crowdfunding campaign. We will discuss what questions should be answered and what problems it needs to solve. They include: how to determine the amount of funds needed, should the firm select crowdfunding or other types of financing, if crowdfunding is selected, what type of crowdfunding, what is the campaign target, AON or KIA?; should the firm prepare a video. The analysis in this section is very basic and is based on a set of simplifying assumptions but is a great starting point. Throughout the book, we will help answer these questions under more realistic conditions.

We begin by preparing a start-up financing plan. This plan will help answer how much funds the firm needs to start its production (among other questions). Start-up financing should cover the costs associated with getting an enterprise up and running. It usually includes one-time costs (sometimes called fixed costs) plus the first few months of operating (sometime called running) costs. It is important for start-ups to coordinate start-up cost calculations with monthly cash flow projections. They need to know the maximum cumulative cash need during the first year(s) of operation. Examples of one-time costs include new buildings for businesses (or extensions to accommodate expanding ones), new machinery, vehicles or equipment (including installation and delivery costs), target market research, initial advertising cost, payments towards insurance costs incurred through staff recruitment and training. Examples of running costs include rent wages and salaries, maintenance, loan repayments, interest on loans, communications (telephone, internet, etc.),

[20] Unlike ICO, STO and IEO, NFTs usually are used for trading purposes. There are however some cases where they were used for raising funding (see e.g. Cases of Stoner Cats and The Gimmicks https://www.lexology.com/library/detail.aspx?g=a2d91fc1-b441-4f6a-9b61-a9a4a14c68a5).

mortgage repayments, advertising, stationery, insurance payments, utilities (electricity, gas, water, etc.) and travel expenses (gas, hotel, insurance). If crowdfunding is selected as a funding option, then one should also add crowdfunding platform fees, video development costs and cost related to the creation of webpages on the crowdfunding platform. The following example provides an illustration of the concept of start-up costs.

John X., founder of the new firm Video Bikes, expects to spend the next half year finishing the development and beginning to sell video equipment for childrens' bicycles and wants to use crowdfunding to fund this. Video Bikes's initial capital consists of $100 cash that was invested by John X who owns 100 shares of stock, which currently means 100% of the company's ownership. John is considering reward-based and debt-based crowdfunding. John wants to be in full control of his business and prefers to keep 100% of the firm's ownership so he does not consider equity-based crowdfunding. On the other hand, John wants to provide some rewards to potential investors (either financial or non-financial) so he does not consider donation-based crowdfunding. John anticipates paying a monthly rent of $800 for space in a local warehouse where Video Bikes's product will be produced. Utility expenses for power and heat are estimated to be $250 per month. John plans a salary of $1,500 per month. Materials needed to build the product are expected to cost $5,000. John anticipates that the costs associated with test marketing Video Bikes will be $7,200 and the crowdfunding platform fee is $100. John would like to estimate his expected profit and decide what crowdfunding type he should select.

First determine the amount of financial capital that John will need during the six months, which is the time it will take to develop and test market Video Bikes products (Table 1.1).

Table 1.1 Firm start-up cost

Monthly expenses:		
Rent	6 months x $800 =	$4,800
Utilities	6 months x $250 =	$1,500
Salary	6 months x $1,500 =	$9,000
One-Time Expenses:		

(continued)

Table 1.1 (continued)

Materials needed	$5,000
Marketing	$7,200
Crowdfunding platform fee	$100
Total Expenses (Required Capital)	$27,600

Video Bikes needs to raise $27,600 – $100 = $27,500 with his crowdfunding campaign. Consider reward-based crowdfunding. John decides that each funder who invests $100 will get the firm's future product. The price of the product on the market is expected to be $120 and John plans to produce 1000 units by the end of the 6-month period. If the campaign is successful and John is able to raise funds from 275 backers, he will cover the firm's cost. Further, out of 1000 total products produced, 275 will be sent to the backers as rewards. John's profit will be the revenue from selling the remaining 1000 – 275 = 725 products for a total of $87,000.

Now consider debt-based crowdfunding (interest rate is 10%) to fund the start-up costs of $27,500. Under this strategy, the following sequence of events occurs: debt-based crowdfunding campaign, production, sales, payment to debt-crowdfunders and finally distribution of dividends to the firm's owner (John). John estimates that it will be 55 backers and each backer will invest $500 becoming one of the firm's co-creditors.

Below we will describe the firm's income statement that shows the firm's earnings/expenses.[21]

Income Statement (Table 1.2).

Table 1.2 Income statement under debt-based crowdfunding

Sales	$120,000
Expenses	$27,600
Earnings	$92,400
Interest	$2,750
Net Earnings	$89,650
Dividends	$89,650
Retained Earnings	$0

[21] Knowledge of accounting strictly speaking is not required in order to understand the materials of this book but some basic knowledge is highly recommended. The reader can read e.g. Wild et al. (2014) or read an appendix for this chapter.

Subtracting expenses from the revenues/sales, we get the earnings of \$92,400. Then we subtract interest payment of \$2,750, and we are left with \$89,650 net earnings that are distributed as dividends to shareholders (John). In addition, John owns \$100 of the remaining capital. If the firm decides to take it as a dividend as well, his total cash income is \$100 + \$89,650 = \$89,750.

Looking at the results of the two different crowdfunding strategies, which one should John choose? Under reward-based crowdfunding, John's profit is \$87,000. Under debt-based crowdfunding John's profit is \$89,750. Based on these numbers debt-based crowdfunding is the better option for John. This is an example of an optimal financing strategy/ optimal crowdfunding type choice that will be often discussed in this book. In reality, the problems are more complicated. For example, how does uncertainty about market demand affect the choice of the crowdfunding price? What if the price is not correctly determined and the firm is not able to raise enough funds to cover start-up costs? How does uncertainty about sales affect the decision? If there are not enough sales to cover the crowdloan under debt-based crowdfunding, what is going to happen?

One of the exercises at the end of this chapter will consider an example of a firm that uses equity-based crowdfunding.

1.6 Crowdfunding in the Public Sector

Crowdfunding in the public sector is a growing area of interest among practitioners and theorists (see for example the book mentioned in the preface[22]). Miglo (2021) mentions that this topic spans two area: crowdfunding campaigns organized by non-profit ventures, for e.g. charities and projects organized by for-profit businesses where the government is actively involved.

Regarding the former, Belleflamme et al. (2013) argue that non-profit organizations can use crowdfunding to help mitigate moral hazard problems. They argue that under crowdfunding the firm founders and managers are less focused on their own profits than they are under traditional business models and traditional financing. As a result, the interests of the managers and investors better aligned. Further, under crowdfunding the funders may be actively involved in the organization, which

[22] Lenart-Gansiniec and Chen (2021).

in turn may increase the level of community benefits provided to funders. For example, in May 2024, Crickhowell FC (a non-profit football club in England) raised £10,410 using crowdfunding. Crickhowell FC is a community-based club and organize non-sporting events such as bonfire nights and car boot sales.[23]

The second area is related to government participation in crowdfunding. Government participation can help increase trust in crowdfunding campaigns as well as increase public benefits from crowdfunding. Other benefits can include improving information about projects and reducing project risk. Governments can help evaluate if a project's aim is to achieve public rather than private goals; the government can help to generate or publish information about the firm and subsequently increase project transparency. Furthermore, there are other potential benefits of government participation in crowdfunding because of the network effects of crowdfunding, for example it can create value for a community without necessarily creating financial reward or profit for individual investors at least in the short run. Often government involvement creates both: some financial rewards for investors and non-financial rewards for the community (see e.g. Belleflamme et al., 2014). Crowdfunding is considered a helpful tool for developing and delivering public goods (see e.g. Adamo et al., 2020; Davies, 2014, 2015; Hudik & Chovanculiak, 2018; Wenzlaff, 2020).

Crowdfunding projects with government involvement may better success rates and attract more funding than comparable projects without government involvement (see e.g. Hong & Ryu, 2019; Lee et al., 2016; Miglietta et al., 2014). For example, since 2021, the Crowdfunding Alberta platform has helped non-profit organizations raise money for their projects, including some help from the Provincial Government. The projects on the platform support and build vibrant communities in Alberta and the Alberta government matches 50% of the raised funds on eligible campaigns (up to a maximum of $5,000 annually). Albertans are also eligible to receive a tax credit on any money they donate. Specifically, they receive a 60% tax credit on the first $200 they donate to a charity

[23] https://www.crowdfunder.co.uk/stories/how-crickhowell-fc-raised-over-10000-for-community-driven-upgrades.

registered with the Canada Revenue Agency and receive a 21% tax credit on every additional dollar donated.[24]

Although there are potential advantages of government involvement, there are some potential issues. Governments can use crowdfunding to privatize public services, which in some cases may create a conflict between public interest and private objectives (e.g. Van Slyke, 2007). Further, some research finds that the use of local taxes may increase fiscal disparity across localities (Afonso, 2015; Zhao & Hou, 2008). A similar issue may emerge regarding the government's use of crowdfunding if fundraising is more successful in high-income communities than it is in low-income communities.

Questions and Exercises

Throughout the book we have four types of questions: "multiple choice", "true–false", "problems" and "mix". For multiple choice questions, choose a letter corresponding to your answer. For true–false questions, the answer is "TRUE" if you agree with the sentence and "FALSE" otherwise. A sentence without options for answers represents a true-false question like question 1 below. This applies to questions in every section. Problems usually require a complete solution.

1. Online crowdfunding platforms are a place where firms can safely secure bank loans.
2. For an entrepreneurial firm, asymmetric information problems between the firm and providers of capital are typically important.
3. In addition to funds invested in a firm during reward-based crowdfunding the backers should also provide the firm with some non-financial gifts or rewards.
4. (select all possible answers) Peter made the decision to finance the purchase of three new vans for his delivery service business with debt. Which of the following sources of financing did Peter use?

    a. personal savings
    b. commercial banks
    c. venture capitalists
    d. IPO

[24] For more details see https://highriveronline.com/articles/crowdfunding-in-alberta-gets-a-boost-from-the-provincial-government.

e. debt-based crowdfunding

5. Crowdfunding is a method for obtaining project funding, by soliciting contributions from a large group of people, and is usually done online via a crowdfunding platform.
6. Equity-based crowdfunding enables people to contribute to projects and receive non–financial rewards in return.
7. John made the decision to finance his business using a modern crowdfunding campaign. To participate in this campaign, potential investors should visit:

   a. A bank.
   b. The Kickstarter website.
   c. John's house

8. Crowdfunding is sometimes ranked as one of the top business innovations of the twenty-first century.
9. AON means that the campaign does not have an established target.
10. Consider the project Video Bikes discussed in the text. Suppose that the founder decides to use equity-based crowdfunding to fund the start-up costs \$27,500. Every backer who invests \$100 will receive one share of the firm. Under this strategy, the following sequence of events occurs: crowdfunding campaign, production, sales and distribution of firm capital to shareholders. Describe the firm's Balance Sheet and Income Statement under this strategy. Look at the results of three different crowdfunding strategies (reward-based, debt-based and equity-based crowdfunding (first two strategies were discussed in the text)) and decide which one should be chosen? Discuss possible limitations of this analysis.
11. Project.

Visit the Kickstarter website. Choose an industry. Find 10 firms from this industry that used Kickstarter to conduct a crowdfunding campaign. Create a table that will show the: name of the project, country of origin, size of campaign and actual amount raised. How many campaigns in your table were successful?

Appendix 1.1. Basics of Accounting

Firms make decisions about investment projects and how to finance them. It is essential for the firm to keep detailed information regarding their projects in order to measure the successes, mitigate failures and adapt to changes. The following are two most important financial statements: Balance Sheet and Income Statement.

The Balance Sheet is a "snapshot" of the firm's assets and liabilities at a given point in time. Assets are listed according to their liquidity and liabilities are listed according to their maturity (short-term liabilities followed by long-term liabilities). The market values of assets and liabilities are not generally equal to their book values: book values are based on historical data, while market values measure current values of assets and liabilities. Founders and Shareholders are often interested in market values since that reflects the current worth of their shares. The identity of the balance sheet is:

$$\text{Assets} = \text{Liabilities} + \text{Shareholders' Equtiy.}$$

Table A.1.1 shows a typical accounting style balance sheet.

Table A.1.1 The balance sheet

Assets		*Liabilities and Shareholders Equity*	
		Liabilities	
Cash	120		
		Accounts Payable	140
Accounts Receivable	78	Long-Term Bank Debt	530
Inventory	45	Bank Loan	2150
Short-Term Investments	30	Bonds	80
		Equity	
Fixed Assets	1200		
		Capital	1073
Intangible Assets	2977	Additional Capital	60
		Retained Earnings	417
Total	4450		4450

The income statement is different from the balance sheet: it's more like a video of the firm's operations, revenues, expenses and net income over a specified period of time. Table A.1.2 is an example of an income statement.

Table A.1.2 Income statement

Income Statement	
Sales	20,000.8
Cost of Goods Sold	18,900.6
Gross Profit (Earnings before interest, taxes, depreciation and amortization/ EBITDA)	1,100.2
Depreciation	110.8
Earnings before interest and taxes (EBIT)	989.4
Interest	108.8
Earnings before taxes	880.6
Taxes	275
Net Income	605.6
Retained Earnings	69.0

From Table A.1.2, we can see that the net income was 605,600. The bulk of the positive income stems from sales which exceed the cost of goods and other expenses. This is a positive sign for investors. It means that core operations are generating income and that there is enough money to make new investments (retained earnings are positive).

References

Adamo, R., Federico, D., Intonti, M., Mele, S., & Notte, A. (2020) Crowdfunding: The case of Italy. In *Banking and finance*. IntechOpen.

Afonso, W. (2015). The equity of local sales tax distributions in urban, suburban, rural, and tourism rich counties in North Carolina. *Public Finance Review, 44*(6), 691–721.

Ahlers, G., Cumming, D., Guenther, C., & Schweizer, D. (2015). Signaling in equity crowdfunding. *Entrepreneurship Theory and Practice, 39*(4), 955–980.

Ahlstrom, D., Cumming, D., & Vismara, S. (2018). New methods of entrepreneurial firm financing: Fintech, crowdfunding and corporate governance implications. *Corporate Governance: An International Review, 26*, 310–313.

Alegre, I., & Moleskis, M. (2016). *Crowdfunding: A review and research agenda* (IESE Research Papers D/1142). IESE Business School.

Allaz, B. (1992). Oligopoly, uncertainty and strategic forward trans-actions. *International Journal of Industrial Organization, 10*(2), 297–308.

Alt, R., Beck, R., & Smits, M. T. (2018). FinTech and the transformation of the financial industry. *Electron Markets, 28*, 235–243.

Ante, L., & Fiedler, I. (2020). Cheap signals in security token offerings (STOs). *Quantitative Finance and Economics, 4*(4), 608–639.

Assenmacher, K. (2017). *Crowdfunding als kommunale Finanzierungsalternative*. Springer. https://www.springer.com/in/book/9783658171520

Babich, V., Marinesi, S., & Tsoukalas, G. (2021). Does crowdfunding benefit entrepreneurs and venture capital investors? *Manufacturing & Service Operations Management, 23*(2), 508–524.

Bachmann, N., Drasch, B., Fridgen, G., Miksch, M., Regner, F., Schweizer, A., & Urbach, N. (2021). Tarzan and chain: Exploring the ICO jungle and evaluating design archetypes. *Electronic Markets, 32*(3), 1725–1748.

Bagwell, K., & Riordan, M. H. (1991). High and declining prices signal product quality. *The American Economic Review, 81*(1), 224–239.

Baker, K., & Martin, G. S. (2011). *Capital structure and corporate financing decisions: Theory, evidence, and practice*. Wiley.

Bao, H., & Roubaud, D. (2022). Non-fungible token: A systematic review and research agenda. *Journal of Risk and Financial Management, 15*, 215. https://doi.org/10.3390/jrfm15050215

BBC Online. (2013, April 24). *The statue of liberty and America's crowdfunding pioneer*. BBC.

Belavina, E., Marinesi, S., & Tsoukalas, G. (2020). Rethinking crowdfunding platform design: Mechanisms to deter misconduct and improve efficiency. *Management Science, 66*(11), 4980–4997.

Belleflamme, P., Lambert, T., & Schwienbacher, A. (2013). Individual crowdfunding practices. *Venture Capital: An International Journal of Entrepreneurial Finance, 15*(4), 313–333.

Belleflamme, P., Lambert, T., & Schwienbacher, A. (2014). Crowdfunding: Tapping the right crowd. *Journal of Business Venturing, 29*(5), 585–609.

Belleflamme, P., Omrani, N., & Peitz, M. (2015). The economics of crowdfunding platforms. *Information Economics and Policy, 33*, 11–28.

Bolton, P., & Scharfstein, D. (1990). A theory of predation based on agency problems in financial contracting. *American Economic Review, 80*(1), 93–106.

Booty, L. (2017). *Equity or reward-based crowdfunding? Hear from both sides to make your mind up*. https://realbusiness.co.uk/equity-reward-based-crowfunding-hear-sides-make-mind/

Brander, J. A., & Lewis, T. R. (1986). Oligopoly and financial structure: The limited liability effect. *The American Economic Review, 76*, 956–970.

Brown, T. E., Boon, E., & Pitt, L. F. (2017). Seeking funding in order to sell: Crowdfunding as a marketing tool. *Business Horizons, 60*(2), 189–195.

Brüntje, D., & Gajda, O. (2016). *Crowdfunding in Europe, state of the art in theory and practice*. Springer. https://www.springer.com/gp/book/9783319180168

Cason, T. N., & Zubrickas, R. (2019). Donation-based crowdfunding with refund bonuses. *European Economic Review, 119*, 452–471.

Chakraborty, S., & Swinney, R. (2020). Signalling to the crowd: Private quality information and rewards-based crowdfunding. *Manufacturing and Service Operations Management Manufacturing & Service Operations Management, 23*(1), 155–169.

Chalmers, D., Fisch, C., Matthews, R., Quinn, W., & Recker, J. (2022). Beyond the bubble: Will NFTs and digital proof of ownership empower creative industry entrepreneurs? *Journal of Business Venturing Insights, 17*, Article e00309. https://doi.org/10.1016/j.jbvi.2022.e00309

Charbit, C., & Desmoulins, G. (2017). *Civic crowdfunding: A collective option for local public goods?* (OECD Regional Development Working Papers 2017/1). OECD Publishing.

Chemla, G., & Tinn, K. (2019). Learning through crowdfunding. *Management Science, 66*(5), 1783–2290.

Cumming, D., & Hornuf, L. (2018). *The economics of crowdfunding startups, portals and investor behavior*. Palgrave Macmillan.

Cumming, D., Hornuf, L., Karami, M., & Schweizer, D. (2023). Disentangling crowdfunding from fraudfunding. *Journal of Business Ethics, 182*(4), 1103–1128.

Cumming, D., & Johan, S. (2017). Crowdfunding and entrepreneurial internationalization. In *The World Scientific reference on entrepreneurship* (pp. 109–126). World Scientific.

Cumming, D., Leboeuf, G., & Schwienbacher, A. (2020). Crowdfunding models: Keep-it-all versus all or nothing. *Financial Management, 49*, 331–360.

Das, S. (2019). The future of FinTech. *Financial Management, 48*(4), 981–1007.

Davies, R. (2014, September 1). *Civic crowdfunding as a marketplace for participation in urban development* (pp. 1–25). Presented at the Internet, Policy & Politics Conference, Stanford, CA, USA.

Davies, R. (2015). Three provocations for civic crowdfunding. *Information, Communication & Society, 18*, 342–355.

de Meza, D., & Reito, F. (2020). Too much waste, not enough rationing: The failure of stochastic, competitive markets. *Journal of Economic Theory, 188*, Article 105067.

Dushnitsky, G., Guerini, M., Piva, E., & Rossi-Lamastra, C. (2016). Crowdfunding in Europe: Determinants of platform creation across countries. *California Management Review, 58*(2), 44–71.

Estrin, S., Gozman, D., & Khavul, S. (2018). The evolution and adoption of equity crowdfunding: Entrepreneur and investor entry into a new market. *Small Business Economics, 51*(2), 425–439.

Graham, J. R., & Harvey, C. R. (2001). The theory and practice of corporate finance: Evidence from the field. *Journal of Financial Economics, 60*, 187–243.

Hall, B. (2009). The financing of innovative firms. *EIB Papers, 14*(2), 8–29.

Hildebrand, T., Puri, M., & Rocholl, J. (2017). Adverse incentives in crowdfunding. *Management Science, 63*(3), 587–608.

Hong, S., & Ryu, J. (2019, November). Crowdfunding public projects: Collaborative governance for achieving citizen co-funding of public goods. *Government Information Quarterly, 36*(1), 145–153.

Horvat, T., & Bobek, V. (2020). Two modern aspects of intangible assets—Protection on blockchain and funding through ICO. In T. Dirsehan (Ed.), *Managing customer experiences in an Omnichannel world: Melody of online and offline environments in the customer journey* (pp. 287–303). Emerald Publishing Limited.

Howell, S., Niessner, M., & Yermack, D. (2020). Initial coin offerings: Financing growth with cryptocurrency token sales. *The Review of Financial Studies, 33*, 3925–3974.

Hudik, M., & Chovanculiak, R. (2018). Private provision of public goods via crowdfunding. *Journal of Institutional Economics, 14*(1), 23–44.

Hughes, J. S., & Kao, J. (1997). Strategic forward contracting and observability. *International Journal of Industrial Organization, 16*(1), 121–133.

Hummel, D. (2016). Civic crowdfunding: A potential test of the voluntary theory of public finance for public capital goods. *Journal of Public Budgeting, Accounting and Financial Management, 28*, 171–195.

Hurst, S. (2016). *Pod Point's Erik Fairbairn reveals why he is investing in Crowdcube.* Crowdfundinsider.com. https://www.crowdfundinsider.com/2016/07/88567-pod-points-erik-fairbairn-reveals-investing-crowdcube/

ICO and IEO Report. (2020). 6th ed. https://www.pwc.ch/en/insights/fs/6th-ico-sto-report.html

Jensen, L. S., & Özkil, A. G. (2018). Identifying challenges in crowdfunded product development: A review of Kickstarter projects. *Design Science, 4*, Article e18.

Kraus, S., Richter, C., Brem, A., Cheng, C. F., & Chang, M. L. (2016). Strategies for reward-based crowdfunding campaigns. *Journal of Innovation and Knowledge, 1*(1), 13–23.

Kuppuswamy, V., & Bayus, B. (2018). A review of crowdfunding research and findings. In P. N. Golder & D. Mitra (Eds.), *Handbook of new product development research*. Elgar.

Lambert, T., & Schwienbacher, A. (2010). An empirical analysis of crowdfunding. *Social Science Research Network, 1578175*(1), 23.

Lee, C. H., Zhao, J. L., & Hassna, G. (2016). Government-incentivized crowdfunding for one-belt, one-road enterprises: Design and research issues. *Financial Innovation, 2*, 2.

Lenart-Gansiniec, R., & Chen, J. (2021). *Crowdfunding in the public sector: Theory and best practices*. Series: Contributions to finance and accounting. Springer.

Li, G., & Wang, J. (2019). Threshold effects on Backer motivations in reward-based crowdfunding. *Journal of Management Information Systems, 36*(2), 546–573.

Mach, T. L. (Board of Governors of the Federal Reserve System, Washington DC, USA). (2014). The role of credit access in firm sustainability: A comparison of the 1998 and 2003 surveys of small business finances. *International Review of Entrepreneurship. IRE, 12*(4), 141–162.

Masiak, C., Block, J., Masiak, T., Neuenkirch, M., & Pielen, K. (2020). Initial coin offerings (ICOs): Market cycles and relationship with bitcoin and ether. *Small Business Economics, 55*(4), 1113–1130.

Miglietta, A., Parisi, E., Pessione, M., & Servato, F. (2014). *Crowdfunding and local governments: A financial opportunity for a new liaison with citizens*. Paper presented at the Toulon-Verona Conference "Excellence in Services".

Miglo, A. (2020). Crowdfunding in a competitive environment. *Journal of Risk and Financial Management, 13*, 39.

Miglo, A. (2021). Crowdfunding: Definitions, foundations and framework. In R. Lenart-Gansiniec & J. Chen (Eds.), *Crowdfunding in the public sector: Contributions to finance and accounting*. Springer.

Miglo, A. (2022). Theories of financing for entrepreneurial firms: A review. *International Review of Entrepreneurship, 20*(2), 301–330.

Miglo, A. (2025). *Capital structure in the modern world*. Palgrave.

Miglo, A., & Miglo, V. (2019). Market imperfections and crowdfunding. *Small Business Economics Journal, 53*(1), 51–79.

Milne, A., & Parboteeah, P. (2016, May). *The business models and economics of peer-to-peer lending* (ECRI Research Report No 17). https://doi.org/10.2139/ssrn.2763682

Mochkabadi, K., & Volkmann, C. (2020). Equity crowdfunding: A systematic review of the literature. *Small Business Economics, 54*, 75–118.

Modigliani, F., & Miller, M. (1958). The cost of capital, corporation finance and the theory of investment. *American Economic Review, 48*(3), 261–297.

Mollick, E. (2014). The dynamics of crowdfunding: An exploratory study. *Journal of Business Venturing, 29*(1), 1–16.

Moores, C. (2015). Note: Kickstart my lawsuit: Fraud and justice in rewards-based crowdfunding. *US Davis Law Review, 49*(1), 385–424.

Moritz, A., & Block, J. H. (2016). Crowdfunding: A literature review and research directions. In D. Brüntje & O. Gajda (Eds.), *Crowdfunding in*

Europe: FGF studies in small business and entrepreneurship. Springer. https://doi.org/10.1007/978-3-319-18017-5_3

Myalo, A. (2019). *Comparative analysis of ICO, DAOICO, IEO and STO: Case study, digital financial assets*. https://doi.org/10.26794/2587-5671-2019-23-6-6-25.

Platt, K. (2020). Corporate bonds and product market competition. *The Journal of Financial Research, 43*, 615–647.

Prescott, E. C. (1975). Efficiency of the natural rate. *Journal of Political Economy, 83*(6), 1229–1236.

Rau, P. R. (2019). *Law, trust, and the development of crowdfunding*. https://ssrn.com/abstract=2989056.

Schaaf, R., & Skiera, B. (2014). Effect of time preferences on optimal prices and probability of advance selling. *Customer Needs and Solutions, 1*(2), 131–142.

Schwienbacher, A. (2018). Entrepreneurial risk-taking in crowdfunding campaigns. *Small Business Economics, 51*(4), 843–859.

Simons, O. (2016, March 11). *Crowdfunding comte*. http://positivists.org/blog/archives/5959

Stiver, A., Barroca, L., Minocha, S., Richards, M., & Roberts, D. (2014). Civic crowdfunding research: Challenges, opportunities, and future agenda. *New Media & Society, 17*, 249–271.

Strausz, R. (2017). Crowdfunding, demand uncertainty, and moral hazard—A mechanism design approach. *American Economic Review, 107*(6), 1430–1476.

Tamburro, A. (2018). Far from madding crowd: Crowdfunding a small business reorganization. *EMORY Bankruptcy Developments Journal, 34*, 521–559.

Thakor, A. (2019). Fintech and banking: What do we know? *Journal of Financial Intermediation, 41*, Article 100833.

The Capital Structure Decisions of New Firms, Kauffman Foundation. (2009). http://www.kauffman.org/what-we-do/research/kauffman-firm-survey-series/the-capital-structure-decisions-of-new-firms

Tönnissen, S., Beinke, J. H., & Teuteberg, F. (2020). Understanding token-based ecosystems—A taxonomy of blockchain-based business models of start-ups. *Electronic Markets, 30*(2), 307–323.

Van Montfort, K., Siebers, V., & De Graaf, F. J. (2021). Civic crowdfunding in local governments: Variables for success in the Netherlands? *Journal of Risk and Financial Management, 14*, 8.

Van Slyke, D. M. (2007). Agents or Stewards: Using theory to understand the government-nonprofit social service contracting relationship. *Journal of Public Administration Research and Theory, 17*(2), 157–187.

Vismara, S. (2016). Equity retention and social network theory in equity crowdfunding. *Small Business Economics, 46*(4), 579–590.

Wenzlaff, K. (2020). Civic crowdfunding: Four perspectives on the definition of civic crowdfunding. In R. Shneor, L. Zhao, & B. T. Flåten (Eds.), *Advances in crowdfunding*. Palgrave Macmillan. https://doi.org/10.1007/978-3-030-46309-0_19

Wild, J., Shaw, K., & Chiappetta, B. (2014). *Fundamental accounting principles*. McGraw-Hill Education.

Williams, J. T. (1995). Financial and industrial structure with agency. *The Review of Financial Studies, 8*(2), 431–474.

Wilson, K. E. (2015). *Policy lessons from financing innovative firms* (OECD Science, Technology and Industry Policy Papers, No. 24). OECD Publishing.

Zhao, Z. J., & Hou, Y. (2008). Local option sales taxes and fiscal disparity: The case of Georgia counties. *Public Budgeting & Finance, 28*, 39–57.

CHAPTER 2

Different Types of Crowdfunding

2.1 Reward-Based Crowdfunding

As was previously mentioned, there are 4 main types of crowdfunding: reward-based crowdfunding, equity-based crowdfunding, debt-based crowdfunding and donation-based crowdfunding. In the case of reward-based crowdfunding, a non-financial reward is expected by the backers in return for their contributions. Rewards can vary from something simple such as a T-shirt with a firm name or logo to a firm's product. Usually a set of pairings (contribution; reward) is associated with a crowdfunding campaign where a higher contribution means a better reward.

Reward-based crowdfunding represents a very active and dynamic informational structure. Unlike traditional financing, one of the main advantages of crowdfunding is "market feedback" i.e. the firms' ability to collect useful information about their campaigns and products.[1] Even if a campaign fails, the entrepreneur may decide to revise the product and go ahead with another project and another crowdfunding campaign. Serial

[1] For more discussion about this idea see Chapter 3.

Supplementary Information The online version contains supplementary material available at https://doi.org/10.1007/978-3-032-10724-4_2.

© The Author(s), under exclusive license to Springer Nature Switzerland AG 2026

A. Miglo and V. Miglo, *The Theories and Developments of Crowdfunding*, https://doi.org/10.1007/978-3-032-10724-4_2

entrepreneurship is a growing area in theory and practice based in the idea of "learning by doing" (see e.g. He et al., 2020). Research shows that prior experience in crowdfunding has a positive effect on crowdfunding success, and it usually finds that entrepreneurs with a high number of successful project campaigns are more successful in subsequent projects (see e.g. Courtney et al., 2016; Greenberg & Gerber, 2014; Janků & Kučerová, 2018; Koch & Siering, 2015, 2019; Zhou et al., 2018).

The history of crowdfunding, in particularly reward-based crowdfunding, is a growing area of research (see e.g. Zhao et al., 2019). Early examples include eighteenth century book writers and musicians when they were gathering money from many investors to publish large pieces of work. Modern crowdfunding is related to the internet. One of the earliest examples is a campaign organized by the British band Marillion that managed to save their 1997 US tour through digital donations totalling $60,000.[2] Another important historical point is 2012, when a legislation (JOBS act or jump start our business start-up act) was adopted in the USA that allowed small businesses to use easier ways to raise funds, including crowdfunding, that require less bureaucracy.[3]

2.1.1 Decisions Related to Reward-Based Crowdfunding

Entrepreneurs who are interested in using reward-based crowdfunding will have to make several important decisions. Some examples include: comparing crowdfunding with other financing strategies, comparing reward-based crowdfunding with other types of crowdfunding, selecting AON or KIA, selecting a platform, creating a video or not, determining the campaign target in case of AON, determining crowdfunding prices/contributions and rewards, deciding on the frequency of campaign website updates. Most of these questions are very important for firms so a lot of ideas/theories related to them have been written in recent years. We will discuss some of these questions below, but many of them are very deep and will be discussed to some extent throughout the book.

To understand the importance and the challenges facing entrepreneurs making these decisions we need to go back to the previous chapter, where we discussed the concept of a perfect financial market versus an

[2] See e.g. https://smallbrooks.com/history-of-crowdfunding/.

[3] More discussion about crowdfunding regulation is in Chapter 8.

imperfect market. Table 2.1 summarizes ideas related to reward-based crowdfunding that we will study in the subsequent chapters in more detail. They are related to the decisions entrepreneurs are making when considering the usage of reward-based crowdfunding.

Table 2.1 Ideas/theories related to reward-based crowdfunding

Ideas/Theories related to reward-based crowdfunding	*Explanation*
Network/community benefits	People are motivated to fund projects on computer-mediated crowdfunding platforms because of social interactions and feelings of connectedness to a community with similar interests
Learning market demand	For entrepreneurs, it is vital to know if there is demand for their products. Intuition is important but to make decisions (production scale, market choice, product price, investments etc.) more concrete knowledge is always useful. Crowdfunding helps with learning demand ("crowd wisdom") before making important decisions (unlike traditional financing). Entrepreneurs often mention that the ability to learn crowd wisdom was the main benefit of using crowdfunding
Cases of moral hazard, incomplete contracts, entrepreneurs' misbehaviour and public trust	Some firms conducting reward-based crowdfunding campaigns are not quality. For example, a very large number of campaigns fail and many of firms that had successful reward-based crowdfunding campaigns do not deliver the promised rewards. This even includes some cases of fraud and can affect the public's trust in crowdfunding. Entrepreneurs should make every effort to avoid any negative impression from their company materials, e.g. explain in detail the way funds will be used and when rewards will be provided

(continued)

Table 2.1 (continued)

Ideas/Theories related to reward-based crowdfunding	*Explanation*
Informational problems in crowdfunding/ asymmetric information between entrepreneurs and funders	Information problems are recognized as an important factor in crowdfunding. It is recommended that entrepreneurs try to signal the quality of their firm/products to the public directly and indirectly in order to improve their chances of success. Direct signals include videos, updates, information about firm quality/risks etc. These signals have their limits as "actions speak louder than words". Indirect signals consist of taking some actions that may be seen favourably by potential investors. For example, selecting AON may have a positive effect in the eyes of the public ("signalling by risk-bearing"). In the next lesson, we will learn how to use excel to collect and analyze data that can help entrepreneurs with decision-making

The following is an example illustrating learning market demand/the market feedback idea. Entrepreneur Marc received the following feedback during his crowdfunding campaign for the web app he is going to develop: "...your app is relatively slow compared to similar apps on the market". John thinks that this was very useful feedback. The learning market demand idea will be discussed in detail in Chapter 3.

Below is an example illustrating network benefits. Helen and Jessica enjoyed learning about Marc's crowdfunding campaign since he suggested a new app to help them find the best clothing store using an interesting search idea based on advertising text analysis that was very well described in his firm's video. They spent hours discussing it online and finally decided to participate in the campaign. The network benefits idea will be further discussed in Chapter 5.

The following illustrates the signalling by risk-bearing idea, which is based on asymmetric information between entrepreneurs and potential investors. Consider the choice between AON and KIA for an entrepreneur who wants to use reward-based crowdfunding. If the entrepreneur selects AON, it takes additional risk because if the sufficient amount of funds is not raised, the campaign fails and the project cannot continue (it can negatively affect the entrepreneur's reputation). This leads to the idea of signalling by risk-bearing. It means that only good quality entrepreneurs can afford to signal their quality by bearing some risk. Low-quality entrepreneurs who are not sure about the strength of their ideas and their campaigns may not be willing to take this additional risk. Why is it important? If investors had the same amount of information as firm founders, they would be able to evaluate the quality of ideas/campaigns before the campaigns are launched so the signalling by risk-bearing would not matter. But because information is imperfect, investors are trying to indirectly assess the quality of campaigns by observing the entrepreneurs' campaign type choices. By observing AON, they can conclude that this campaign is run by a high-quality entrepreneur/project as the entrepreneur is willing to take the campaign failure risk. This is indirectly consistent for example with the slightly higher percentage of successful crowdfunding campaigns on Kickstarter (which uses AON) than on Indiegogo (see e.g. Cumming et al., 2020). The logic here is that bad quality entrepreneurs will not be able to mimic the strategy of high-quality entrepreneurs because for them the risk of failure is higher.

The practical challenge and the theoretical beauty of crowdfunding is that on one hand there are a lot of relatively simple and intuitive ideas behind it but at the same time it seems unlikely one theory can explain everything (similar to capital structure where unlike many other areas of finance, a lot of disagreements exist between theorists and practitioners about which theory is dominant). For example, there are plenty of examples of good quality campaigns on Indiegogo. The challenge for researchers is to continue to develop ideas and build models incorporating different factors attempting to explain a large number of empirical observations. We will discuss the signalling idea in more detail in Chapter 3.

Next, we discuss the selection of a crowdfunding platform. Of course to a large extent it depends primarily on whether an entrepreneur chooses AON or KIA because some reward-based crowdfunding platforms offer only one of these models. In addition, a platform's country can play a role. Although theoretically, an online method of raising funds using crowdfunding does not have physical borders so it should not matter but as practice shows some bias can still exist for potential backers and some of them may lean towards local platforms. We will discuss geographical biases along with other behavioural aspects of crowdfunding in Chapter 5. In addition, the entrepreneur may check if the platform offers other services like helping entrepreneurs with bank connections as well as check the platform's statistics like, for example, the percentage of successful campaigns. Some examples of crowdfunding platforms that offer reward-based crowdfunding as the only type of crowdfunding, or along with other types, are presented in Table 2.2. It includes information about the type of crowdfunding used on these platforms as well as their country of origin. Entrepreneurs should also check platform fees. Usually, fees range from 5 to 15% of the amount raised. Anything above this range would be considered a little too expensive. Also, different platforms may have slightly different fee structures depending on what kind of payments they adopt e.g. flat vs. variable fees.

Kickstarter and Indiegogo are the two largest crowdfunding platforms in the world and they both use reward-based crowdfunding. Consider a typical crowdfunding campaign webpage on Kickstarter.[5] It usually contains information about the amount of funds raised ($273,855 as of July 15, 2025), the number of backers (548) and the campaign target ($10,000). The existence of a campaign target means that Kickstarter uses the AON method and firms need to establish a target for funds

Table 2.2 Examples of crowdfunding platforms that use reward-based crowdfunding

Platform	*AON/KIA*	*Country of the platform origin; website*
Kickstarter	AON	USA; https://www.kickstarter.com/
Indiegogo	KIA[4]	USA; https://www.indiegogo.com/
Booomerang	AON	Denmark; https://boomerang.dk/
Produzioni Dal Basso	AON, KIA	Italy; https://www.produzionidalbasso.com/
Fongogo	AON	Turkey; https://www.fongogo.com/
Zaar	AON	Malta; https://zaar.com.mt/
Verkami	AON	Spain; https://www.verkami.com/

[4] Some research argues that while Indiegogo allows the entrepreneur to choose between KIA and AON, the vast majority of campaigns choose KIA (Cumming et al., 2020). In recent months, Indiegogo has changed their campaign model where instead of allowing an entrepreneur to directly choose a KIA campaign, they are allowed to add intermediate funding thresholds. https://www.indiegogo.com/en/blog/post/no-more-flexible-funding-heres-why-you-wont-miss-it.

[5] The campaign name is Gaming Chair Redefined. See https://www.kickstarter.com/projects/120942733/tgif-t0-revolutionize-gaming-chairs-with-ergonomic-design.

raised during the campaign. If this amount is not reached, Kickstarter will return the funds to the funders. You can usually also find a video about the campaign, the description of rewards, information about the duration of the campaign and some comments. Note that the total duration of a typical reward-based crowdfunding campaign is usually short. Some data shows that the average duration of a campaign on Kickstarter is around 30 days.[6] This is consistent with what we discussed previously, i.e. that it takes less bureaucracy to create and approve the campaign as compared to traditional methods of raising funds. Also, it is easier to reach a large number of potential investors quickly via the Internet. For more information about the duration of the different stages of firm activities related to launching a campaign, see for example Ananian (2025).[7] Next we will discuss the factors of crowdfunding campaign success.

2.1.2 *Factors of Crowdfunding Campaign Success*

Factors of crowdfunding campaign success is a popular topic in crowdfunding literature (see e.g. Cordova & Dolci, 2015; Paakkarinen, 2016). From practical point of view, knowing the factors of crowdfunding campaign success should help entrepreneurs make decisions related to crowdfunding campaigns. From a theoretical point of view, it connects theories with data and helps evaluate theories and their consistency with empirical evidence. For example, as we mentioned previously, asymmetric information plays an important role in crowdfunding. Investors do not have the same information as the entrepreneur, and they usually lack investment knowledge and experience, making it difficult for them to select high-quality projects for investment (Lui, et al., 2023). In order to attract more investors, entrepreneurs are often interested in mitigating the problem of asymmetric information. They can do it either directly or indirectly. The former includes, for example, putting more information about their projects online, creating a good video about the project, providing information about company risks and providing more updates

[6] See e.g. https://www.sendfromchina.com/NewsCenter/how-long-should-you-run-crowdfunding-campaign.html.

[7] https://www.tcf.team/blog/how-long-should-crowdfunding-campaign-last#:~:text=in%20the%20cold.-,Sweet%20Spot%20for%20Campaign%20Length,project%20types%20and%20funding%20goals.

during the campaign. These direct actions indeed improve the likelihood of campaign success (see e.g. Koch & Siering, 2019). High-quality campaigns often contain detailed project descriptions and appealing visual elements (images or videos), provide investors with a more visual description of the project etc. (Lui, et al., 2023). This can attract backers who can also promote the project to additional potential backers or external media enhancing the project's attractiveness (Mollick, 2014). Additionally, detailed project descriptions and visual presentations can effectively showcase a project's readiness and appeal, reducing uncertainty in investment decisions. Meanwhile, the emotional content in project narratives also influences backers' decisions, where positive sentiment can boost investors' confidence in the project (Koch & Siering, 2019). Using at least 500 words to introduce a project can also help a campaign. Furthermore, Kim et al. (2022) observed that the presence of a video pitch reduces the likelihood of being funded on Indiegogo. Nonetheless, creative videos still had a positive impact on crowdfunding efforts on Kickstarter (Calic & Mosakowski, 2016).

Indirect methods to attract investors in an environment with asymmetric information is a growing area of research. It may include signalling by risk-bearing as mentioned previously, in particular selecting AON vs. KIA, and choosing a specific type of crowdfunding. As was previously mentioned that there is some evidence that AON campaigns have a higher probability of success than KIA campaigns (see e.g. Cumming et al., 2020; Zhou et al., 2018). Josefy et al., (2016) found that projects on the Kickstarter platform are more likely to achieve crowdfunding success compared to those on GoFundMe. More research is expected in this direction.

Founder characteristics also significantly impact project success. Their history of success and expertise can increase a project's credibility (Skirnevskiy et al., 2017). Koch and Siering (2019) found that experienced founders can use their extensive experience and reputation to reduce the need for information and risk disclosure as they are already a strong signal of a project's feasibility. Zvilichovsky et al. (2013) believe that founders with a successful fundraising record will be more successful in subsequent crowdfunding activities because fundraisers with fundraising experience are better able to win the trust and support of investors (Lui, et al., 2023). Moreover, the relationship between the founder's nationality and the project's geographical location shows that backers tend to support local projects. For example, Borrero-Domínguez et al. (2020) analyze data on the Spanish Goteo platform and found that entrepreneurs with previous successful experience have a higher rate of crowdfunding success. They also found that projects based in Spain have a higher success rate than those based abroad, indicating that supporters prefer to fund projects that are geographically closer. Huang et al. (2022) found that the credibility of the entrepreneur can compensate even for project quality and facilitate crowdfunding success.

Social networks can help enhance the reputation and legitimacy of start-ups and can serve as a signal of quality (Song et al., 2021). Granovetter (1983) noted that information obtained through social networks is often more valuable than information retrieved through formal networks as social networks help build trust. In the high-noise environment of crowdfunding, signal theory emphasizes the importance of reducing information asymmetry and enhancing the confidence of potential investors (Huang et al., 2022). Moreover, teams have a higher likelihood of raising money than individuals in crowdfunding campaigns (Liu, et al., 2021). This is because project fundraisers with team size have certain social network connections, which helps facilitate the completion of the project. Additionally, large teams possess more knowledge, skills and a stable organizational structure (Liu, et al., 2021). Zheng et al. (2014) also suggested that team experience plays an important role in enhancing the success rate of projects. Lagazio and Querci (2018) suggested that it is better to have more than 5 members for fundraising teams to be able to handle a crowdfunding campaign, which takes a lot of time and effort. Courtney et al. (2016) found that third-party information such as media and positive evaluations from supporters can enhance the impact of a founder's experience on project success.

Additionally, founders need to pay special attention to gain early success in their crowdfunding campaigns as it was found on Kickstarter that successful campaigns raised the majority of their funds in the first one-sixth of their campaign time (Colombo et al., 2015). Some fundraisers on a Polish crowdfunding platform even invested their own funds to increase their chances of success, highlighting the importance of early success (Galuszka & Brzozowska, 2016).

If the firm selects AON, the next step is to select the campaign target. There are advantages in setting a lower target as well as setting a higher target. The primary factor is the amount of start-up costs that the entrepreneur needs to cover. Another factor can be signalling by risk-bearing where an entrepreneur signals its quality by setting a high target and showing they are confident in their campaign. On the other hand, a lower target reduces the risk of campaign failure, which can be advantageous to entrepreneurs who's start-up requirements are flexible. For more analysis on the role of target selection (see e.g. Chakraborty & Swinney, 2020). Data shows that the benefits of a lower target tend to outweigh the benefits of setting a high target and usually leads to attracting more supporters. For instance, Felipe et al. (2022) analyzed campaigns on the Brazilian Catarse platform, and suggested that campaigns with lower goals and more rewards are more successful. Lagazio and Querci (2018) used data from Indiegogo and found that the larger the funding amount requested, the less likely it is to be raised. Therefore, they suggested that entrepreneurs with large-scale projects should consider raising funds in multiple stages, launching several rounds of financing with relatively modest funding targets. Similarly, Meer (2014) claimed that the cost of rewards should not be too high because setting higher prices can decrease the chances of a project receiving funding on a reward-based platform. Further, setting too high a financing goal may lead to not achieving the funding target within the specified time and longer fundraising periods may be viewed by investors as a sign of low confidence (Mollick, 2014). Similarly, Härkönen (2014) made the point that longer durations may be unhelpful; he noted that longer crowdfunding campaigns give investors more time to think about and potentially forget about the crowdfunding campaign. Most investors prefer to support projects requiring less funding and shorter periods to reduce potential financial risks (Lui, et al., 2023).

2.2 Equity-Based Crowdfunding

Equity-based crowdfunding is a financing method where backers acquire an equity stake in a firm via an on-line crowdfunding platform. Equity-based crowdfunding shares a lot of commonalities with traditional equity financing, but there are some innovative elements as well (see Table 2.3). One of the differences with traditional equity financing is that equity investments in crowdfunding do not have an active secondary market although some crowdfunding platforms have been recently working on improving in this area as we mentioned previously. The main advantage of equity-based crowdfunding compared to traditional equity is the smaller amount of bureaucracy involved. In addition, it is usually much less expensive to organize a crowdfunding campaign than to issue traditional equity issues, and crowdfunding campaigns have the advantage of quickly reaching a large number of potential investors around the world using the internet via online platforms. The fact that shares sold during equity-based crowdfunding provide ownership interest to their holders (and respectively dilute the ownership of the firm founders) does not constitute a difference between equity-based and traditional equity (the same applies to the first equity-based crowdfunding campaign but also to the second, third etc.) in case the firm uses multiple equity-based crowdfunding campaigns.

Miglo (2021) argues that entrepreneurs can use equity-based crowdfunding as a learning tool. Entrepreneurs can learn the value of the project they develop by observing the demand during the crowdfunding stage. Under some conditions, equity-based crowdfunding can even be more efficient as a learning tool than reward-based crowdfunding since the entrepreneur can learn the value of the project before committing to any production decisions.

In terms of equity-based crowdfunding history, one should of course note the 2012 JOBs Act. To understand the importance of this act for crowdfunding, note that prior to that any issues of equity to the public would be extremely hard/impossible for small entrepreneurial firms as companies had to present a lot of documents before a financial authority/ agency regulating equity markets. Issuing equity publicly represents one of the most significant events in the life of any firm and often takes place on a large public exchange e.g. the London Exchange or the New York Stock Exchange. A significant amount of bureaucracy exists because historically one of the reasons behind the major financial crises, such as

Table 2.3 Comparing equity-based crowdfunding with traditional equity

Equity-based crowdfunding	*Traditional equity*
– Ownership interest – Does not require registration with a government agency, e.g. the Securities Exchange Commission in the USA – Firms usually use an equity-based crowdfunding platform to quickly reach a large number of potential investors around the world	– Ownership interest – Usually requires registration with the Securities Exchange Commission or a similar regulatory authority – Usually requires the service of a professional firm (underwriter) that is usually very expensive and often costs between 5–15% – After a successful issue of shares there is usually a liquid secondary market for firm shares

the Great Depression in 1929–1933 and the Great Recession in 2007–2009, was the lack of regulation. One of the main ideas of strengthening regulation in the area of the public issues of securities was making sure that companies provide a significant amount of information to investors. But on the negative side, the whole process has become quite bureaucratic, expensive and time consuming. Under these circumstances, using equity financing as a major financing strategy has become not feasible for many small entrepreneurial and innovative firms. The JOBs Act in 2012 was an important milestone to address these negative effects and led to the adaption of crowdfunding, especially equity-based crowdfunding.

Note a couple of interesting points related to the JOBs act. First note that Title II of this act allows for "crowdfunding" by so-called "accredited investors". Although it does not involve the same level of bureaucracy as before, this is still quite restrictive since to become an accredited investor, an investor needs to satisfy a number of conditions. Title III of the JOBs Act, however, allows for "crowdfunding" by all investors (i.e. accredited and non-accredited) within certain parameters. Specifically, an issuer may sell up to $1,000,000 of its securities every 12 months, and depending upon their net worth and income, investors will be permitted to invest up to $100,000 in crowdfunding issues every 12 months. The proposed equity crowdfunding rules under Title III were clarified by the SEC in October 2013. This was a major development in public equity issues by simplifying the procedure and reducing costs, which is consistent with the overall spirit of FinTech developments. We will provide more discussion related to the regulation of crowdfunding in Chapter 8.

2.2.1 Equity-based Crowdfunding platforms

Selecting a platform to conduct a campaign is an important step for entrepreneurs who have decided to use equity-based crowdfunding. Table 2.4 contains a list of equity-based crowdfunding platforms that shows each platform's country of origin as well as some additional features.

A typical webpage of an equity-crowdfunding campaign is to a large extent similar to a typical one under reward-based crowdfunding. Consider for example the campaign Nich Mobility on Crowdcube.[8] This

[8] https://www.crowdcube.com/companies/niche-mobility-s-l/pitches/ZNEDol.

Table 2.4 Equity-based crowdfunding platforms

Platform	*Features*	*Platform country of origin and website*
Crowdcube	Develops secondary market elements; some campaigns offer rewards	UK; https://www.crowdcube.com/
Republic	Secondary market; asset tokenization[9]	USA; https://republic.com/
Republic Europe (former Seedrs)	Seedrs nominee—the platform takes care of all the administrative shareholder work—with any financial benefit (e.g. the right to dividends, capital returns on an exit and any tax relief); asset tokenization	USA, UK[10]; https://europe.republic.com/
Frontfundr[11]	Campaigns usually have targets; has the concept of a closing target	Canada; https://www.frontfundr.com/
Wefunder[12]	Provides investor education services (Investor School); there are restrictions on investors from certain countries	USA; https://wefunder.com/
StartEngine[13]	Secondary market; good for larger investments; Pre-IPO	USA; https://www.startengine.com/

[9] We discuss tokens in Chapter 9.

[10] Initially was created as Seedrs (UK); was acquired by Republic (USA) in 2021. See https://en.wikipedia.org/wiki/Seedrs.

[11] The platform explains that they use equity-based crowdfunding on their website see e.g. https://support.frontfundr.com/en/articles/7217328-crowdfunding-vs-equity-crowdfunding.

[12] The term crowdfunding is used on their page FAQ. See e.g. https://help.wefunder.com/#/investor/getting-started-for-investors (then click the question What is Wefunder?).

[13] The term crowdfunding is used on their page Investor-FAQ. See e.g. https://blogstartenginecom.kinsta.cloud/blog/regulation-a-what-entrepreneurs-need-to-know/.

is one of the largest and probably one of the most famous UK platforms in terms of equity-based crowdfunding; the UK has a very good reputation in terms of FinTech development in general and especially equity-based crowdfunding.[14] One difference in equity-crowdfunding campaign pages compared to reward-based crowdfunding pages is information about share price (it was 6.83 euros for Nich Mobility on July 17, 2025). Another difference is that equity-crowdfunding pages have a pre-money valuation of the project (for Nich Mobility it was 3,040,000 euros on July 17, 2025). This is crucial for potential investors as it provides an explanation for the value of their investments. This would not be too important in reward-based crowdfunding campaigns as the key information for investors is more related to the rewards and contribution-reward pairings.

The analysis of success factors of equity-based crowdfunding campaigns[15] is similar to that of reward-based crowdfunding campaigns, which we discussed previously.[16] Some of these factors are: providing regular updates (Block et al., 2018), third-party signals (Bapna, 2017), association with a venture capitalist support (Colombo & Shafi, 2025) and human capital attributes (Piva & Rossi-Lamastra, 2018). These are all consistent with the asymmetric information idea and direct signalling to mitigate the effects of asymmetric information. Further, the size of the target is negatively associated with the likelihood of success (see e.g. Vulkan et al., 2016; Wachira & Wachira, 2022).[17] Among factors that are unique to equity-based crowdfunding note, for example, the effect of the fraction of equity retained by entrepreneurs. A higher percentage of equity offered to investors implies a lower fraction remaining for the entrepreneur and vice versa. Usually, the literature finds an entrepreneur retaining a larger fraction of equity has a positive effect on the likelihood of the campaign's success (see e.g. Ralcheva & Roosenboom, 2020;

[14] Another large equity-based crowdfunding platform Seedrs (recently renamed to Republic Europe) is also UK-based.

[15] For a review of related literature (see e.g. Mochkabadi & Volkmann, 2018). Also See Signori and Vismara (2018) and Hornuf & Schmitt, (2016) for the analysis of equity-based crowdfunding campaign on firm after-campaign activities and performance.

[16] For more discussion on the differences between equity-based crowdfunding and traditional equity financing, see Coakley and Lazos (2021).

[17] To some extent, this is related to Ahlers et al. (2015) that finds that larger equity share offerings have a negative impact on the number of backers.

Vismara, 2016). This result is consistent with the spirit of the results regarding the size of the target on the campaign success since a lower target implies a higher equity fraction for the entrepreneur, other things being equal. Li et al. (2018) show that the minimum initial investment amount has a significant negative impact on financing efficiency. The minimum initial investment amount represents the investment threshold for investors wanting to invest in an equity-crowdfunding project. A lower minimum initial investment amount can reduce the investor's investment threshold and enable them to spread their own portfolio investment risk. This is consistent with the spirit of the idea that reducing bureaucracy may be a good factor for crowdfunding. In the past, investment in public equity has often been done by so-called large or accredited investors (see our earlier discussion on crowdfunding regulation; we will provide more discussion in Chapter 8). Li et al. (2018) also find that early investment affects the decision-making behaviour of investors later in the process via the herding effect (behavioural factors will be discussed in more detail in Chapter 5).

In addition, there has been a study that has analyzed different types of crowdfunding comparatively showing that smaller fundraising targets are better suited to reward-based campaigns, while larger funding targets are more dominant in equity crowdfunding (Belleflamme et al., 2014). Some research also finds that subsequent campaigns, by the same entrepreneurs, may have a higher probability of success than initial campaigns and that the size of these subsequent equity-based crowdfunding campaigns increases over time (see e.g. Ralcheva & Roosenboom, 2020). Li et al. (2018) find that a more mature project stage means greater willingness to invest by investors, indicating that projects in the profitable stage are more popular and favoured by investors. A larger team size also leads to a greater willingness to invest by investors.

2.2.2 Evaluating Shares

Organizing an equity-based crowdfunding campaign is to a large extent similar to the process of organizing a reward-based campaign except that the entrepreneur should decide on the fraction of equity offered to investors, which is in turn related to the problem of evaluating the value of the firm. Now let's talk about evaluation methods. In general, there exist several methods of evaluating a firm's equity (see e.g. Chastenet & Marion, 2015; Damodaran, 2009). The same holds for crowdfunding.

The different methods of valuation that can be used by firms conducting equity-based crowdfunding campaigns are discussed, for example, in Noopila (2019). The method we will describe in this section is consistent with the spirit of the other methods. The idea is that one estimates the firm's value sometime in the future and then makes a fair comparison of the estimated future return and today's investment. This is based on the traditional concept used in finance called the present value idea. This idea is contingent on using appropriate discount rates, which is usually quite challenging but as argued in Estrin et al. (2018), investors appear to understand and appropriately evaluate the risks that they are bearing.[18]

Summary of Steps.

- Estimate the firm's value by projecting the firm's profit at some point in the future and multiply by the P/E ratio for comparable firms

$$VX = \frac{P}{E} E_t$$

Here VX is the firm's value in the future; $\frac{P}{E}$ is the price earnings ratio that is calculated by dividing the price per share by earnings per share. One can use for example industry multiples; E_t is the firm's earnings estimation at time t. It can be based on the firm's business and financial projections; t is the period of time.

- Next find the present value of the firm's value VX

$$V = \frac{VX}{(1+r)^t}$$

where V is the firm's present value; r is the discount rate (or required rate of return)

- Next divide today's cash investment required by the firm's present value. This will be equal to the per cent ownership that needs to be sold in order to expect to provide the investor's target return

$$A = \frac{I}{V}$$

[18] Note that Hornuf and Neuenkirch (2017) analyze the factors of pricing in equity-based crowdfunding and argue that it can be very informative.

Here A is the requested percentage of ownership by the crowd (investors/ backers) and I is the amount of investment by the crowd.

- Finally, one can calculate the number of shares the firm has to issue and the share price:

$$n = \frac{m * A}{1 - A}$$

and $p = \frac{I}{n}$

Here m is the number of initial shares; n is the number of shares issued during the crowdfunding campaign and p is the share price.

Consider the following example. A firm is owned by an entrepreneur who holds 2000 shares. The firm plans to conduct an equity-based crowd-funding for its development and wants to raise \$1,000,000. To determine the number of shares offered during the campaign as well as the share price of the firm, the entrepreneur estimates the firm's income in 5 years to be \$1,000,000. Additional market research showed that potential backers expect a 50% annualized return and that similar firms have share prices of £20,000,000.

Solution. First estimate P/E. It equals \$20,000,000/ \$2,000,000 = 10. Next find A:

$$A = \frac{I}{\frac{\frac{P}{E} E_t}{(1+r)^t}} = \frac{1{,}000{,}000}{\frac{\frac{10}{1} 1{,}000{,}000}{(1+0.5)^5}} = 75.93\%$$

Next find n:

$$n = \frac{m * A}{1 - A} = \frac{2,000,000 * (0.759375)}{0.240625} = 6,311.688$$

And finally, p:

$$p = \frac{I}{n} = \frac{\$1,000,000}{6,311.688} = \$158.43622$$

One can use a similar procedure for subsequent campaigns as well. Firms can also mix equity-based crowdfunding with other ways of raising funds, including venture capital or angel financing.

2.3 Debt-Based Crowdfunding

In the case of debt-based crowdfunding an entrepreneurial firm (borrower) applies for a loan using a debt-based crowdfunding platform. Usually, the application is reviewed and then listed on the platform. Investors then decide to support the borrower or not. Similarly to other types of crowdfunding, the entrepreneurial firm is supported by a pool of investors. Under debt-based crowdfunding, investors make money from interest and the platform makes money by taking a percentage of the loan and a loan servicing fee.

The following table illustrates the differences between debt and equity, which will help us understand the differences between debt-based crowdfunding and equity-based crowdfunding (Table 2.5).

Table 2.5 Differences between debt and equity

Debt	*Equity*
– The return is usually known (fixed interest rate) – The maturity is usually known – Not an ownership interest – Creditors do not have voting rights – Interest is considered a cost of doing business and is tax deductible – Creditors have legal recourse if interest or principal payments are missed – Excess debt can lead to financial distress and bankruptcy	– The rate of return and the maturity are usually not fixed – Ownership interest – Common stockholders vote on the board of directors and other issues – Dividends are not considered a cost of doing business and are not tax deductible – Dividends are not a liability of the firm and stockholders have no legal recourse if dividends are not paid – An all-equity firm cannot go bankrupt

Let's discuss a couple of the differences indicated in the table starting with the fixed interest on debt. In the case of equity, a fixed interest rate is usually not promised by the issuer. This main difference between debt and equity holds true when comparing debt-based and equity-based crowdfunding.[19] The second important difference between debt and equity is that in the case of equity, investors usually get ownership rights and

[19] An interesting area of research is Islamic-based debt that has common features with both debt and equity and where fixed interests are usually prohibited. We discuss more regional aspects of crowdfunding in Chapter 8.

respectively voting rights in the firm. An interesting area in practice and research is the control rights of debtholders, where debtholders can influence decisions of the firm without formally having any ownership rights. Banks, for example, often play an important role in the financing of firms and as a result can receive seats on the Board of Directors and are often involved in what is called outside monitoring activities. You will not expect the same level of control rights from crowdloan holders since they are usually small and dispersed. This is however an interesting line for future developments. The third difference that is very important between debt and equity (at least on the level of large firms [corporations]) is the firm's ability to use interest on debt to reduce its corporate income tax by subtracting interest payments from firm profits. This is a common element of financial regulation around the world, particularly in developed countries. The same difference should be seen between debt and equity-based crowdfunding however, crowdfunding is not very often used by large corporations so to what extent this difference plays an important role remains an open question. In contrast, dividends on equity are not considered a cost of doing business and cannot be used to reduce a firm's profit for taxation purposes. The logic here is that since a firm is owned by its shareholders, the dividends are considered a firm objective rather than a cost.

2.3.1 Some History

Debt-based crowdfunding arose with the founding of Zopa in the UK in 2005 and with the launches of Lending Club and Prosper.com. in the USA in 2006. There are a variety of ways a debt-based crowdfunding platform can be organized and different platform even use different terminology like "peer-to-peer lending", "P2P", "marketplace lending", "crowdsourcing", "microfinance" and "crowdlending". In some cases, the platform is actively involved in the initial screening of borrowers (similar to a bank) e.g. Crowd2Fund—one of the largest platforms in the UK; in some cases the platform connects with a lending partner (e.g. Kiva) that may disburse/lend funds to a borrower upfront and provide other services. The terminology denoting the technology used on each platform can also be different including such terms as private placement memorandum, promissory note and unsecured loan. We also observe different ways in which interest rates are determined (e.g. auctions on Prosper) and different interest rate-related terminology (yield, effective yield etc.).[20] In general, the two key features of debt used on most crowdfunding platforms are one, interest rates are known (fixed) and two, loans are less secured than loans taken by large corporations. The latter is not related to the quality of platforms used but rather that large firms can use their assets as collateral which makes their loans much more secured than those taken by start-up entrepreneurial small firms, who do not have as many assets, especially tangible assets.

Prosper and LC closed in 2008 due to regulatory uncertainty and litigation. In 2008–2009, these platforms reopened after SEC registration. In 2012 and 2014, respectively, LC and Prosper became profitable and in 2014 LC went public. The size of the global debt-based (P2P) crowdfunding market is estimated at USD 4.38 billion in 2024 and is projected to reach USD 4.98 billion in 2025 and USD 14.02 billion by 2033.[21] Interestingly, in the beginning of the COVID-19 crisis some data showed an increase in debt-based crowdfunding. Some experts explain that a quick source of debt was a good option for many companies during that period.[22]

2.3.2 Comparing Debt-Based Crowdfunding and Traditional Debt

See Table 2.6.

Table 2.6 Differences between debt-based crowdfunding and traditional debt

Debt-based crowdfunding	*Traditional debt*
– Many small creditors with small pieces of the overall loan – No credit history required – No geographic barriers	– Usually one large creditor e.g. a commercial bank – Often credit history or a credit rating required – Credit providers (e.g. commercial banks) are often actively involved in firm monitoring

[20] See e.g. https://www.prosper.com/investor/glossary.

[21] https://www.businessresearchinsights.com/market-reports/debt-based-p2p-crowdfunding-market-104948.

[22] https://www.argaam.com/en/article/articledetail/id/1671143.

In contrast to traditional debt financing where the debtor usually faces one creditor such as, for example, a commercial bank, in the case of debt-based crowdfunding, there are multiple creditors, which creates a different dynamic in the case of financial distress.[23] The main advantage of debt-based crowdfunding compared to traditional debt is the smaller amount of bureaucracy involved and the ability to quickly reach a large number of potential investors around the world. The main advantage of traditional debt is that, unlike in crowdfunding, credit providers (e.g. commercial banks) are often actively involved in firm monitoring. This can be an advantage as entrepreneurs are often subject to moral hazard problems (see Chapter 4 for more discussions). Moral hazard also makes traditional debt costlier. Traditional debt is often not available to risky small firms due to the credit rationing idea (see e.g. Stiglitz & Weiss, 1981).

Even though crowdfunding platforms do not usually monitor borrowers like commercial banks do, they often conduct some screening of loans applications. They may look at a firm's financial plans for example. The UK's largest debt-based crowdfunding platform, Crowd2fund screen borrowers in great detail by looking at keywords and using lender partners. The platform Kiva also uses lending partners because they help with screening borrowers, providing quick fund disbursements, collecting repayments, and they also often provide business counselling, entrepreneurial training and literacy skills. Lending partners can also help with making payments, collecting payments from entrepreneurs and can be involved in educational activities for entrepreneurs, which many find to be extremely helpful.

2.3.3 Organizing a Debt-Based Crowdfunding Campaign

To a large extent organizing a debt-crowdfunding follows similar steps to organizing other types of crowdfunding campaigns. An important step is selecting an appropriate platform. Table 2.7 shows some popular platforms along with their countries of origin and some additional features.

Kiva is for example one of the largest debt-based crowdfunding platforms supporting entrepreneurs around the world. From their website: "…Kiva uses crowdfunded microloans as a force for good, creating a

[23] For an analysis of economics of debt-based crowdfunding see e.g. Milne and Parboteeah (2016).

Table 2.7 Debt-based crowdfunding platforms

Platform	*Features*	*Platform country of origin; website*
Kiva	Field partner-analysis; local expertise; relending; no fees for investors or borrowers	USA; https://www.kiva.org/
Prosper	Platform establishes borrower scores that affect their interest rates (previously used auctions)[24]; a minimum $25 investment for crowdloan participants; borrowers can apply for up to $50,000	USA; https://www.prosper.com/
Crowd2Fund	Also offer equity-based and donation-based crowdfunding services to entrepreneurs; due diligence team; credit risk indicator	UK; https://www.crowd2fund.com/
Lendosphere	No fees for investors; uses the ideas of community development	France; https://lendosphere.com/

24 Kräussl et al. (2025).

space where people can have one-to-one impact, and together, expand financial access for all…".[25] Interestingly, they use the term crowdfunded microloans, which confirms that debt-based crowdfunding generally use a variety of terms yet it does not change the meaning of the main idea. They argue on their website why debt-based crowdfunding should be used as opposed to traditional debt or donations/donation-based crowdfunding: "…If you needed to buy a delivery truck for your business, you probably wouldn't ask for donations; you'd apply for a loan. ….But what about the billion people without access to traditional finance? That's where you—and Kiva—come in. Kiva loans give people the power and resources to build the life they choose. By crowdfunding smaller amounts—called microloans—we can help more borrowers get funded…" Further, Kiva uses some interesting ideas including relending when lenders can use the same amount to participate in loans to different borrowers; using field partners for analyzing loan applications etc. "…Kiva partners with microfinance institutions, nonprofits, and other organizations to disburse loans in the communities we serve. We choose partners who have fair, non-predatory lending practices and prioritize social good…".[26]

Prosper is another popular platform. The approach they use is similar to debt-based crowdfunding. For example, they explain on their website: "…You can invest in small portions of a variety of loans…".[27] It implies that there is a group of lenders behind their loans. Further, they received the Best Peer-to-Peer Lending Platform 2024 Fintech Breakthrough Award.[28]

2.3.4 Bankruptcy, Organizational form and Debt-based Crowdfunding

The issue of potential bankruptcy, a situation when sales are not sufficient to cover the firm's debt, is directly related to a firm's decision to use crowdfunding especially debt-based crowdfunding since it affects the firm total amount of debt. Firms can be divided into two large groups depending on the scenario at hand: firms with unlimited liability

[25] https://www.kiva.org/about/how.

[26] https://www.kiva.org/about/how#why-loans.

[27] https://www.prosper.com/invest#sec-3.

[28] https://www.prosper.com/about.

(usually includes sole proprietorships and partnerships), where owners are not protected and may have to resort to selling their own assets to repay a debt and firms with limited liability (includes corporations and some types of partnerships) where owners' assets are protected.[29] So an interesting question is how should the entrepreneur optimally select the organizational form for their business taking into account potential bankruptcy costs associated with debt-based crowdfunding (it may also affect the choice of reward-based crowdfunding). In capital structure theory bankruptcy costs are a very important area that significantly determines the firm's choice between debt and equity. Similar considerations arise with regard to crowdfunding.

The second interesting issue connecting firm bankruptcy and crowdfunding is related to the growing evidence that firms use crowdfunding to help them solve their financial difficulties. For example, firms can use donation-based crowdfunding (we will discuss it in the next section) or reward-based crowdfunding (see e.g. Tamburro, 2017) to combat financial difficulties. It makes sense if crowdfunding has less bureaucracy and as a result has lower entry costs for firms in financial distress. There are several interesting questions here. For example, what is the seniority order. What place do crowdfunders hold in relation to other claimholders, which may include not only debt-based crowdfunding but also reward-based crowdfunding participants. In most cases, reward-based crowdfunders seem to be treated as non-secured debtholders.

2.4 Donation-Based Crowdfunding

Under donation-based crowdfunding the donor is not expected to give any rewards or financial returns to investors/donors. The motivation of backers is an interesting area of debate among theorists and practitioners. One idea is that backers are driven by so-called behavioural aspects like the idea of helping entrepreneurs in need and other philanthropic ideas. An example is Support your KWSymphony Musicians campaign organized on the GoFundMe platform.[30] This is also an example of firms in financial distress using crowdfunding, which, as mentioned previously, is a growing area of interest among theorists and practitioners. Another idea is that

[29] For more details see Miglo (2025).

[30] https://www.gofundme.com/f/support-your-kwsymphony-musicians.

investors can potentially benefit from the community benefits offered by donation-based crowdfunding campaigns/platforms.[31] An example is the football club campaign mentioned previously. Certain data shows that this type of crowdfunding is quite popular around the world (see e.g. Wade, 2023[32]). Literature on donation-based crowdfunding is not as numerous as literature on other types of crowdfunding but is growing (see e.g. Cason & Zubrickas, 2019).

2.4.1 *Comparing Donation-Based Crowdfunding and Traditional Donations*

We will compare donation-based crowdfunding to traditional donations in a similar manner to how we compared equity- and debt-based crowdfunding to traditional equity and debt financing. In practice, charities and social entrepreneurs/non-profit organizations face this choice between donation-based crowdfunding and traditional donations.[33] As found in Nesta's Crowdfunding Good Causes report, many charities are interested in learning and implementing crowdfunding. However, to our knowledge the choice between crowdfunding and traditional charity fundraising has not been extensively studied in the existing literature.[34] The early successes of crowdfunding in providing public goods Crowdfunding captured the attention of worldwide policy makers through its early success of providing public goods to communities (Belleflamme et al., 2013; Best et al., 2013).

Compared with traditional charitable fundraising strategies, donation-based crowdfunding provides a way for potential donors to reach people/groups in need of help without the constraints of physical distance/geographical reach. In practice, traditional charities as well as social

[31] There exists empirical evidence that donors in crowdfunding enjoy these types of "community" benefits (see e.g. Bone & Baeck, 2016; Boudreau et al., 2021; Chen et al., 2019; Zhao & Shneor, 2020). There are different ways of modellings. For example, one can assume that donors get some satisfaction if they donate the same amount as the previous donor (conformity effect in donation-based crowdfunding) se e.g. Sasaki (2019).

[32] See also https://doublethedonation.com/nonprofit-fundraising-statistics/.

[33] See e.g. https://charitydigital.org.uk/topics/topics/charities-should-do-more-to-tap-into-crowdfunding-potential-3974.

[34] For an empirical comparison of donation-based crowdfunding and traditional fundraising see e.g. Salido-Andrés et al. (2019).

entrepreneurs/non-profit organizations face this problem. Furthermore, donation-based crowdfunding usually has lower transaction costs and allows for better interactions with investors/donors. Both traditional charity fundraising and donation-based crowdfunding do not provide direct financial rewards. Donation-based crowdfunding campaigns typically use the AON feature, which means that if a sufficient amount of funds is not collected, contributions are returned to the donors (see e.g. Cason & Zubrickas, 2019). The all-or-nothing feature of crowdfunding (the refund bonuses in the case of donation-based crowdfunding) can improve campaign outcomes. Its main idea is to offer an additional refund bonus to people who agreed to contribute if the campaign fails. In other words, if the fundraising campaign misses the target, the contributors who offered funds are not only fully refunded but also receive additional bonuses. Donation-based crowdfunding campaign donors can usually observe the other donor contribution amounts. Participants of donation-based crowdfunding campaigns often enjoy additional benefits such as communication benefits.

Both traditional charity fundraising and donation-based crowdfunding represent methods of public good provisioning.[35] Multiple equilibria and free riding are typical problems in the provision of public goods. Argo et al. (2020) argue that the uncertainty around the firm/recipient's ability to collect the necessary amount of funds and/or private benefits from the fact of making a deciding contribution to the projects can improve the campaign outcome.

2.4.2 *Factors of Campaign Success*

In contrast to other types of crowdfunding, Alazazi et al. (2020) found that a larger campaign target positively contributed to the average number of donations as well as to individual donation size. They also find that longer campaign durations are associated with a lower amount of funds raised. The authors suggest that donors are less willing to fund campaigns that have received a large amount of contributions. This plays out in higher donor enthusiasm at the beginning of each fundraising campaign and lower contribution as donor enthusiasm wears off. As a result, the

[35] A public good is the opposite to a private good since its consumption is available to the public not only to private individuals. For more about public goods see McConnell et al. (2025).

average daily amount received decreases as a campaign continues (see also Burtch et al., 2013). Alazazi et al. (2020) also found that more social media presence does not significantly affect investor willingness to contribute but the number of likes on a campaign's social media post is positively associated with its success. Note also Zhang et al. (2020) who analyze the effect of behavioural factors on donation-based crowdfunding campaign success. Among other things, they find that platform trust, website reputation and information quality are important factors in campaign success.

2.4.3 Donation-Based Crowdfunding Platforms

Table 2.8 provides examples of crowdfunding platforms specializing in donation-based crowdfunding.

Table 2.8 Donation-based crowdfunding platforms

Platform	*Features*	*The platform country of origin; website*
GoFundMe	Trust and safety experts	USA; https://www.gofundme.com/
FundRazr	Crowdfunding advisors and implementation teams	Canada; https://fundrazr.com/
WhyDonate	Donor management dashboard	Netherlands; https://whydonate.com/

Donation-based crowdfunding requires special skills and an understanding of the types of people not looking for direct financial or physical rewards, and what types of projects attract those people. Platform creators put a lot of effort in providing a comfortable, trustworthy and high-quality on-line environment for investors/donors. Features may include, for example, creating a high efficiency donor management dashboard on the WhyDonate platform and the trust and safety team on Gofundme. Another example is FundrazR providing advanced tools for different types of campaigns including quickstart fundraising, peer-to-peer types, perks wishlist crowdfunding, microprojects and special website templates.

Questions and Exercises

1. Reward-based crowdfunding campaigns usually use a tiered system where the more you invest the better the reward you receive.
2. The following is usually not an advantage of reward-based crowdfunding:

   a. Exchange of comments with peers
   b. Feedback from backers
   c. Marketing tool for new products
   d. High risk of failure

3. Early crowdfunding dates back to the eighteenth century when writers were raising funds from many investors to help them write and publish.
4. KIA is used by Kickstarter—the largest crowdfunding platform in the world.
5. Decisions related to reward-based crowdfunding include all of the following except:

   a. Select KIA or AON
   b. Select the campaign target
   c. Select crowdfunding price
   d. Decide to create a video or not
   e. Determine the fraction of equity offered to backers
   f. Establish the percentage of ownership sold to backers

6. The following is not one of the factors that is usually considered important in crowdfunding, which affects the entrepreneur's decisions as well as the outcome of a reward-based crowdfunding campaign.

a. Network/community benefits
b. Learning market demand
c. Moral hazard
d. Information between investors and entrepreneurs is usually symmetric.

7. Based on the analysis of success factors what campaign is more likely to be successful:

Factor	*TallFan*	*Jonnybot*
Entrepreneur's prior experience	1[36]	0
Target	3,000	5,000
Risk information	1	0
Number of backers	309	17
Instagram	0	0
Facebook	1	0
Twitter	1	0
Type of crowdfunding	Reward	Reward
Type of campaign	AON	AON

8. Continue with the project from Chapter 1 #8. Add an additional 20 campaigns. Find the connection between the target and the likelihood of campaign success, and the connection between the presence of video and campaign success. Use excel.[37] Create a chart with the target on the x-axis and the success variable on the y-axis.
9. Describe and explain why reward-based crowdfunding is beneficial to entrepreneurs from the firm control point of view.
10. How common is fraud in reward-based crowdfunding markets?
11. A firm announced its crowdfunding campaign for developing a new type of computer. The campaign is organized on Kickstarter and the firm announced that it will have to raise at least $10,000 otherwise the funds will be returned back to the funders. The firm was able to get contributions from 300 backers with an average contribution of $30. What kind of financing was most likely used? Was it successful?
12. Under debt-based crowdfunding, businesses seeking financing apply through a platform uploading their pitch, with members of the crowd taking small chunks of the overall loan.

[36] In this table "1" means yes to the presence of the factor in the crowdfunding campaign and "0" stands for "No".

[37] The skills of deep knowledge of MS Excel prior to reading this book is not required. However, familiarity with the basics can help as it is the case for most finance related topics. For basics of MS Excel the reader can use Benninga & Mofkadi (2018) or check the Appendix of this chapter.

13. Under equity-based crowdfunding a platform does not formally make any investment decisions unlike traditional financial intermediaries but the platform provides technical support to entrepreneurs e.g. it is responsible for the documentation of the deal as well as the pass through of information to investors.
14. In the USA the SEC adopted rules pursuant to Title III of the JOBS Act that permit equity crowdfunding to be used by non-accredited investors.
15. Equity-based crowdfunding enables people to contribute to projects and receive a fixed interest in return.
16. Which of the following equity-based crowdfunding campaigns dilutes the ownership of founders?

    a. only the first campaign
    b. only the second campaign
    c. any campaign
    d. neither campaign

17. Kiva is a US-based equity-based crowdfunding platform.
18. Kiva uses lending partners because they help with screening borrowers, quick funds disbursement, collecting repayments and often business counselling, entrepreneurial training and literacy skills.
19. Under debt-based crowdfunding, loans are always well secured with borrower collateral.
20. Donation-based crowdfunding is a great opportunity to build support and enthusiasm both within your group and in the greater community.
21. Use the information below about two firms to analyze the following question: which campaign would rather select equity-based crowdfunding and which one would more likely select reward-based crowdfunding?

    a. XX is a special events organizing company. The founder mentioned that the idea of diluting his ownership is not very comfortable for him.
    b. YY produces equipment for electric vehicles. The founder thinks that it would be appealing to the wider community if people passionate about electric vehicles would be long-term partners of our firm.

22. Your start-up is considering raising money through equity crowd-funding. The goal is to raise £400,000 and you need to decide what share of the company you should sell. The crowdfunding platform charges a 2% fee that you are going to pay using the funders' investments. You forecast that the company will have a Net Income in year 5 of £1.8 million. A similar firm was recently sold for £28 million and had annual earnings of £2 million. The company currently has 1000 shares outstanding. Given the risk of failures in this industry, you promote that in the event of a successful outcome, investors should expect to receive a 30% rate of return. What share of the company should you offer to the crowd? How many shares should you offer to the backers, and what is the estimated share price?
23. Continue with previous question. How many shares would that offering comprise in an equity-crowdfunding campaign? What would be the appropriate price per share?
24. Discuss refund bonuses in donation-based crowdfunding.
25. (Excel) Consider the crowdfunding campaigns (AON) in the table below. Graphically illustrate the connection between the campaign target/goal and the likelihood of campaign success. Discuss. Find all factors that seem to be positively related to the campaign's success and illustrate graphically. Discuss. Which factor(s) seem(s) to have an ambiguous effect on the likelihood of success. Discuss.

Project	*Percentage of reached goal*	*Com ments*	*Risk infor mation*	*Pic ture*	*Upd ates*	*Goal*	*Video*	*Prior experience (number of prior campaigns)*
Simple LED tester	1050%	82	1	1	8	450	1	3
TurtlTeck	835%	7	1	1	22	1000	1	2
The 3 faces of Flowza	865%	170	1	1	9	1600	1	1
The fume Fan—oldering Fume Extractor	513%	86	1	1	11	3000	1	1

(continued)

(continued)

Project	*Percentage of reached goal*	*Com ments*	*Risk infor mation*	*Pic ture*	*Upd ates*	*Goal*	*Video*	*Prior experience (number of prior campaigns)*
Low-cost open-source arsenic detector for drinking water	36%	120	1	0	4	3000	0	0
Globe—See through the Earth	7%	52	1	1	3	3600	0	0

Appendix 2.1. About Microsoft Excel

Over the last 25–30 years finance professors have been actively using Microsoft Excel in the classroom to help students make calculations involving present and future values and related problems. For a good reference, see Benninga & Mofkadi (2018). Using Excel helps with crowdfunding related problems including numerical problems or problems involving data analysis. The knowledge of such aspects of Excel as Creating formulas, basic functions including NPV, SUM etc. can help with many questions. Below is an example of calculating the percentage of equity that an entrepreneur should issue during an equity-based crowdfunding campaign. The theory was discussed in Sect. 2.2.

Table A.2.1 shows an Excel worksheet used to solve this problem. Each cell in the table has its "address" that consists of a column letter and a row number. Cells A1:B8 contain the initial information about the firm and other useful information. Calculations are made in cells B10:B14. Some formulas used for calculations are shown in cells D10:D14. Cells D10 and D11 show the calculations of the total value of funds needed including the platform fee. Cell D12 contains the formula to evaluate the firm's expected value in 5 years; cell D13 shows the calculation of the firm's present (current) value, and cell D14 shows the calculation of the percentage of equity that should be issued.

Table A.2.1 Calculating the value of equities under equity-based crowdfunding

	A	*B*	*C*	*D*
1	Number of shares held by founders	1,000		
2	New investment required (from the crowd)	400,000		
3	Platform fee	2%		
4	Exit (horizon) time	5		
5	Required rate of return	0.3		
6	Firm annual income per year @ exit	1,800,000		
7	Similar firm sold for	28,000,000		
8	Similar firm income for last year	2,000,000		
9				
10	Platform fee, $	8,000		= C3*C4
11	Total investment	408,000		= C3 + C11
12	Firm future value	25,200,000		= C8/C9*C7
13	Present value	6,787,092.67		= C13/(1 + C6)^C5
14	Issued %	0.0589354		= C3/C14

Below is an example of finding the value of a debt-based crowdfunding related investment solved using Excel.

A funder participates in a debt-based crowdfunding campaign. The total value of the crowdloan is 50,000. The funder's fraction in this loan is 10%. The interest rate is 7% and the maturity is 10 years. However, the funder made his/her own forecast of future market interest rates as indicated and wants to know if the investment is worth it. The funder makes an estimation of the present value of future expected payments using market rates and compares it with the initial investment.

Table A.2.2 shows an Excel worksheet used to solve the above problem. Cells A1:B8 contain initial information about the loan, the funder's fraction of the loan and the interest rates. Calculations are made starting at line 10. Some formulas used for calculations are shown in the cells in column E and also in cell C23. For example, cell B23 (formula displayed in cell C23) contains the present value of future payments using the interest rate 7% and uses the Excel function NPV which calculates the present value of a stream of payments.

Table A.2.2 Excel worksheet

	A	B	C	D	E
1	Interest rate	7%			
2	Total value of crowdloan	50,000			
3	fraction of the funder	10%			
4	Loan maturity (years)	10			
5	Expected market interest rate				
6	Year 1–3	7%			
7	Year 4–6	10%			
8	Year 7–10	6.80%			
9					
10	Value of funder investment	5000			
11					
12	Year	Payment	Expected market interest rate	PV	
13	1	350	7%	327.102804	= C14/(1 + D14)^B14
14	2	350	7%	305.703555	= C15/(1 + D15)^B15
15	3	350	7%	285.704257	= C16/(1 + D16)^B16
16	4	350	10%	239.054709	= C17/(1 + D17)^B17
17	5	350	10%	217.322463	= C18/(1 + D18)^B18
18	6	350	10%	197.565876	= C19/(1 + D19)^B19
19	7	350	7%	220.835697	= C20/(1 + D20)^B20
20	8	350	7%	206.774997	= C21/(1 + D21)^B21
21	9	350	7%	193.609548	= C22/(1 + D22)^B22
22	10	5,350	7%	2771.03018	= C23/(1 + D23)^B23
23	PV of future payments using current rate (7%)	5,000	= NPV(C2,C14:C23)		

(continued)

Table A.2.2 (continued)

	A	*B*	*C*	*D*	*E*
24	PV of future payments using market rates			4964.70408	= SUM(E14:E23)
25					

References

Ahlers, G., Cumming, D., Günther, C., & Schweizer, D. (2015). Signaling in equity crowdfunding. *Entrepreneurship Theory and Practice, 39*(4), 955–980.

Alazazi, M., Wang, B., & Allan, T. (2020). Success factors of donation-based crowdfunding campaigns: A machine learning approach. *Proceedings of the 53rd Hawaii International Conference on System Sciences*. https://scholarspace.manoa.hawaii.edu/server/api/core/bitstreams/57db49a1-b730-444b-96f2-10710a86ba91/content

Argo, N., Klinowski, D., Krishnamurti, T., & Smith, S. (2020). The completion effect in charitable crowdfunding. *Journal of Economic Behavior & Organization, 172*, 17–32.

Bapna, S. (2017). Complementarity of signals in early-stage equity investment decisions: Evidence from a randomized field experiment. *Management Science, 65*(2), 933–952.

Belleflamme, P., Lambert, T., & Schwienbacher, A. (2013). Individual crowdfunding practices. *Venture Capital: An International Journal of Entrepreneurial Finance, 15*(4), 313–333.

Belleflamme, P., Lambert, T., & Schwienbacher, A. (2014). Crowdfunding: Tapping the right crowd. *Journal of Business Venturing, 29*(5), 585–609.

Benninga, S., & Mofkadi, T. (2018). *Principles of finance with excel* (Vol. 3). Oxford University Press.

Best, J., Lambkin, A., Neiss, S., Raymond, S., & Swart, R. (2013). *Crowdfunding's potential for the developing world (English)*. InfoDev and World Bank Group. http://documents.worldbank.org/curated/en/409841468327411701

Block, J., Hornuf, L., & Moritz, A. (2018). Which updates during an equity crowdfunding campaign increase crowd participation? *Small Business Economics, 50*(1), 3–27.

Bone, J., & Baeck, P. (2016). Crowdfunding good causes. *Nesta (Issue June)*, 1–51. Retrieved March 2, 2016 from www.nesta.org.uk

Borrero-Domínguez, C., Cordón-Lagares, E., & Hernández-Garrido, R. (2020). Analysis of success factors in crowdfunding projects based on rewards: A way to obtain financing for socially committed projects. *Heliyon, 6*, Article e03744. https://doi.org/10.1016/j.heliyon.2020.e03744

Boudreau, K. J., Jeppesen, L. B., Reichstein, T., & Rullani, F. (2021). Crowdfunding as donations to entrepreneurial firms. *Research Policy, 50*(7), Article 104264.

Burtch, G., Ghose, A., & Wattal, S. (2013). An empirical examination of the antecedents and consequences of contribution patterns in crowd-funded markets. *Information Systems Research, 24*(3), 499–519.

Calic, G., & Mosakowski, E. (2016). Kicking off social entrepreneurship: How a sustainability orientation influences crowdfunding success. *Journal of Management Studies, 53*(5), 738–767. https://doi.org/10.1111/joms.12201

Cason, T., & Zubrickas, R. (2019). Donation-based crowdfunding with refund bonuses. *European Economic Review, 119*, 452–471.

Chakraborty, S., & Swinney, R. (2020). Signalling to the crowd: Private quality information and rewards-based crowdfunding. *Manufacturing and Service Operations Management, 23*(1), 155–169.

Chastenet, E., & Marion, A. (2015). Valuation using industry multiples: How to choose the most relevant multiples. *Business Valuation Review, 34*(4), 173–183.

Chen, Y., Dai, R., Yao, J., & Li, Y. (2019). Donate time or money? The determinants of donation intention in online crowdfunding. *Sustainability, 11*(16), 4269.

Coakley, J., & Lazos, A. (2021). New developments in equity crowdfunding: A review. *Review of Corporate Finance, 1*(3–4), 341–405.

Colombo, M. G., Franzoni, C., & Rossi-Lamastra, C. (2015). Internal social capital and the attraction of early contributions in crowdfunding. *Entrepreneurship Theory and Practice, 39*(1), 75–100.

Colombo, M. G., & Shafi, K. (2025). Firms' venture capital affiliation, platforms' "skin in the game" and the success of equity crowdfunding campaigns. *Journal of Industrial and Business Economics*. https://doi.org/10.1007/s40812-025-00350-7

Cordova, J., & Dolci, G. (2015). The determinants of crowdfunding success: Evidence from technology projects. *Procedia—Social and Behavioral Sciences, 181*, 115–124.

Courtney, C., Dutta, S., & Li, Y. (2016). Resolving information asymmetries: Influence of media and crowd sentiment on crowdfunding success. *Academy of Management Proceedings, 14663*. https://doi.org/10.5465/AMBPP.2016.14663abstract

Cumming, D., Leboeuf, G., & Schwienbacher, A. (2020). Crowdfunding models: Keep-it-all versus all or nothing. *Financial Management, 49*, 331–360.

Damodaran, A. (2009). *Valuing young, start-up and growth companies: Estimation issues and valuation challenges*. Available at SSRN: https://ssrn.com/abstract=1418687

Estrin, S., Gozman, D., & Khavul, S. (2018). The evolution and adoption of equity crowdfunding: Entrepreneur and investor entry into a new market. *Small Business Economics, 51*(2), 425–439.

Felipe, I., Mendes-da-Silva, W., Leal, C. C., & Santos, D. (2022). Reward crowdfunding campaigns: Time-to-success analysis. *Journal of Business Research, 138*, 214–228.

Galuszka, P., & Brzozowska, B. (2016). Crowdfunding and the democratization of the music market. *Media, Culture & Society, 39*(6), 833–849. https://doi.org/10.1177/0163443716674364

Granovetter, M. (1983). The strength of weak ties: A network theory revisited. *Sociological Theory, 1*, 201–233.

Greenberg, M., & Gerber, E. (2014). Learning to fail: Experiencing public failure online through crowdfunding. *Proceedings of the SIGCHI Conference on Human Factors in Computing Systems* (pp. 581–590).

Härkönen, J. (2014). *Crowdfunding and its utilization for startup finance in Finland–Factors of a successful campaign*. Lappeenranta University of Technology, School of Business. https://lutpub.lut.fi/handle/10024/96798

He, H., Bai, Y., & Xiao, X. (2020). How past failure predicts subsequent entrepreneurial intention: A comparative study of mainland China and Taiwan. *Sustainability, 12*(6), 2331.

Hornuf, L., & Neuenkirch, M. (2017). Pricing shares in equity crowdfunding. *Small Business Economics, 48*(4), 795–811.

Hornuf, L., & Schmitt, M. (2016). Success and failure in equity crowdfunding. *Cesifo DICE Report, 14*(2), 16–22.

Huang, S., Pickernell, D. G., Battisti, M., & Nguyen, T. (2022). Signalling entrepreneurs' credibility and project quality for crowdfunding success: Cases from the Kickstarter and Indiegogo environments. *Small Business Economics, 58*, 1801–1821.

Janků, J., & Kučerová, Z. (2018). Successful crowdfunding campaigns: The role of project specifics, competition and founders' experience. *Finance a Uver, 68*, 351–373.

Josefy, M., Dean, T. J., Albert, L. S., & Fitza, M. A. (2016). The role of community in crowdfunding success: Evidence on cultural attributes in funding campaigns to "save the local theater." *Entrepreneurship Theory and Practice, 41*(2), 161–182.

Kim, K., Park, J., Pan, Y., Zhang, K., & Zhang, X. (2022). Risk disclosure in crowdfunding. *Information Systems Research, 33*(3), 1023–1041.

Koch, J.-A., & Siering, M. (2015). Crowdfunding success factors: The characteristics of successfully funded projects on crowdfunding platforms. *Proceedings of the 23rd European Conference on Information Systems (ECIS 2015)*. Muenster, Germany. Available at SSRN: https://ssrn.com/abstract=2808424

Koch, J.-A., & Siering, M. (2019). The recipe of successful crowdfunding campaigns An analysis of crowdfunding success factors and their interrelations. *Electronic Markets, 29*, 661–679.

Kräussl, R., Kräussl, Z., Pollet, J. M., & Rinne, K. (2025). The Performance of Prosper Marketplace Lending Platform: Evidence from Proprietary Payment Data. *Available at SSRN 5098048.*

Lagazio, C., & Querci, F. (2018). Exploring the multi-sided nature of crowdfunding campaign success. *Journal of Business Research, 90*, 318–324.

Li, Y., Cao, H., & Zhao, T. (2018). Factors affecting successful equity crowdfunding. *Journal of Mathematical Finance, 8*(2), 446.

Liu, Y., Chen, Y., & Fan, Z. P. (2021). Do social network crowds help fundraising campaigns? Effects of social influence on crowdfunding performance. *Journal of Business Research, 122*, 97–108.

Lui, S. S., Zhu, Z., Liu, J. (2023). Success of crowdfunding: A trust-worthiness perspective. *Asia Pacific Journal of Management, 40*(2), 681–706.

McConnell, C. R., Flynn, S. M., Brue, S. L., Barbiero, T., & Eslami, K. (2025). *Microeconomics* (17th ed.). McGraw Hill.

Meer, J. (2014). Effects of the price of charitable giving: Evidence from an online crowdfunding platform. *Journal of Economic Behavior & Organization, 103*, 113–124.

Miglo, A. (2021). Crowdfunding under market feedback, asymmetric information and overconfident entrepreneur. *Entrepreneurship Research Journal, 11*(4), 20190018.

Miglo, A. (2025). *Capital structure in the modern world* (2nd ed.). Palgrave.

Milne, A., & Parboteeah, P. (2016, May). *The business models and economics of peer-to-peer lending* (ECRI Research Report No 17).

Mochkabadi, K., & Volkmann, C. (2018). Equity crowdfunding: A systematic review of the literature. *Small Business Economics, 54*(1), 75–118. https://doi.org/10.1007/s11187-018-0081-x

Mollick, E. R. (2014). The dynamics of crowdfunding: An exploratory study. *Journal of Business Venturing, 29*(1), 1–16.

Noopila, T. (2019). *The role of valuation in equity crowdfunding*. https://aaltodoc.aalto.fi/items/06b6a07d-bf7e-4940-9f5d-ab11e29e8e75

Paakkarinen, P. (2016). *Success factors in reward based and equity based crowdfunding in Finland*. https://core.ac.uk/download/pdf/80719599.pdf

Piva, E., & Rossi-Lamastra, C. (2018). Human capital signals and entrepreneurs' success in equity crowdfunding. *Small Business Economics, 51*(3), 667–686.

Ralcheva, A., & Roosenboom, P. (2020). Forecasting success in equity crowdfunding. *Small Business Economics, 55*, 39–56.

Salido Andrés, N., Rey García, M., Álvarez González, L. I., & Vázquez Casielles, R. (2019). Determinants of success of donation-based crowdfunding through digital platforms: The influence of offline factors. *Ciriec-España Revista De Economía Pública Social Y Cooperativa, 95*, 119–141.

Sasaki, S. (2019). Majority size and conformity behavior in charitable giving: Field evidence from a donation-based crowdfunding platform in Japan. *Journal of Economic Psychology, 70*, 36–51.

Signori, A., & Vismara, S. (2018). Does success bring success? The post-offering lives of equity-crowdfunded firms. *Journal of Corporate Finance, 50*, 575–591.

Skirnevskiy, V., Bendig, D., & Brettel, M. (2017). The influence of internal social capital on serial creators' success in crowdfunding. *Entrepreneurship Theory and Practice, 41*(2), 209–236.

Song, Y., Dana, L. P., & Berger, R. (2021). The entrepreneurial process and online social networks: Forecasting survival rate. *Small Business Economics, 56*, 1171–1190.

Stiglitz, J. E., & Weiss, A. (1981). Credit rationing in markets with imperfect information. *The American Economic Review, 71*(3), 393–410.

Tamburro, A. (2017). Far from the madding crowd: Crowdfunding a small business reorganization. *Emory Bankruptcy Developments Journal, 34*, 521.

Vismara, S. (2016). Equity retention and social network theory in equity crowdfunding. *Small Business Economics, 46*(4), 579–590.

Vulkan, N., Åstebro, T., & Sierra, M. F. (2016). Equity crowdfunding: A new phenomena. *Journal of Business Venturing Insights, 5*, 37–49.

Wachira, V. K., & Wachira, E. W. (2022). Equity based crowdfunding—Determinants of successful campaign: The case of crowdcube platform in the United Kingdom. *Public Finance Quarterly= Pénzügyi Szemle, 67*(1), 130–149.

Wade, M. (2023). 'The giving layer of the internet': A critical history of GoFundMe's reputation management, platform governance and communication strategies in capturing peer-to-peer and charitable giving markets. *Journal of Philanthropy and Marketing, 28*(4), Article e1777.

Zhang, Y., Tan, C. D., Sun, J., & Yang, Z. (2020). Why do people patronize donation-based crowdfunding platforms? An activity perspective of critical success factors. *Computers in Human Behavior, 112*, Article 106470.

Zhao, L., & Shneor, R. (2020). Donation crowdfunding: Principles and donor behaviour. In *Advances in crowdfunding: Research and practice* (pp. 145–160). Springer International Publishing.

Zhao, Y., Harris, P., & Lam, W. (2019). Crowdfunding industry—History, development, policies, and potential issues. *Journal of Public Affairs, 19*(1). https://doi.org/10.1002/pa.1921.

Zheng, H., Li, D., Wu, J., & Xu, Y. (2014). The role of multidimensional social capital in crowdfunding: A comparative study in China and US.

Information & Management, 51(4), https://doi.org/10.1016/j.im.2014.03.003.

Zhou, M., Lu, B., Fan, W., & Wang, G. A. (2018). Project description and crowdfunding success: An exploratory study. *Information Systems Frontiers, 20*(2), 259–274.

Zvilichovsky, D., Inbar, Y., & Barzilay, O. (2013). Playing both sides of the market: Success and reciprocity on crowdfunding platforms. In *International Conference on Information Systems (ICIS 2013)*.

CHAPTER 3

Crowdfunding, Learning "Crowd Wisdom" and Signalling

3.1 Two Brilliant Ideas

This chapter considers two of the main ideas of crowdfunding: *learning market demand and signalling*. Learning market demand means that firms can use crowdfunding campaigns (or some stages of the crowdfunding process) to learn information ("crowd wisdom") about the market (Catalini & Gans, 2018; Chemla & Tinn, 2019; Ellman & Hurkens, 2019; Miglo, 2021b; Schwienbacher, 2018; Strausz, 2017). Learning can take different forms. Firms can learn from observing pre-orders under reward-based crowdfunding, by observing the share price under equity-based crowdfunding, by observing the results of the crowdfunding campaigns of their competitors, and by receiving direct feedback from market participants. With reward-based crowdfunding, if a firm uses an AON campaign, the campaign self-screens in the sense that if the demand for the product is too low, the target is not reached and no funds are raised. In this case, according to most platform rules, the campaign will be cancelled and money will be returned to investors. The advantage

Supplementary Information The online version contains supplementary material available at https://doi.org/10.1007/978-3-032-10724-4_3.

© The Author(s), under exclusive license to Springer Nature Switzerland AG 2026

A. Miglo and V. Miglo, *The Theories and Developments of Crowdfunding*, https://doi.org/10.1007/978-3-032-10724-4_3

of this scenario for firms is that it minimizes the entrepreneur's potential losses/damages if demand for the product is low. These losses could potentially be very large if a firm continues to develop and produce a product or service whose demand is low. Similar opportunities do not typically exist under traditional financing methods, like bank financing for example. Martin Källström, CEO of Memoto, a company that used Kickstarter to conduct a crowdfunding campaign, argues that one the most important objective of a crowdfunding campaign is to get feedback from market participants. He said[1]: "..Crowdfunding is the perfect entrepreneurial launch tool – for us it meant an opportunity to do a market estimation (or at least validate product demand)".

Signalling project quality using crowdfunding is another interesting idea. The projects of innovative firms and small- and medium- sized firms are in most cases projects with a very high degree of uncertainty regarding their quality. Unlike large established firms, these firms or products do not have large media or analyst coverage. In these conditions firms try to signal their quality. This can be done directly by explaining the quality of their projects on a company website or a crowdfunding campaign webpage or it can be done indirectly by undertaking some actions that can be interpreted as credible signals of their quality (Chakraborty & Swinney, 2020; Kim et al., 2022; Miglo & Miglo, 2019; Sayedi & Baghaie, 2017). Firms can use different tools and ideas for signalling including an appropriate choice and design of their financing method. This includes the choice between traditional and new financing methods, the choice between different types of crowdfunding, and the choice of a campaign target.

3.2 Learning Market Demand

This section discusses learning market demand and its implications. The following model illustrates the point.[2] Consider a firm with an innovative product or service. The expected market price of the product is p. The required investment to start production is B. The entrepreneur has sufficient funds to cover this cost but is considering different financing

[1] https://djksar.wordpress.com/2012/11/14/kickstarter-campaigns-interview-with-martin-kallstrom-ceo-of-memoto/.

[2] In the spirit of Miglo (2020).

strategies. Assume that the operating cost of production is negligibly small.[3] The demand for the product is Q and is unknown to the entrepreneur. The firm can also use a crowdfunding campaign (the product price during the campaign is p_c i.e. a backer contributes an amount p_c during the campaign and the firm promises to deliver the firm's future product as a reward). Suppose that the cost of using crowdfunding (the crowdfunding platform fee) is f and that the discounting and waiting costs are negligibly small. The latter implies that potential consumer/backers would be interested in purchasing the product during the crowdfunding campaign as long as crowdfunding price is lower than the expected market price and vice versa.

Without crowdfunding, the entrepreneur's net profit is

$$Qp - B \tag{3.1}$$

Here Qp is the firm's revenue and B is the cost. The problem is that if Q is relatively small, more specifically if $Q < B/p$, the entrepreneur sustains losses. Now suppose that the firm conducts a crowdfunding (reward-based crowdfunding) campaign using AON with a target B and a crowdfunding price p_c that is slightly lower than p i.e. the crowdfunding price is lower than the expected market price of the product. Let $p_c = p - \varepsilon, \varepsilon > 0$. In this case, all consumers are interested in participating in crowdfunding because the crowdfunding price is smaller than the expected market price of the product. Two scenarios are possible. (1) $Q < B/(p - \varepsilon)$. Then the target will not be achieved, the campaign will be cancelled, and the entrepreneur's net profit is $-f$. (2) $Q \geq B/(p - \varepsilon)$. . Then the campaign is successful and the entrepreneur will collect funds, start production and deliver rewards (products) to funders. The entrepreneur's net profit in this case is $Q(p - \varepsilon) - B - f$.

Let us now compare the entrepreneur's results with and without crowdfunding. First note that in the scenario $Q < B/(p - \varepsilon)$ if f is sufficiently small (which is usually the case), the entrepreneur definitely benefits from the advantages of crowdfunding as it provides that the demand is not sufficiently high and it is not worth going ahead with

[3] Such an assumption is not crucial for the conclusions but simplifies the analysis. Also note that it is not an unusual assumption in crowdfunding models. Consider for example a firm developing an innovative internet app. The amount of one-time cost (writing codes, creating technology, registering patent etc.) is typically much higher than costs related to selling the app online for example.

production. In the scenario $Q \geq B/(p - \varepsilon)$ the entrepreneur's profit is slightly lower under crowdfunding however, again assuming that f and ε are negliageably small, the difference between the profits with and without crowdfunding is negligibly small.

More formally, suppose P_1 is the probability that $Q < B/p$, P_2 is the probability that $B/p \leq Q < B/(p - \varepsilon)$ and P_3 is the probability that $Q \geq B/(p - \varepsilon)$. Then the entrepreneur expected profit under the "no-crowdfunding" strategy is $EQp - B$, where EQ is the expected value of Q. It means that the firm will invest B and the expected revenues are EQp. With crowdfunding the firm's expected profit is

$$-f(P_1 + P_2) + P_3(EQ_3(p - \varepsilon) - B - f) = P_3(EQ_3(p - \varepsilon) - B) - f \tag{3.2}$$

where EQ_3 is the expected demand when $Q \geq B/(p-\varepsilon)$. This is because $Q < B/(p - \varepsilon)$, the crowdfunding campaign will not collect sufficient funds and the entrepreneur sustains a loss f. And if $Q \geq B/(p - \varepsilon)$, the firm's profit is $P_3(EQ_3(p - \varepsilon) - B - f)$.

Proposition 3.1 *If ε and f are sufficiently small, crowdfunding provides a higher payoff for the entrepreneur.*

Proof Without crowdfunding the firm expected profit is

$$(P_1EQ_1 + P_2EQ_2 + P_3EQ_3)p - B \tag{3.3}$$

where EQ_1 is the expected demand when $Q < B/(p-\varepsilon)$ and EQ_2 is the expected demand when $\frac{B}{p} \leq Q < \frac{B}{p-\varepsilon}$. The difference between (3.3) and (3.2) is

$$P_1(EQ_1p - B) + P_2(EQ_2p - B) + P_3EQ_3\varepsilon + f \tag{3.4}$$

Now consider the extreme case $\varepsilon = f = 0$. Then $P_2 = 0$ and (3.4) is equal to $P_1(EQ_1p - B)$ which is strictly negative because $EQ_1 < B/p$ so the profit under crowdfunding is higher and by the continuity of (3.4) it is also negative when ε and f are sufficiently small.

The above analysis has several implications. First, it justifies the usage of crowdfunding in some conditions like in the presence of demand uncertainty. Secondly, suppose that $\varepsilon = 0$ i.e. no discounting/waiting cost is negligibly small. Note that this implies $P_2 = 0$. Then (3.4) equals $P_1(EQ_1p - B) + f$. The likelihood that this expression is negative increases with P_1 (given that $EQ_1p < B$) and also decreases with EQ_1. Recall that if (3.4) is negative it means that crowdfunding should be used. A possible interpretation of an increase in P_1 and a decrease in EQ_1 is an increase in the extent of demand uncertainty. Indeed P_1 is the probbalility that the demand is very low. In a sense if $P_1 = 0$ there is no big problem for an entrepreneur since at least the demand is sufficiently high to run the firm profitably. A higher P_1 means a higher likelihood of troubles related to demand uncertainty (similar logic applies to a decrease in EQ_1). A possible implication of this analysis is that crowdfunding should be used when the degree of demand uncertainty increases.[4] This is intuitive, for example, if there is no demand uncertainty at all and the entrepreneur knows for sure the demand level for his/her firm's products, then there is no need to use crowdfunding! This scenario is quite unrealistic of course!

Further (3.4) is positive only if f is relatively small. If we assume that platform fees are positively related to the size of the campaign then this result leads to the prediction that crowdfunding should be the preferred strategy for relatively small investment projects.

In Chemla and Tinn (2019), entrepreneurs receive information about their projects when conducting a reward-based crowdfunding campaign. They observe the demand from a sample of backers. Chemla and Tinn (2019) suggest that a higher degree of uncertainty is positively correlated with the benefits of crowdfunding. They discuss some data that supports their conclusion by comparing technology firms (with a higher degree of demand uncertainty) and theatre firms. Further, a smaller campaign size (they equate this to a shorter campaign duration) is associated with a higher probability of crowdfunding success and, as such, is positively correlated with the attractiveness of crowdfunding. These predictions are consistent with the spirit of the findings in Xu (2017) and Mollick (2014).

Schwienbacher (2018) studies the uncertainty of market demand. Reward-based crowdfunding provides valuable information as during these campaigns entrepreneurs base their decisions on the overall profitability of the project and not on consumption, as it would be under

[4] Note that this is quite an important point in general and will be used in different settings and with different modifications throughout the book.

traditional financing. Schwienbacher (2018) also finds that crowdfunding is more likely when demand uncertainty is higher.[5]

3.3 Asymmetric Information Problem and Crowdfunding

Imperfect information problems have been long recognized as an important issue in crowdfunding. The main reason is that investors do not have complete information about firms conducting crowdfunding and their projects (see e.g. Ahlers et al., 2015; Belleflamme et al., 2014; Chakraborty & Swinney, 2020; Hildebrand et al. 2017; Miglo & Miglo, 2019; Vismara, 2016). Further, the degree of campaign failure is very high in crowdfunding. Many of these failures are related to the inability of entrepreneurs to provide sufficient information about their projects' qualities and respectively about potential problems and risks in a convincing fashion in order to attract potential funders.

Early empirical papers on crowdfunding discovered that reward-based crowdfunding is subject to imperfect information and that mitigating this problem contributes to the success of projects (e.g. Mollick, 2014). Crowdfunding success appears to be linked to project quality, in that projects that signal a higher quality level are more likely to be funded. Ahlers et al. (2015) find similar results in equity-based crowdfunding. Other papers considering similar issues include Hildebrand et al. (2017), Block et al. (2018), Piva and Rossi-Lamastra (2018) and Vismara (2016).

Theoretical literature then started to create and analyse different models of crowdfunding to analyse the ways in which firms can mitigate asymmetric information problems using both direct and indirect methods and began making suggestions about the implications of asymmetric information. One of the most significant areas of discussion is the exact nature of asymmetric information, i.e. what aspects of entrepreneurial activities are subject to a high degree of asymmetric information and what is the extent of the impact of asymmetric information on crowdfunding as compared to other financing methods that are also affected by asymmetric information. Figure 3.1 illustrates the different types of asymmetric information that take place in theory and in the practice of crowdfunding.

[5] Other notable works that are related to learning market demand idea include Ellman and Hurkens (2019), Chen et al. (2018) and Sahm (2019).

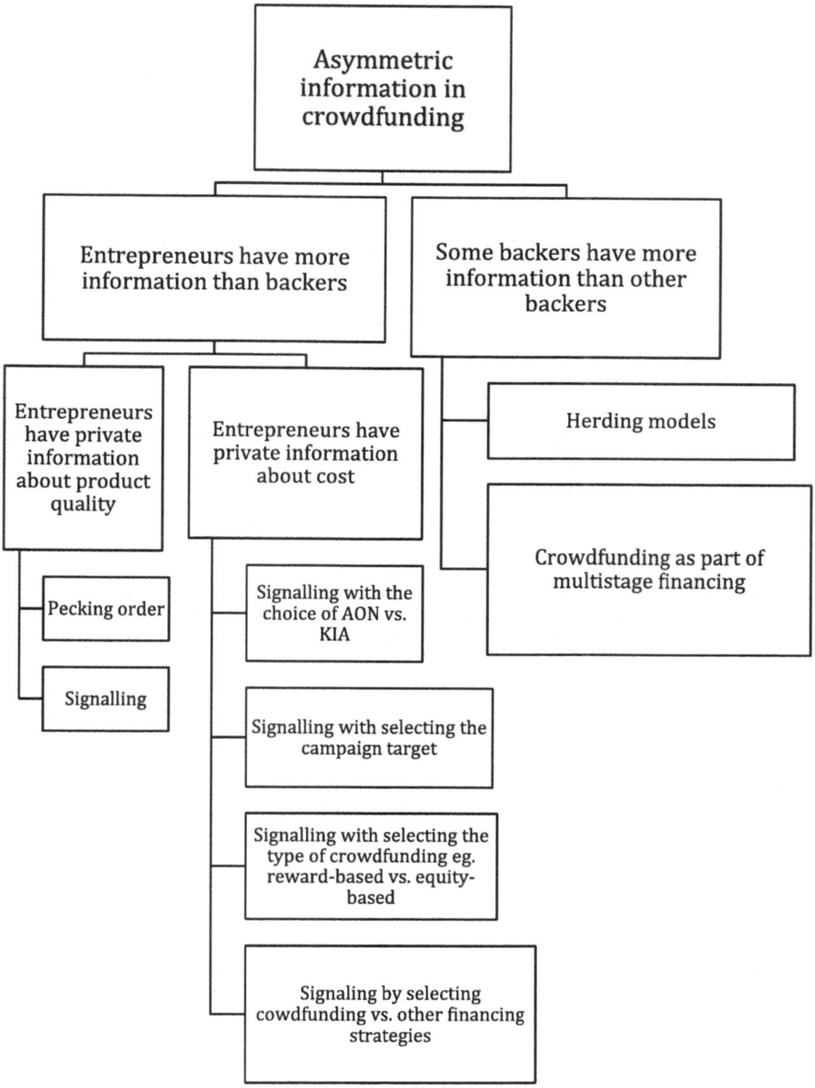

Fig. 3.1 Asymmetric information in crowdfunding

A possible scenario under crowdfunding is when firm founders have more information than backers. This scenario is very intuitive given the nature of most firm products (innovative) and the type of firms using crowdfunding (small, entrepreneurial). As discussed before, the public does not have the same amount of information about these firms as they do about large public firms.

A possible problem in this scenario is that potential funders are hesitant to invest in projects, even high-quality projects. Researchers and practitioners working in this area actively try to find ideas on what founders should do to mitigate the effects of imperfect information.[6] There are two approaches to how this can be done. One is based on the idea that firms can try to eliminate asymmetric information between them and their backers by communicating to the public the description of their activities and new projects, publishing information, providing regular updates etc. This will be referred to as direct signalling (see e.g. Miglo, 2021b). In reality, even if an entrepreneur of a young firm puts a good amount of effort into describing his/her business to the public, it is very hard/impossible to completely eliminate asymmetric information. As a result, entrepreneurs resort to using indirect actions to signal their quality to potential investors. This can be done, for example, by selecting actions that may be viewed upon favourably by potential investors. Most theoretical literature in this area actually uses the second approach (similar to the traditional debt/equity choice under asymmetric information). There are several reasons for this emphasis on the indirect approach. First is the general rule that "actions speak louder than words"[7] (with regard to crowdfunding actions may include, for example, the choice between crowdfunding and other types of financing, the choice of crowdfunding type, and the choice of threshold). Second, it has been found in some recent empirical papers (e.g. Liang et al., 2020) that publishing more information may not necessarily have a linear/positive effect on the probability of success, which again plays in favour of the indirect approach.

[6] For classical papers analysing asymmetric information problems in other areas of finance and economics see e.g. Akerlof (1970) and Spence (1974).

[7] The former has its limits i.e. "actions speak louder than words". See Lincoln (1856). https://www.bookbrowse.com/expressions/detail/index.cfm/expression_number/151/actions-speak-louder-than-words. See also Grinblatt and Titman (2001) and Miglo (2021a).

There are two groups of articles analysing the role of asymmetric information in crowdfunding. One assumes that an entrepreneur's private information is mostly related to the quality of the product that his/her firm develops. The other assumes that the private information is mostly related to the cost of production. Among the first group note Miglo (2024), which considers a model of a firm's choice between traditional debt, equity and reward-based crowdfunding where the entrepreneur has private information about the firm's quality. Under very general assumptions, the paper argues that a pecking order[8] exists where firms prefer debt, followed by equity and followed by reward-based crowdfunding. This is generally consistent with the relatively lower volume of crowdfunding compared to traditional debt and equity. The first preference, namely that under asymmetric information firms prefer traditional debt over equity, is generally consistent with one of the most important theories in capital structure, the so-called pecking-order theory (Myers & Majluff, 1984). Among other papers, note Chakraborty and Swinney (2020) that considers a crowdfunding model where product quality is known to the entrepreneur but not to some contributors. It suggests that a larger campaign target can be used by high-quality firms as a signalling device. Belleflamme et al. (2014) argue that asymmetric information reduces the value of reward-based crowdfunding to entrepreneurs. Uncertainty about a project's quality only partly hurts investors under equity-based crowdfunding since they count on long-term benefits but has a much more substantial negative impact on them under reward-based crowdfunding. Hakenes and Schlegel (2014) analyse a model that compares traditional bank financing and debt-based crowdfunding where asymmetric information exists about the firm's quality. Obtaining information about projects' qualities is costly for investors/households. The authors argue that good projects have more opportunities to receive funding with crowdfunding than with traditional loans. On the other hand, under crowdfunding entrepreneurs will establish low loan rates and low thresholds that will generate too much information which is costly.[9]

Papers that assume that private information is mostly related to the cost of production include Miglo and Miglo (2019) that considers a situation

[8] The pecking-order idea in crowdfunding will be further discussed in more details in Chapter 6.

[9] Also see Belavina et al. (2020).

with two consecutive rounds of financing and argues that reward-based crowdfunding can be used as a signal of quality when there is asymmetric information concerning either the cost of production or product quality. Low-quality firms may not be interested in mimicking high-quality firms when the latter uses AON campaigns because the risk of their projects failing may be too high, which can be costly in the second round. Strausz (2017) uses asymmetric information about cost as an additional feature when analysing a crowdfunding model where the focus is on learning market demand under moral hazard problem. Strausz (2017) argues that the presence of asymmetric information can depend on moral hazard problems. Without moral hazard asymmetric information in Strausz (2017) is irrelevant since revealing the wrong information about the cost or investment will not matter to the entrepreneur since the entrepreneur does not steal investor funds. However, under moral hazard private information becomes relevant.[10]

Empirical evidence is usually consistent with the pecking-order idea in a sense that the volume of debt in general exceeds the volume of equity as well as the volume of crowdfunding. Cumming, et al. (2020) find that KIA campaigns are less successful than AON campaigns in meeting their fundraising goals. For example, the rate of success of campaigns on Kickstarter, which only uses AON, is higher than it is on Indiegogo.[11] We will discuss this idea in the next section in more details. Also note that Ahlers et al. (2015) finds that under equity-based crowdfunding a larger fraction of equity taken by an entrepreneur is associated with a higher project quality. This is consistent with the spirit of signalling by retaining larger fraction of equity as in Leland and Pyle (1977), for example. Overall, it seems like a gap exists between theoretical papers and empirical papers testing these theories so in the future more research with the idea of filling this gap is expected. Also, empirical evidence usually confirms the positive effects of direct signalling in crowdfunding e.g. improving information release about projects by entrepreneurs increases the likelihood of crowdfunding success. This includes information quantity i.e. words, pictures and videos (see e.g. Bi et al., 2017; De Larrea et al., 2019; Kunz et al., 2017; Lagazio & Querci, 2018; Moy et al., 2018; Xu, 2017; Yeh

[10] Among other papers analysing asymmetric information related to crowdfunding note Sayedi and Baghaie (2017), Kim et al. (2022), Chen et al (2018) and Miglo (2020).

[11] See, for example: http://crowdfunding.cmf-fmc.ca/facts_and_stats/how-likely-is-your-crowdfunding-campaign-to-succeed.

et al., 2019; Zhou et al., 2018), and information quality i.e. to what extent the project information is readable, measured for example by readability and the frequency of information update, information attitude, i.e. the backers' opinions or questions about the projects and the creators' replies, comments, information about the entrepreneurs' experience with crowdfunding. (see e.g. Zhou et al., 2018; Mollick, 2014; Davies & Giovannetti, 2018; Shahab et al., 2019; De Larrea et al., 2019; Yeh et al., 2019; Lagazio & Querci, 2018; Bi et al., 2017). As we mentioned previously though some recent research find mixed evidence about opportunities for successful direct signaling in crowdfunding and some research find an inverted U-shape relationship between the amount of information and the probability of project success (see e.g. Liang et al., 2020).

Another line of literature assumes that some investors are better informed than others. This literature usually focuses on the analysis of third-party signals in crowdfunding and phenomena like backer herding behaviour. Theoretical papers include Cong and Xiao (2018) who focus on investor learning during crowdfunding campaigns. They consider an AON campaign using a classical model of information cascade.[12] They find that the campaign target plays an important role in imitating preceding agents' rejections. Åstebro et al. (2024) analyse herding in equity crowdfunding. They argue that when investors see that a particular project supported by a large number of investors, they begin to express interest in the project as well. Kleinert et al. (2020) provides evidence that prior financing certifies firm quality to investors and reduces information asymmetries in equity crowdfunding. Kim et al. (2022) present a model of choice of backer behaviour on a large crowdfunding platform and show that the funding status positively affects the backer's utility before the funding goal is met. Alaei et al. (2016) consider a model of crowdfunding in which funders arrive sequentially and decide whether to invest or not. Funders prefer not to invest if they think the campaign will not succeed. This can lead to cascades where a campaign fails to reach the threshold even when the product is socially efficient. Du et al. (2022) also consider

[12] An information cascade appears when individuals make a choice based on the observed actions of others, potentially ignoring their own information. See e.g. Easley and Kleinberg (2010).

a model where backers arrive sequentially at a crowdfunding project. They show that there exists a "cascade effect" on funders' contributions.[13]

Another interesting line of literature analyses opportunities for signalling by platforms themselves (Johan & Reardon, 2024; Mataigne et al., 2025). The idea is that a platform acquires information about entrepreneurs during their campaign preparation and registration and uses this information to indirectly signal their quality to outside investors. One signalling method a platform may use is to have platform members purchase shares in a company is has gathered positive information on. Empirical evidence of this, however, is mixed. Some papers find confirming evidence of this idea (see e.g. Johan & Reardon, 2024) while others suggest that platforms may engage in so-called "false signalling" where platform members invest in firms with weaker post-campaign outcomes (see e.g. Mataigne et al., 2025). In general, this issue is also related to agency problems, which we will discuss in the next chapter.

The signalling by platforms area of research is also related to the area of research that studies how theoretical ideas can affect different platforms differently (see e.g. Rossi et al., 2021). For example, platforms where campaigns are organized by large and mature firms may demonstrate different signalling effects than platforms with younger and smaller firms. Rossi et al. (2021) find that signalling via patents is less important on platforms with smaller and younger entrepreneurs than on platforms with larger and more mature firms. The paper argues that this is consistent with the idea that standardization (i.e. having a patent) is more important for large mature firms than differentiation (the quality of initial ideas), which is more important for small young firms (based on Rajan, 2012).

3.4 Using Online Opportunities for Signalling

This section provides some illustration of how entrepreneurs can use crowdfunding to signal their quality. Consider a firm with an innovative product or service. The investment cost equals B. There are two firms: a high-quality firm (H) and a low-quality firm (L). To finance the production of the product, firms can use crowdfunding (AON or KIA). The probability of running a successful crowdfunding campaign in terms of reaching B (if AON is selected) is p_h for H and p_l for L, $p_h > p_l$. If

[13] See also Chan et al., (2020), Courtney, Dutta and Li (2017), Kim and Viswanathan, (2019).

the firm runs an AON campaign the expected amount of funds raised is V_2 and if KIA then V_1. We assume that $V_2 > V_1$ because of the market's confidence in AON campaigns is higher since backers understand that the project will not move forward unless a sufficient amount of funds is raised. The trade-off for the entrepreneur is that if AON is selected there is a risk of campaign failure. When selecting the type of crowdfunding (AON or KIA) the entrepreneur maximizes his/her objective function which is the expected value of funds raised during the campaign minus the investment cost. Potential backers can provide financing or buy securities as long as the expected earnings cover the investment. It is usually justified by the assumption that the investor is risk-neutral and that the risk-free interest rate is zero.[14]

Typically, in finance theory when considering a situation with asymmetric information game theory is used as the main tool.[15] Usually the equilibrium concept is used to solve a game including games with asymmetric information. An equilibrium is a situation where no participants have an incentive to deviate from the equilibrium given the strategies played by the other players.

Consider an equilibrium where H selects AON and L selects KIA. Since each type of firm selects a different strategy, it is called a signalling equilibrium where the market participants use indirect signals (in our case the firms' choices of crowdfunding type) to determine firm quality. Suppose that potential backers believe that if a firm selects AON it is a high-quality firm and vice versa if a firm selects KIA it is a low-quality firm. Then H's expected profit equals $V_2 p_h - B$. Since firms can signal their quality, the situation is equivalent to a case with perfect (symmetric) information. H raises an amount V_2 with probability p_h so the expected amount raised during the campaign is $V_2 p_h$. We should subtract the investment cost to arrive at the amount of profit. Similarly, L's profit is $V_1 - B$. Analogously we can calculate the firm's payoff when considering a potential equilibrium where H selects KIA and L selects AON.

Proposition 3.2 *An equilibrium where H selects AON dominates one where H selects KIA.*

[14] This assumption is quite typical in financing models and will be used in most models throughout the book unless specified otherwise.

[15] For some review of game theory see e.g. Fudenberg and Tirole (1991); also see Appendix to this chapter for some basic terminology/concepts.

Proof Indeed, consider the existence conditions for the former. L should not be interested in mimicking (selecting the strategy chosen by H i.e. AON) H or

$$V_2 p_l - B < V_1 - B \tag{3.5}$$

Indeed, if L selects AON, it is perceived by potential backers as type H and therefore it will be able to collect V_2. The probability of a successful campaign for type L is p_l so the expected amount of raised funds is $V_2 p_l$.

Also, H should not be interested in mimicking L or

$$V_2 p_h - B > V_1 - B \tag{3.6}$$

Now consider an equilibrium where H selects KIA.

L should not be interested in mimicking H or

$$V_2 p_l - B > V_1 - B \tag{3.7}$$

Also, H should not be interested in mimicking L or

$$V_2 p_h - B < V_1 - B \tag{3.8}$$

The last two conditions (3.6) and (3.7) cannot hold simultaneously since $p_h > p_l$ and the LHS[16] of (3.8) should be greater not less than the LHS of (3.7) while (3.5) and (3.6) can hold under some conditions namely if $V_2 p_h - B > V_1 - B > V_2 p_l - B$.

This analysis implies that high-quality entrepreneurs can use AON to signal their quality. This prediction has not been directly tested but as was previously mentioned is consistent with the spirit of Cumming et al. (2020) that find that KIA campaigns are less successful in meeting their fundraising goals compared to AON campaigns. Similar results can be found in Zhou et al. (2021).[17]

Further, the above analysis has some implications regarding signalling and the extent of asymmetric information (uncertainty about project

[16] Stands for left-hand side; respectively RHS means right-hand side.

[17] See also Xu and Zhang (2021).

quality). Equations (3.5) and (3.6) predict that signaling opportunities exist when the extent of asymmetric information is large enough. Indeed, for any given value of p_l, the farther p_h is from p_l the more likely it is that a separating equilibrium exists. Similarly for a given value of p_h an equilibrium exists if p_l is farther from p_h or if p_l is sufficiently small. Some empirical research suggests that it is very typical in crowdfunding for projects to attract very low or negligibly small amounts of funds (see, for example, Cordova & Dolci, 2015; Desjardins, 2016; Mollick, 2014). Therefore, the condition that p_l should be sufficiently small is not unrealistic.

Questions and Exercises

1. The term "crowd wisdom" is often associated with an environment with demand uncertainty and an entrepreneur's opportunity to learn about market demand for his/her products/services.
2. Two of the main assumptions behind learning market demand / the crowd wisdom idea are: information about market demand is imperfect, and funds collected during a reward-based crowdfunding campaign are related to the market demand for future products because backers often receive a firm's future products as a reward.
3. Direct signalling, as applied to crowdfunding, includes all of the following except:

   a. Creating a video about the firm
   b. Providing regular updates on the campaign website
   c. Providing information about campaign risk
   d. Selecting reward-based or equity-based type of crowdfunding

4. Indirect signalling includes:

   a. Selecting AON vs. KIA
   b. Creating a video about the firm

5. An entrepreneurial firm owns an innovative project. The firm is organized with unlimited liability. The firm is owned by an entrepreneur who owns personal assets in the amount 400. To run the project, an investment of 300 is required (a fixed cost that is invested in tangible assets that fully depreciate by the time the firm completes the project; variable cost is negligible small). The demand for the good is 70 items at the price of 10 if demand is high (with probability 50%) and 10 items at the price of 1 if demand is low. The

firm is planning to use reward-based crowdfunding (AON) or debt-based crowdfunding (under this strategy the firm will have to return to the backers the amount of funds collected i.e. 300 along with the interest rate of 10%). Under reward-based crowdfunding, the firm announces the crowdfunding price and the campaign target.

a. Discuss the "learning market demand" idea.
b. Suppose that the demand is high. Calculate the entrepreneur's profit is the firm uses debt-based crowdfunding (the platform fee is 10).
c. Continue to assume that the demand is high. Calculate the entrepreneur's profit if the firm uses reward-based crowdfunding assuming that the firm announces the campaign target 300 and collects 70 pre-orders/contributions of 10 each from 70 backers. Also assume that the platform charges a fee of 50.
d. What strategy is optimal for the entrepreneur? Comment why.
e. Now suppose that the demand is uncertain. Assume that the entrepreneur maximizes his/her expected profit and the value of his/her own assets is 400 (which he/she does not plan to use for firm financing since it will be inconvenient to sell assets etc.). Calculate the profits under both strategies.
f. Discuss your result in the previous question.

6. Consider a firm with an innovative product or service. The predicted sales of the product are A. There are two firms: a low-cost (high-quality) firm (L) and a high-cost (low-quality) firm (H). The cost of production is c_h for H and c_l for L, $c_h > c_l$. The firm does not have any initial resources. To finance the production of the product, firms can use reward-based crowdfunding (where backers will receive rewards; for simplicity assume that the value of rewards is fair i.e. equal to the amount of investment provided by backers; also assume that the discount rate is negligibly small i.e. all consumers are indifferent whether to participate in crowdfunding and receive the reward or buy the product on the spot market later on) or equity-based crowdfunding. Show that under perfect information, the choice of the crowdfunding type is irrelevant. Now suppose that information is asymmetric. Analyse the equilibrium.
7. Consider a firm with an innovative product or service. The cost of production equals 50. There are two firms: a high-quality firm (H) and a low-quality firm (L). The probability of running a successful

crowdfunding campaign with a target of 50 is 0.9 for H and 0.3 for L. The firm does not have any initial resources. To finance the production of the product, firms can use crowdfunding (AON or KIA). If the firm uses AON it will be able to collect 70 and if KIA then it will collect 50. When selecting AON or KIA, the entrepreneur maximizes his/her objective function which is the expected amount of funds raised during the campaign minus the investment cost. Analyse the equilibrium.

Appendix: Introduction to Basic Terminology/Concepts of Game Theory

In most cases we will consider cases with two so-called players. Each player must decide how he or she will play the game. The goal of each player is to maximize his/her payoff. A player's payoff is the amount (points, money, or anything a player values) a player receives from a particular outcome of a game. To solve a game usually means to find an equilibrium. An equilibrium (Nash equilibrium) is a pair of strategies (one for each player) such that player A's strategy gives A the best payoff if player B selects his/her strategy and vice versa.

For example, suppose two players are playing a game in which they can choose between A and B with the payoffs given in the game matrix in Table 3.1.

For example, if player 1 selects strategy A and player B selects strategy A their payoffs are 100 and 100. The solution of the game is A, A and the respective payoffs are 100 and 100. Indeed, if player 1 deviates and plays strategy B instead his payoff is 0 and if player 2 deviates and plays B his payoff is 10. No other scenario is an equilibrium. Consider, for example,

Table 3.1 Payoff matrix

		Player 2	
		A	B
Player 1	A	(100,100)	(−10,10)
	B	(0,20)	(−1,11)

the case when player 1 plays A and Player 2 plays B. The players' payoffs are −10 and 10, respectively. If player 2 deviates and plays A his payoff is 100 which is greater than 10 so Player 2 would deviate. Similar reasoning can be applied to other cases as well.

References

Ahlers, G., Cumming, D., Günther, C., & Schweizer, D. (2015). Signaling in equity crowdfunding. *Entrepreneurship Theory and Practice, 39*(4), 955–980.

Akerlof, G. A. (1970). The market for "Lemons": Quality uncertainty and the market mechanism. *The Quarterly Journal of Economics, 84*(3), 488–500.

Alaei, S., Malekian, A., & Mostagir, M. (2016). *A dynamic model of crowdfunding* (Ross School of Business Paper No. 1307). Available at SSRN. https://ssrn.com/abstract=2737748

Åstebro, T., Fernández, M., Lovo, S., & Vulkan, N. (2024). Herding in equity crowdfunding. *The RAND Journal of Economics, 55*(3), 403–441.

Belavina, E., Marinesi, S., & Tsoukalas, G. (2020). Rethinking crowdfunding platform design: Mechanisms to deter misconduct and improve efficiency. *Management Science., 66*(11), 4980–4997.

Belleflamme, P., Lambert, T., & Schwienbacher, A. (2014). Crowdfunding: Tapping the right crowd. *Journal of Business Venturing, 29*(5), 585–609.

Bi, S., Liu, Z., & Usman, K. (2017). The influence of online information on investing decisions of reward-based crowdfunding. *Journal of Business Research, 71*, 10–18.

Block, J., Hornuf, L., & Moritz, A. (2018). Which updates during an equity crowdfunding campaign increase crowd participation? *Small Business Economics, 50*(1), 3–27.

Catalini, C., & Gans, J. S. (2018). *Initial coin offerings and the value of crypto tokens* (NBER Working Paper, 24418).

Chakraborty, S., & Swinney, R. (2020). Signalling to the crowd: Private quality information and rewards-based crowdfunding. *Manufacturing and Service Operations Management, 23*(1), 155–169.

Chan, C. R., Parhankangas, A., Sahaym, A., & Oo, P. (2020). Bellwether and the herd? Unpacking the u-shaped relationship between prior funding and subsequent contributions in reward-based crowdfunding. *Journal of Business Venturing, 35*(2), Article 105934.

Chemla, G., & Tinn, K. (2019). Learning through crowdfunding. *Management Science, 66*(5), 1783–1801.

Chen, R. R., Gal-Or, E., & Roma, P. (2018). Reward-based crowdfunding campaigns: Informational value and access to venture capital. *Information Systems Research, 29*, 679–697.

Cong, L., & Xiao, Y. (2018). Up-cascaded wisdom of the crowd. *SSRN Electronic Journal*.

Cordova, J., & Dolci, G. (2015). The determinants of crowdfunding success: Evidence from technology projects. *Procedia—Social and Behavioral Sciences, 181*, 115–124.

Courtney, C., Dutta, S., & Li, Y. (2017). Resolving information asymmetry: Signaling, endorsement, and crowdfunding success. *Entrepreneurship Theory and Practice, 41*(2), 265–290.

Cumming, D., Leboeuf, G., & Schwienbacher, A. (2020). Crowdfunding models: Keep-it-all versus all or nothing. *Financial Management, 49*, 331–360.

Davies, W. E., & Giovannetti, E. (2018). Signalling experience & reciprocity to temper asymmetric information in crowdfunding evidence from 10,000 projects. *Technological Forecasting and Social Change, 133*, 118–131.

De Larrea, G. L., Altin, M., & Singh, D. (2019). Determinants of success of restaurant crowdfunding. *International Journal of Hospitality Management, 78*, 150–158.

Desjardins, J. (2016, July 14). *19 weird crowdfunding campaigns that failed spectacularly*. http://www.visualcapitalist.com/19-weird-crowdfunding campaigns-failed/

Du, L., Hu, M., & Wu, J. (2022). Contingent stimulus in crowdfunding. *Production and Operations Management, 31*(9), 3543–3558.

Easley, D., & Kleinberg, J. (2010). *Information cascades. Networks, Crowds, and Markets: Reasoning about a Highly Connected World*. Cambridge University Press.

Ellman, M., & Hurkens, J. P. M. (2019). Optimal crowdfunding design. *Journal of Economic Theory., 184*, Article 104939.

Fudenberg, D., & Tirole, J. (1991). *Game theory*. MIT Press.

Grinblatt, M., & Titman, S. (2001). *Financial markets & corporate strategy* (2nd ed.). McGraw-Hill Higher Education.

Hakenes, H., & Schlegel, F. (2014). *Exploiting the Financial Wisdom of the Crowd—Crowdfunding as a Tool to Aggregate Vague Information* (Working paper).

Hildebrand, T., Puri, M., & Rocholl, J. (2017). Adverse incentives in crowdfunding. *Management Science, 63*(3), 587–608.

Johan, S., & Reardon, R. S. (2024). The role of platform stakes in equity crowdfunding success. *Finance Research Letters, 69*, Article 106097.

Kim, J.-H., Newberry, P., & Qiu, C. (2022). The role of information signals in determining crowdfunding outcomes. *Journal of Empirical Finance, 67*, 168–181.

Kim, K., & Viswanathan, S. (2019). The experts in the crowd. *MIS Quarterly, 43*(2), 347-A9.

Kleinert, S., Volkmann, C., & Grünhagen, M. (2020). Third-party signals in equity crowdfunding: The role of prior financing. *Small Business Economics, 54*, 341–365.

Kunz, M. M., Bretschneider, U., Erler, M., & Leimeister, J. M. (2017). An empirical investigation of signaling in reward-based crowdfunding. *Electronic Commerce Research, 17*(3), 425–461.

Lagazio, C., & Querci, F. (2018). Exploring the multi-sided nature of crowdfunding campaign success. *Journal of Business Research, 90*, 318–324.

Leland, H. E., & Pyle, D. H. (1977). Information asymmetries, financial structure, and financial Intermediation. *Journal of Finance, 32*, 371–387.

Liang, X., Hu, X., & Jiang, J. (2020). Research on the effects of information description on crowdfunding success within a sustainable economy—The perspective of information communication. *Sustainability, 12*(2), 650.

Mataigne, V., Meoli, M., Vanacker, T., & Vismara, S. (2025). False signaling by platform team members and post-campaign venture outcomes: Evidence from an equity crowdfunding platform. *Journal of Business Venturing, 40*(1), Article 106457.

Miglo, A., & Miglo, V. (2019). Market imperfections and crowdfunding. *Small Business Economics, 53*(1), 51–79.

Miglo, A. (2020). Crowdfunding in a competitive environment. *Journal of Risk and Financial Management, 13*(3), 39 (Special Issue on Crowdfunding. Ed. D. Cumming and S. Johan).

Miglo, A. (2021a). Crowdfunding: Definitions, foundations and framework. In R. Lenart-Gansiniec & J. Chen (Eds.), *Crowdfunding in the public sector: Theory and Best Practices. Series: Contributions to finance and accounting* (pp. 1–19). Springer. ISBN 9783030778408.

Miglo, A. (2021b). Crowdfunding under market feedback, asymmetric information and overconfident entrepreneur. *Entrepreneurship Research Journal, 11*(4), 20190018.

Miglo, A. (2024). Crowdfunding, asymmetric information and pecking order. *Journal of Economic Studies 14 August 2025, 52*(6), 1156–1170. https://doi.org/10.1108/JES-03-2024-0194

Mollick, E. R. (2014). The dynamics of crowdfunding: An exploratory study. *Journal of Business Venturing, 29*(1), 1–16.

Moy, N., Chan, H. F., & Torgler, B. (2018). How much is too much? The effects of information quantity on crowdfunding performance. *PLoS ONE, 13*(3), Article e0192012.

Myers, S., & Majluf, N. (1984). Corporate financing and investment decisions when firms have information that investors do not have. *Journal of Financial Economics, 13*, 187–222.

Piva, E., & Rossi-Lamastra, C. (2018). Human capital signals and entrepreneurs' success in equity crowdfunding. *Small Business Economics, 51*(3), 667–686.

Rajan, R. G. (2012). Presidential address: The corporation in finance. *The Journal of Finance, 67*(4), 1173–1217.

Rossi, A., Vanacker, T., & Vismara, S. (2021). Equity crowdfunding: New evidence from US and UK markets. *Review of Corporate Finance, 1*(3–4), 407–453.

Sahm, M. (2019). Advance-purchase financing of projects with few buyers. *Review of Industrial Organization., 57*, 909–933.

Sayedi, A., & Baghaie, M. (2017). Crowdfunding as a marketing tool. Available at SSRN. https://ssrn.com/abstract=2938183

Schwienbacher, A. (2018). Entrepreneurial risk-taking in crowdfunding campaigns. *Small Business Economics, 51*(4), 843–859.

Shahab, Y., Ye, Z., Riaz, Y., & Ntim, C. G. (2019). Individual's financial investment decision-making in reward-based crowdfunding: Evidence from China. *Applied Economics Letters, 26*(4), 261–266.

Spence, M. (1974). Competitive and optimal responses to signals: An analysis of efficiency and distribution. *Journal of Economic Theory, 7*(3), 296–332.

Strausz, R. (2017). Crowdfunding, demand uncertainty, and moral hazard—A mechanism design approach. *American Economic Review, 107*(6), 1430–76.

Vismara, S. (2016). Equity retention and social network theory in equity crowdfunding. *Small Business Economics, 46*(4), 579–590.

Xu, T. (2017). *Learning from the Crowd: The feedback value of crowdfunding* (University of British Columbia working paper).

Xu, S., & Zhang, Z. (2021). Choosing a crowdfunding model considering strategic customer behaviour. *Total Quality Management & Business Excellence, 33*(7–8), 862–883.

Yeh, T. L., Chen, T. Y., & Lee, C. C. (2019). Investigating the funding success factors affecting reward-based crowdfunding projects. *Innovation, 21*(3), 466–486.

Zhou, M., Lu, B., Fan, W., & Wang, G. A. (2018). Project description and crowdfunding success: An exploratory study. *Information Systems Frontiers, 20*(2), 259–274.

Zhou, S., Ma, T., & Liu, Z. (2021). Crowdfunding as a screener for collective investment. *Electronic Commerce Research, 21*(1), 195–221.

CHAPTER 4

Crowdfunding and Moral Hazard Problems

4.1 Agency Problems and Moral Hazard Problems in Crowdfunding

Moral hazard refers to situations where the actions of managers/entrepreneurs are not observable and/or not verifiable by investors. Sometimes it is called the agency problem referring to a theoretical framework when one party (principal) hires another party (an agent) to perform some tasks and the interests of parties are not perfectly aligned.[1] As we discussed in the previous chapters one of the main advantages of crowdfunding compared to traditional financing methods is a significantly smaller amount of required bureaucracy. The downside is that entrepreneurs have more freedom and less obligations to register their projects and disclose details about their plans. In general, most entrepreneurs have interesting innovative ideas and have no intentions to disappoint the crowd by not working hard enough or running illegal

[1] For a general overview of principal-agent theories see e.g. Bolton and Dewatripont (2004) or Laffont and Martimort (2002).

Supplementary Information The online version contains supplementary material available at https://doi.org/10.1007/978-3-032-10724-4_4.

© The Author(s), under exclusive license to Springer Nature Switzerland AG 2026

A. Miglo and V. Miglo, *The Theories and Developments of Crowdfunding*, https://doi.org/10.1007/978-3-032-10724-4_4

schemes to divert money without fulfilling their promises and obligations. However, this sometimes changes when things are not going well. Moral hazard problems have emerged as an important issue in crowdfunding. This is because of lack of information about the firm it is hard to imagine that the firm activities especially in early stages would be highly transparent or that investors would be able to fully control or control to a significant extent the actions of entrepreneurs. Appio et al. (2020) argue that bad decisions by entrepreneurs and fraud can explain why many crowdfunding campaign fail to deliver products and rewards to their backers. Bakri et al. (2021) argue that the entrepreneurial effort and performance expectancy affect backer decision-making.

For large firms, the moral hazard problem is closely related to the problem of corporate governance. Firm financing strategies and ownership structures are generally a part of corporate governance mechanisms. In general, corporate governance represents the set of rules (informal and formal) used by firms around the world to improve manager incentives and align manager interests with the interests of shareholders and other claimholders. Although these issues are typically less important for small firms where there is less separation between ownership and management (e.g. founders are often top managers) they are still sometimes analysed (see e.g. Abor & Adjasi, 2007). Interestingly the connection between corporate governance and crowdfunding is a growing area of interest (see e.g. Cumming et al., 2021; Verret, 2016 or Kourabas, 2021).

Several ideas have been developed in practice and in the literature to align the interests of shareholders and decision-makers (e.g. firm managers). These include the controlling role of large shareholders, the activities of boards of directors, the role of external auditors, the influence of external analysts, a threat of takeovers, the incentives created by firm financial structure, the use of stock options as a reward for decision-makers (see Bolton & Dewatripont, 2004 for a review). We will discuss some of these ideas below and their relevance to firms that use crowdfunding.

One of the methods to incentivize managers of large firms is through the threat of a takeover (called stock market discipline). The idea is that if managers do not act in the interest of shareholders, i.e. do not maximize the value of the firm's shares, the firm's share price is likely to go down. If this happens, the firm is more likely be taken over by a large external investor(s) since it is cheaper for them to buy a large portion of the firm's equity. Further, if the company is taken over, there is a very large chance that the top managers will lose their jobs (see e.g. Franks & Mayer, 1996). This mechanism creates a strong incentive for managers of large firm to act in the interest of shareholders. Can this idea apply to small firms and to firms that use crowdfunding?! As we discussed previously, for most firms that use crowdfunding, including equity-based crowdfunding, a secondary market of shares does not exist so this method may not work well, especially in the in the early stages of firm development. Similarly, we know that for crowdfunding firms methods like constant monitoring by external analysts may not exist either because analysts are usually interested in following firms for which they can observe and analyse certain financial indicators like the stock price, which they cannot do for most start-up firms. As we mentioned before, some platforms are working to create a secondary market for shares of crowdfunding firms (e.g. Republic Europe[2]). This would help mitigate the problems described above for crowdfunding firms.

Another idea in corporate governance is monitoring by large shareholders/investors. For example, if we compare equity-based crowdfunding with venture capital financing, venture capital firms are usually much more actively involved in different aspects of firms management than equity-crowdfunding investors. In the case of equity-based crowdfunding, the firm usually gets a large number of small "unprofessional" investors that do not have a significant portfolio of firm shares. Further, it is usually quite challenging for small shareholders to coordinate their interests and decisions to try to control the entrepreneur or other decision-makers of the firm. Similarly in the context of debt financing, if a firm receives traditional debt from a bank, the bank will usually monitor how the firm uses its funds. In some countries banks even have seats on the board of directors (see e.g. Panicker et al., 2023). In the case of debt-based crowdfunding, the creditors behind the crowdload naturally face difficulties in coordinating their efforts to monitor the entrepreneur.

So what opportunities in this area exist for crowdfunding firms? One idea is to attract professional investors. This may be beneficial because they have more experience, knowledge, and expertise, so they can help the firm not only raise more funds (by investing themselves), but also to attract more small shareholders who do not have the same amount of

[2] https://europe.republic.com/invest/marketplace.

information and are interested in following big investors. This is consistent with the spirit of some findings that firms that have support from professional investors are more likely to succeed (see e.g. Chang et al., 2021).

In a similar spirit, another idea is the nominee model (see e.g. Coakley et al., 2022). It is used by Crowdcube, Seedrs and SyndicateRoom (among other platforms). The way it works for equity-based crowdfunding for example, is that backers (shareholders) do not invest directly in the firm, but they invest in a company called a Special Purpose Vehicle (SPV). It manages the shares of all equity crowd investors. This has some advantages because it simplifies tasks for the small shareholders to deal with the technical side of their investments like constant account monitoring, dividends and other major decisions that may be limited by the coordination problems between crowd investors. SPVs can help with these issues and can facilitate coordination between the small shareholders. On the hand, we get a sort of intermediary (SPV) between investors and firms here which is not entirely consistent with the spirit of one of basic ideas of Fintech that we discussed previously: the "no-middle-man" idea. In addition, note that the presence of an SPV may create new agency problems between this nominee and the shareholders, because its interests may not necessarily be 100% aligned with the interests of the small shareholders. As we can see, there are advantages and disadvantages in this co-investment or nominee model. Coakley et al. (2022) argue that this model is generally beneficial by arguing that that nominee firms exhibit better short run and long run performance.

Another related topic is opportunities for an entrepreneur to run a crowdfunding campaign to separate (at least to some extent) the cash flow rights and control rights of crowdfunding participants (mostly in the case of equity-based crowdfunding). This idea lends itself from venture capital research where this phenomenon is quite frequently observed (see e.g. Kaplan & Strömberg, 2003). The idea is to design securities that will mitigate moral hazard issues. Some literature suggests that optimal securities should not be straight equity i.e. where 1% of firm ownership means 1% of everything (cash flow rights, voting rights etc.). In the case of venture firms these often take the shape of convertible securities (see e.g. Schmidt, 2003). In the case of crowdfunding, some investors may have the opportunity to give more voting rights to other investors that can be in charge of controlling/monitoring the entrepreneur's activities. In a similar vein, large companies have the opportunity to release dual shares.

Alibaba, a famous Chinese firm, tried to make an IPO in Hong Kong and one the biggest problems it faced was issuing these dual-class shares (different shares have different voting rights) so they had to go public in the US instead. In crowdfunding, Crowdcube allows entrepreneurs to use dual-class shares when running an equity-based crowdfunding campaign. In practice, what firms usually do is determine a threshold for investments in shares and if an investor wants more votes (class B shares), they need to contribute an amount that is greater than the indicated threshold. There are advantages and disadvantages when cash flow rights and voting rights are separated and these are to a large extent similar to the ones in the nominee model. Empirical papers find mixed evidence regarding the efficiency of dual-class shares in crowdfunding (see e.g. Cumming et al., 2020).

Crowdfunding research and practice show that there are two important types of moral hazard that emerge: costly effort taken by the entrepreneur (in the spirit of Jensen & Meckling, 1976) and the possibility of funds being diverted by the entrepreneur (in the spirit of Jensen, 1986). Among the theoretical papers studying the costly effort of the entrepreneur, note Schwienbacher (2018), Babich et al. (2021) and Miglo and Miglo (2019). For papers analysing the potential misusage of funds received during crowdfunding campaigns note Strausz (2017), Belavina et al. (2020) and Chemla and Tinn (2019).

A costly effort problem usually applies to situations where the decision-maker can deliberately choose the level of effort and this level is difficult to observe or control by third parties. One of the main ideas here is that decision-makers weigh the costs and benefits when making their decisions and the problem is that the decision-maker often bears the full cost of his/her actions but is rewarded only partially. There are many factors that can create a situation like this. One is the fraction of ownership belonging to the decision-maker. Usually if the decision-maker fully owns the firm, the problem of optimal effort is not very significant since the interests of the firm and the decision-maker are perfectly aligned. This means that if delivering the optimal effort level maximizes the firm's profit it usually means that that same effort level maximizes the entrepreneur's own benefit. In most cases, when the decision-maker does not own 100% of the firm, the decision-maker's efforts may be suboptimal from the firm's point of view. This problem has been extensively studied in classic corporate finance literature leading to the ideas of rewarding managers with bonuses and stock options. Similar issues can arise in crowdfunding when the firm uses for example equity-based crowdfunding since the fraction of the entrepreneur's equity in the firm is reduced. Similar problems do not typically arise when the firm uses other types of crowdfunding. The problem here is that small start-up firms usually lack the tools used to improve decision-makers/entrepreneur's incentive such as using a board of directors and stock market discipline. We will provide more discussion in Sect. 4.3.

Entrepreneurs may also divert the funds raised during a crowdfunding campaign. Early empirical papers (e.g. Cumming et al., 2023) discovered that many campaigns suffered from funds embezzlements. Several factors contribute to this phenomenon. One is the early stages of bankruptcy concepts being developed in crowdfunding (we will provide discussions about connections between bankruptcy and crowdfunding in Chapter 8). Another factor is the nature of reward-based crowdfunding and how the entrepreneur practically sells future products of the firm before the production process even starts so the economic incentive to start production is weakened. There exists a risk of potential funds expropriation/misuse, and a perfect monitoring and control system of start-up entrepreneurial firms conducting crowdfunding campaigns is difficult to implement. We will provide more discussion in Sect. 4.2.

Another interesting moral hazard issue is the moral hazard problems related to crowdfunding platforms. Although the magnitude of these problems is not as large as it is in banking, for example, (since banks actually use their clients' funds while crowdfunding platforms do not) they are still relevant. As we mentioned in the previous chapter, one such moral hazard issue is that platforms may engage in "false signalling" where the platform members invest in firms with weaker post-campaign outcomes (see e.g. Mataigne et al., 2025). In general, crowdfunding platform moral hazard issues arise because platform earnings (and ultimately their existence) depend on the success of their campaigns, which incentivizes platform members to become involved in campaign success. For more discussion on the underlying problems of crowdfunding platforms, including informational problems, see e.g. Belleflamme et al. (2015).

4.2 Crowdfunding and the "Cash-In-and-Run" Problem

The following model illustrates the importance of the cash-in-and-run problem in crowdfunding. Consider a firm with an innovative product or service. The firm estimates that the project requires an investment cost I. In order to raise the required amount I, the firm plans a crowdfunding campaign. The firm estimates that it will be able to generate earnings V from the sales of the product. Further let α be the fraction of the firm's earnings that belongs to the entrepreneur after the crowdfunding campaign, for example in the case of equity-based crowdfunding α is the fraction of equity that belongs to the entrepreneur, in the case of reward-based crowdfunding some fraction of the firm's products should be delivered to the backers as reward instead of being sold on the market. The firm is owned and run by an entrepreneur that is subject to moral hazard. More specifically we assume that the entrepreneur is able to divert the funds received during the crowdfunding campaign. In this case the entrepreneur's profit equals βI, where I is the amount of funds raised during crowdfunding campaign and β is the probability of not beign caught (a parameter that reflects the institutional strength).

With moral hazard, after finishing the crowdfunding campaign and raising an amount I but before making the investment the entrepreneur faces the following choice. If he continues with the project, the profit equals:

$$I - I + \alpha V \tag{4.1}$$

If the entrepreneur diverts funds, the profit equals

$$\beta I \tag{4.2}$$

If the following holds

$$\alpha V < \beta I \tag{4.3}$$

then (4.2) is greater than (4.1), the entrepreneur has an incentive to divert funds. Funders will anticipate this and the campaign will not be successful.

Project/Campaign size. The likelihood that (4.3) holds increases with I. . This implies that crowdfunding is likely to be used (i.e. (4.3) does not hold) if the required investment is relatively small and respectively the campaign size is relatively small. Generally, this is consistent with other theories and predictions as discussed previously.

Regulation. As follows from (4.3), if β increases the likelihood that (4.3) holds increases and thus decreases the likelihood that crowdfunding is used. This implies that regulation efficiency can improve the likelihood of entrepreneurs using crowdfunding. Further, let's assume that the entrepreneur is able to divert funds not only at the end of the crowdfunding campaign but also during the campaign. Then condition (4.3) becomes:

$$0 < \beta F \tag{4.4}$$

where F is the amount of funds raised (4.4) always holds since the firm is not able to start the project without raising the full required amount (that's why the LHS of (4.4) equals zero). The implication is that until the end of the campaign the entrepreneur always has an incentive to "steal" funds. Strausz (2017) argues that deferred payments should be a part of the optimal mechanism i.e. entrepreneurs should not be able to access funds until the end of campaign. This condition is used in practice by most crowdfunding platforms.[3] This is also consistent with the idea of using AON vs. KIA since it forces the firm to use condition (4.3) rather than (4.4).

Several theoretical papers analyse moral hazard issues in crowdfunding together with the learning demand idea by counterbalancing the advantages of the latter and the disadvantages of the former. Strausz (2017) suggests that crowdfunding should be preferred if the required investment is smaller than the expected profit by a significant margin and that deferred payments should be a part of the optimal mechanism. Belavina et al. (2020) look in more detail at specific deferred mechanisms that should be used by the platforms to mitigate the risk of funds misappropriation. They analyse reward-based crowdfunding (AON) by analysing a model where entrepreneurs have the ability to misappropriate campaign funds either at the end of the campaign or after attempting some product development efforts (and observing poor development results). The entrepreneur makes decisions after observing the size of

[3] See e.g. https://help.kickstarter.com/hc/en-us/articles/360010120934-If-my-project-is-successfully-funded-how-do-I-receive-my-funds-.

the potential market. They also consider the case where there is asymmetric information between the entrepreneur and backers. The authors argue that moral hazard and asymmetric information can reinforce their negative effects when taken together. The authors suggests that platforms should take actions to mitigate these effects by, for example, forcing entrepreneurs to stop campaigns once their threshold is reached and/or escrowing the funds received after the target is reached. Chemla and Tinn (2019) analyse a model that combines the cash-in-and-run problem and the learning market demand idea. They suggest that AON dominates KIA in mitigating moral hazard problems. The idea is that under AON the firm should set a target high enough to self-commit to not be interested in stealing funds at the end of campaign. If the target is not high enough the incentive to steal increases in some cases. Similar logic applies to KIA. The authors argue that in order to incentivize backers to support the project under KIA, the firm should offer large discounts during the campaign, which is suboptimal. Among more recent papers see e.g. Miglo (2020, 2023).

In general, the literature makes some useful suggestions for explaining some features of crowdfunding campaigns and regulations e.g. the usefulness of establishing a threshold and delaying the releasing of funds to entrepreneurs, which is generally used by crowdfunding platforms that use AON. However, there still exists a large gap between empirical and theoretical papers. Most theoretical papers have not yet been directly tested.

4.3 Crowdfunding and Entrepreneurial Effort

The following model illustrates the role of moral hazard when an entrepreneur selects his/her level of effort in crowdfunding. Consider a firm with an innovative product or service. The firm is run by an entrepreneur who can provide either a high or low level of effort during a crowdfunding campaign. Let c be the cost of effort. If effort is high ($c = e$), the firm can raise an amount A. . If effort is low ($c = 0$), the firm raises B, where $B < A$. . We assume that both strategies have a positive net present value (NPV), i.e.

$$A > e \quad \text{and} \quad B > 0 \tag{4.5}$$

In addition, if the campaign is successful, there will be a second period of production during which the firm will generate profit x, where x depends on the crowdfunding campaign threshold. If the company sets a high threshold during the campaign it can generate more profits in period 2 as it creates more trust in the firm (and its product). The firm has 3 strategies: KIA; AON with threshold A; and AON with threshold B. We assume that $x = b$ if the threshold is B and $x = a$ if the threshold is A, where $a > b \geq 0$. $x = 0$ in the case of KIA.

The firm's expected payoff under KIA is

$$A - e \tag{4.6}$$

if the effort is high and

$$B \tag{4.7}$$

if the effort is low. The firm's expected payoff under AON with threshold A is

$$A + a - e \tag{4.8}$$

if the effort is high and 0 if the effort is low (a high threshold will not be reached if the effort is low).

Finally, under AON with a threshold B the profit is

$$A + b - e \tag{4.9}$$

if the effort is high and

$$B + b \tag{4.10}$$

if the effort is low.

(4.5) implies that (4.8) is positive and therefore there is no sense to set a high threshold and put in low effort because in this case the entrepreneur's payoff is zero. Next, note that (4.8) is greater than (4.9), which implies that there is no sense to put in a high effort and set a low threshold.

Two cases are possible. First consider $A - B \geq e.$. This means that (4.6) is greater than (4.7) and implies that a high effort under KIA is better than a low effort. It also means that (4.9) is greater than (4.10) so the optimal choice for the entrepreneur is AON with high effort (threshold A) since (4.9) is greater than (4.6).

Now consider $A - B < e$. Two cases are possible. First consider $A + a - e > B + b$. Then the choice is between AON with high effort and threshold A and KIA with low effort. The former is preferred if

$$A + a - e > B \tag{4.11}$$

Second consider $A + a - e < B + b$. Then the choice is between AON with low effort and threshold B and KIA with low effort. The former is preferred.

Level of effort and crowdfunding type. The main prediction of the above analysis is that the only case when the entrepreneur selects different levels of efforts for different types of crowdfunding is when he selects a high level of effort under AON (and a high threshold) and a low level of effort with KIA. Cumming et al (2020) suggest that KIA campaigns are less successful in achieving their objectives, which is consistent with the spirit of the above results. For example, the expected probability of success on Kickstarter, which uses AON, is usually higher than it is on Indiegogo.

Cost of effort and the extent of continuation benefits. The above choice (between AON with a high threshold and a high level of effort) and KIA with a low level of effort depends on (4.11). As follows from (4.11), AON is more likely when the cost of effort is relatively low. Under AON, the entrepreneur's payoff is risky so when he/she chooses his/her effort level, he/she faces a trade-off between the marginal cost of effort (the entrepreneur bears 100% of the cost increase) and expected benefits that are weighted by the risk of campaign failure. In these conditions, entrepreneurs of high-quality ventures tend to provide more effort than those of low-quality ventures.

Schwienbacher (2018) analyses a model of choice between crowdfunding and venture capital that is based on moral hazard problems. Similar to the spirit of the above analysis, the paper finds that under AON the best strategies are either to have a large target and deliver a high level of effort or a small target and a low effort. Entrepreneur prefers the former if the effort cost is relatively low or when demand uncertainty is high. Schwienbacher (2018) then compares crowdfunding with venture capital financing. We will provide more discussion in Chapter 6.

Miglo and Miglo (2019) analyse the roles of different market imperfections in crowdfunding including the effect of moral hazard issues on pricing and production strategies. Under equity-based crowdfunding the fraction of shares retained by the entrepreneur is reduced (in the spirit of Jensen & Meckling, 1976). Miglo and Miglo (2019) suggest that prices can be higher and quantity produced can be lower under equity-based crowdfunding than under reward-based crowdfunding. This seems to be indirectly consistent with Paakkarinen (2016) in that equity-based crowdfunding may have fewer customers but higher margins. In more general terms, moral hazard issues related to entrepreneurial effort may be more important under equity-based crowdfunding (see, for example, Gabison, 2015 and Paakkarinen, 2016, which notes that equity-based crowdfunding is more constricted in comparison to other forms of crowdfunding; see also Babich et al., 2021).

Questions and Exercises

1. Why can equity-based crowdfunding reduce an entrepreneur's incentives and create/amplify moral hazard problems? Discuss.
2. The threat of a takeover and a secondary market for shares are usually not available for crowdfunding firms as disciplinary tools.
3. Under the nominee model, equity-based crowdfunding platforms require firms to provide rewards to backers.
4. Crowdcube offers the possibility for campaigns to offer dual stock structures where class A shares have more voting rights than cash flow rights.
5. Mixed evidence exists regarding whether the separation of ownership and control is beneficial for crowdfunding campaign success.
6. An entrepreneur's incentive to misappropriate funds received from a crowdfunding campaign can be described as a trade-off between the size of the post-campaign market for the firm's product (a larger size reduces the incentive to cash-in-and-run) and the strength of the regulatory environment (stronger punishment for funds misappropriation reduces the incentive for it).
7. (based on problem 5 from Chapter 3 with the addition of moral hazard) An entrepreneurial firm owns an innovative project. The firm is organized with unlimited liability. An investment of 400 is required (fixed cost that is invested in tangible assets that fully depreciate by the time the firm completes the project; the variable cost is negligible small). The demand for the good is 70 items for the price of 10 if the demand is high (with probability 60%) and 20 items for the price 5 if the demand is low. Under

crowdfunding the entrepreneur is subject to moral hazard (cash-in-and-run problem). The entrepreneur can divert funds received during the crowdfunding campaign and not use them for the purposes announced during the campaign. Suppose that the probability of being caught in this case is 50% and all "stolen" funds are returned to the government in this case. Also assume that the entrepreneur suffers a disutility level -100 in this scenario (reputation loss, legal responsibility etc.). The firm is planning to use either reward-based crowdfunding (AON) or traditional funding in the form of a bank loan with an interest rate of 10%. Under reward-based crowdfunding, the firm announces the crowdfunding price and the campaign target.

a. Critically discuss the cash-in-and-run problem in crowdfunding.
b. Suppose the demand is high for sure. Calculate the entrepreneur's profit if the firm uses bank financing.
c. Continue to assume that the demand is high for sure and that the entrepreneur is totally honest, so he/she does not consider diverting funds. Calculate the entrepreneur's profit if the firm uses crowdfunding assuming that the firm announces a campaign target of 400 and collects 40 pre-orders/contributions of 10 each from 40 backers and sell 30 items for the price 10 on the spot market after the campaign is finished. Also assume that the platform charges a fee of 50.
d. What strategy is optimal for the entrepreneur? Comment why.
e. Now suppose that the demand is uncertain, and the entrepreneur is subject to a moral hazard problem. Also assume that the entrepreneur maximizes his/her expected profit and the value of his/her own assets is 500 (which he/she does not plan to use for firm financing since it will be inconvenient to sell assets etc.). Calculate profits under both strategies (bank loan and crowdfunding). As before assume that under crowdfunding the firm announces a campaign target of 400 and the crowdfunding price is 10. If demand is high the firm collects 40 pre-orders/contributions of 10 each from 40 backers and sells 30 items for the price of 10 on the spot market after the campaign is finished. If the demand is low the firm will not collect any funds.
f. Discuss your result in the previous question.

8. Consider a firm with an innovative product or service. The firm is run by an entrepreneur who can provide either a high or low level of effort during the campaign of raising funds. Let c be the cost of effort. If the effort is high ($c = e$), the firm can raise an amount of A with probability p_h and 0 otherwise. If the effort is low ($c = 0$), the firm can raise A with probability p_l and 0 otherwise, $p_l < p_h$.
   In addition, if the campaign is successful, there will be a second period of production during which the firm will generate profit $X + x$, where x depends on the crowdfunding campaign threshold. Suppose that if the company sets a threshold during the campaign (AON) it can generate more profits in period 2 since it creates more trust in the firm (and its product). The firm has 2 strategies: KIA or AON (with threshold A); $x = a$ if AON is selected and $x = 0$ otherwise, $a > 0$. What strategy is the best?
9. Consider a firm with an innovative product or service. The firm plans to make an investment I and then sell the product for two periods. The production is $q_t, t = 1{,}2$. The cost per item equals c. In each period, the demand is $p_t = a - q_t$ and the firm selects the optimal price to maximize its profit (the spot price in period 2 and the crowdfunding price in period 1, assuming that funders receive an item as a reward when they pay the crowdfunding price). The firm is single-owned and run by an entrepreneur.

   a. Determine the entrepreneur's optimal strategy. Determine the entrepreneur's profit.
   b. Now suppose that the entrepreneur is subject to moral hazard. After the crowdfunding campaign, the entrepreneur is able to divert funds received during the campaign. In this case the entrepreneur's profit equals aF, where F is the amount of funds raised during the crowdfunding campaign and a is the probability of not being caught (a parameter that reflects the institutional strength). Suppose that the entrepreneur uses the prices determined in question a. Find the condition that determines whether the entrepreneur will divert funds. Analyse the effect of I on the entrepreneur's incentive. Find the conditions and describe the threshold. Analyse the role of regulation (a).
   c. What strategy can the entrepreneur use to try to mitigate the moral hazard problem?

References

Abor, J., & Adjasi, C. (2007). Corporate governance and the small and medium enterprises sector: Theory and implications. *Corporate Governance, 7*(2), 111–122.

Appio, F. P., Leone, D., Platania, F., & Schiavone, F. (2020). Why are rewards not delivered on time in rewards-based crowdfunding campaigns? An empirical exploration. *Technological Forecasting and Social Change, 157*, Article 120069.

Babich, V., Marinesi, S., & Tsoukalas, G. (2021). Does crowdfunding benefit entrepreneurs and venture capital investors? *Manufacturing & Service Operations Management, 23*(2), 508–524.

Bakri, M. H., Radzai, M. S. M., & Rasid, A. M. M. (2021). Technology acceptance in crowdfunding among retailers. *Studies of Applied Economics, 39*(5).

Belavina, E., Marinesi, S., & Tsoukalas, G. (2020). Rethinking crowdfunding platform design: Mechanisms to deter misconduct and improve efficiency (2020). *Management Science, 66*(11), 4980–4997.

Belleflamme, P., Omrani, N., & Peitz, M. (2015) The economics of crowdfunding platforms. *Information Economics and Policy, 33*(C), 11–28.

Bolton, P., & Dewatripont, M. (2004). *Contract theory*. MIT Press.

Chang, C., Lee, Y., & Tien, H. (2021). Does venture capital affect crowdfunding performance?. Economic Review. *Journal of Economics and Business, 19*(2), 53–64.

Chemla, G., & Tinn, K. (2019). Learning through crowdfunding. *Management Science, 66*(5), 1783–1801.

Coakley, J., Cumming, D., Lazos, A., & Vismara, S., (2022). *Corporate governance with crowd investors in innovative entrepreneurial finance: Nominee structure and coinvestment in equity crowdfunding* (Essex Finance Centre Working Papers 33709). University of Essex.

Cumming, D., Hornuf, L., Karami, M., & Schweizer, D. (2023). Disentangling crowdfunding from fraudfunding. *Journal of Business Ethics, 182*, 1103–1128.

Cumming, D., Leboeuf, G., & Schwienbacher, A. (2020). Crowdfunding models: Keep-it-all versus all or nothing. *Financial Management, 49*, 331–360.

Cumming, D., Vanacker, T. R., & Zahra, S. A. (2021). Equity crowdfunding and governance: Toward an integrative model and research agenda. *Academy of Management Perspectives, 35*(1), 69–95.

Franks, J., & Mayer, C. (1996). Hostile takeovers and the correction of managerial failure. *Journal of Financial Economics, 40*(1), 163–181.

Gabison, G. (2015). *Understanding Crowdfunding and its Regulations*. http://publications.jrc.ec.europa.eu/repository/bitstream/JRC92482/lbna26992enn.pdf

Jensen, M. (1986). Agency costs of free cash flow, corporate finance, and takeovers. *American Economic Review, 76*, 323–329.

Jensen, M., & Meckling, W. (1976). Theory of the firm: Managerial behavior, agency costs and ownership structure. *Journal of Financial Economics, 3*, 305–360.

Kaplan, S. N., & Strömberg, P. (2003). Financial contracting theory meets the real world: An empirical analysis of venture capital contracts. *The Review of Economic Studies, 70*(2), 281–315.

Kourabas, S. (2021). Corporate governance implications of equity crowdfunding. A. Godwin, R. Langford & P. W. Lee (Eds.), *Technology and corporate law: How innovation shapes corporate activity*. Edward Elgar.

Laffont, J. J., & Martimort, D. (2002). *The theory of incentives: The principal-agent model*. Princeton University Press.

Mataigne, V., Meoli, M., Vanacker, T., & Vismara, S. (2025). False signaling by platform team members and post-campaign venture outcomes: evidence from an equity crowdfunding platform. *Journal of Business Venturing, 40*(1).

Miglo, A., & Miglo, V. (2019). Market imperfections and crowdfunding. *Small Business Economics, 53*(1), 51–79.

Miglo, A. (2020). Crowdfunding in a Competitive Environment. *Journal of Risk and Financial Management, 13*(3), 39 (Special Issue on Crowdfunding. Ed. D. Cumming and S. Johan).

Miglo, A. (2023). *A theory of crowdfunding under asymmetric information and discounting cost*. Available at SSRN. https://ssrn.com/abstract=4659368.

Paakkarinen, P. (2016). *Success factors in reward based and equity based crowdfunding* (Finland Master's thesis).

Panicker, V. S., Upadhyayula, R. S., & Mitra, S. (2023). Lender representatives on board of directors and internationalization in firms: An institutionalized agency perspective. *Journal of Management and Governance, 27*, 75–98.

Schmidt, K. M. (2003). Convertible securities and venture capital finance. *The Journal of Finance, 58*(3), 1139–1166.

Schwienbacher, A. (2018). Entrepreneurial risk-taking in crowdfunding campaigns. *Small Business Economics, 51*(4), 843–859.

Strausz, R. (2017). Crowdfunding, demand uncertainty, and moral hazard—A mechanism design approach. *American Economic Review, 107*(6), 1430–1476.

Verret, J. W. (2016). Uber-ized corporate law: Toward a 21st century corporate governance for crowdfunding and app-based investor communications. *Journal of Corporation Law, 41*(4), 101–143.

CHAPTER 5

Crowdfunding, Network Benefits and Behavioural Biases

5.1 Crowdfunding and Network Benefits

There are several ideas related to the role of networks benefits for crowdfunding firms. First, by definition, crowdfunding is an online method of raising funds where backers can potentially be connected with each other via e.g. forums on crowdfunding platforms. Second, the new generation of investors may have slightly different priorities compared to previous generations. Younger investors are better at using online communication tools and generally have better developed habits in terms of not only using online tools because of cost efficiency but also because of their innovative benefits. People are motivated to participate in crowdfunding because of social interactions and feelings of connectedness to a community with similar interests (Belleflamme et al., 2014; Gerber et al., 2012). Theoretically, this idea has interesting interpretations e.g. an important problem in game theory is the multiplicity of possible equilibria (see e.g. Borkovsky et al., 2015), in other words an absence of a clear solution. As

Supplementary Information The online version contains supplementary material available at https://doi.org/10.1007/978-3-032-10724-4_5.

© The Author(s), under exclusive license to Springer Nature Switzerland AG 2026
A. Miglo and V. Miglo, *The Theories and Developments of Crowdfunding*, https://doi.org/10.1007/978-3-032-10724-4_5

we saw before game theory is often a useful tool to analyse the outcome of crowdfunding related problems. The following provides an illustration.[1]

Suppose there are two perspective consumers/buyers of a firm's product. Suppose the firm sells the product on the spot market and the price of the product is p. Each consumer receives a value/benefit v if they purchase the product and $v + s$ if and only if the other consumers also buy the product where s is the network benefit (exchange of ideas, community sense etc.). Let us consider the game where each consumer decides whether to purchase the product. Each player has two strategies: to buy or not to buy. The matrix of payoffs is (Table 5.1).

Table 5.1 The matrix of payoffs in a game of purchasing a product

Player 1/Player 2	*Buy*	*Not buy*
Buy	$v + s - p, v + s - p$	$v - p, 0$
Not buy	$0, v - p$	0,0

What explains the payoffs? Consider, for example, the case when both players decided to buy. Then each of them receives the standalone value v minus the product price p and also the additional benefit s given that the second player has also purchased the product. If one of the players decides not to puy this player's payoff is zero by definition. If the other player decides to purchase his/her payoff is $v - p$ (no additional benefits exist in this case since the other player did not buy the product). There are two Nash equilibria in this (coordination) game.[2] if

$$v < p < v + s \tag{5.1}$$

either both investors purchase the product, or neither does. Indeed, consider for example the case when both players buy the product. No player is interested in deviating because it can only reduce their payoffs. For example, if one of the players decides not to buy his/her payoff becomes 0 which is smaller than $v + s - p$ given (Eq. 5.1). Similarly suppose that no one buys the product. This is an equilibrium indeed since if one of the players deviates, their payoff becomes $v - p$ which is negative

[1] In the spirit of Miglo (2021a).

[2] Formally, the structure of the game is similar to the classical coordination game (see e.g. Tomassini & Pestelacci, 2010).

because of (Eq. 5.1) and hence smaller than the equilibrium payoff so no player has an incentive to deviate. The multiplicity of equilibria opens the door for social value loss. The problem with having two possible equilibria is that one may be a good equilibrium where both participants buy the product and one may be a "bad" equilibrium where neither participant buys.

This analysis implies that crowdfunding can improve the equilibria/equilibrium. If instead of using spot sales the firm pre-sells the product using crowdfunding, potential buyers/funders can observe other funders' strategies (e.g. crowdfunding campaigns update information about the number of pre-sold items). In this case, we can assume that the game becomes dynamic (and not strategic as described above). In this case the only equilibrium is the one where both consumers participate.[3]

Further, crowdfunding is more likely to be used for products with large community benefits. Indeed if s is sufficiently large then (Eq. 5.1) is more likely to hold for given values of p and v. It is observed that crowdfunding is especially popular in sectors or segments of the market with large network benefits (Brown et al., 2019; Kromidha & Robson, 2016; Mourao et al., 2018.

(Eq. 5.1) also implies that coordination problems under crowdfunding can be avoided if the production cost of the firm is either very small or very high. Indeed, suppose that the cost per product is c. The product price should at least cover this cost. If the cost is not sufficiently small and not very large, i.e. if, for example, $v + s > c > v$ then the only situation where an entrepreneur can make a profit is if $v < p < v + s$. Indeed $v > p$ would imply $p < v < c$ making production unprofitable since the price of the product is less than its cost. If $p > v + s$ then no participants would be interested in purchasing the product. So (Eq. 5.1) should hold to ensure an equilibrium multiplicity. A similar situation can arise if the fixed cost of the campaign or the crowdfunding fees are not sufficiently small.

Deb et al. (2024) study reward-based crowdfunding campaigns. In their model two types of funders exist: some of them want to consume the product ("buyers") while others just want the firm to be successful. There is a coordination problem between buyers. The paper describes

[3] Similar to the idea of the prisoner's dilemma which is played statically (with a bad equilibrium) vs. dynamic game where a good equilibrium can be sustainable (see e.g. Akin, 2016).

the possible equilibria in the game and provides a comparative analysis of factors affecting the probability of campaign success. The paper also suggests that projects that finish close to the deadline are usually driven by the second type of funders while projects that finish early are primarily driven by the first type.

Among other ideas note the following. In Belleflamme et al. (2014), participants of crowdfunding campaigns enjoy community benefits. It is argued that equity-based crowdfunding should be preferred by large projects while reward-based should be preferred for small projects.

So far we have discussed the network as a large set of potential investors or a large set of consumers/firm product buyers. Since crowdfunding is used by many small firms, one can also consider the potential benefits of firms operating in a competitive network with multiple producers.[4] The following illustrates the idea. Consider a firm that can choose between selling its product on the spot market (the product value is v) and via reward-based crowdfunding. Suppose that if the firm uses the reward-based crowdfunding the price is $v - \beta$. This means that the backers who invested this amount will receive the firm's future product as a reward. Campaign backers are rewarded a benefit β for waiting, $\beta < v$, compared to consumers on the spot market. Further, assume that the firm gets an additional benefit s when conducting a crowdfunding campaign e.g. it receives feedback from potential buyers, which it can use for its other projects for example. For simplicity suppose that the total number of potential consumers/backers is 4. Without crowdfunding, the firm's expected profit is $4v$. Further, assume that if the firm decides to use both crowdfunding and spot sales, consumers will be split 50–50 between the crowdfunding campaign and spot sales i.e. two backers will participate in the crowdfunding campaign, and two consumers will buy the product on the spot market. Then the firm's expected profit equals $4v - 2\beta + s$. If $s < 2\beta$ crowdfunding is useless in the model since the spot price is greater than the crowdfunding price, crowdfunding is useless in this model with one firm that we can call a monopoly.

Now consider the case with two firms. Suppose that if two firms are on the spot market, buyers are split 50–50 between firms. The following situations can occur: both firms select spot sales (denote this strategy S); both firms select crowdfunding followed by spot sales (denote this

[4] In the spirit of Miglo (2020).

strategy CF); Firm 1 selects CF and Firm 2 selects S; Firm 2 selects CF and Firm 1 selects S. If both firms select S, the equilibrium firms' profits are $\pi_1 = \pi_2 = 2v$. If both firms select CF, the equilibrium firms' profits are $\pi_1 = \pi_2 = 2v - \beta + s$. . Indeed, in this case each firm gets two buyers one of whom pre-orders the product during the crowdfunding campaign. Now consider the case when one firm (suppose Firm 1) selects CF and Firm 2 selects S. During crowdfunding Firm 1 pre-sells two goods and on the spot market the 2 remaining buyers are split 50–50 between the firms. So Firm 1's profit equals $3v - \beta + s$ and Firm 2's profit equals v.

The payoff matrix for this game is then (Table 5.2).

Table 5.2 The matrix of payoffs in a game with two firms

Firm 1/Firm 2	*S*	*CF*
S	$2v, 2v$	$v, 3v - \beta + s$
CF	$3v - \beta + s, v$	$2v - \beta + s, 2v - \beta + s$

If $v > \beta - s$, the only equilibrium is where both firms use crowdfunding. Indeed, consider a situation where both firms select the spot market strategy. Consider Firm 1. Its payoff is $2v$. If it deviates to CF then its payoff is $3v - \beta + s$, whichis greater than $2v$ so Firm 1 would deviate making situation (S,S) not an equilibrium. Similarly, a situation where one firm selects S and one firm selects CF is not an equilibrium because the former would deviate to CF. The only equilibrium is (CF,CF) where no firms have an incentive to deviate. Further $v > \beta - s$ implies that $s > \beta - v > \beta$, which implies that the total social surplus when there are two firms (which is equal to $4v - 2\beta + 2s$ is greater than the total social suplus when there is only one firm (which is $4v$).

There is a new and growing line of research related to donation-based crowdfunding that also uses coordination problems and network effects ideas. Argo et al. (2020) argue that the non-observability of other donor contributions implies an uncertainty about the recipient's ability to collect the necessary amount of funds that combined with private benefits of donors from the fact of making a deciding contribution to the projects can improve the campaign outcome for donation-based crowdfunding. Cason and Zubrickas (2019) argue that the all-or nothing feature of crowdfunding (refund bonuses) can also improve coordination problems and ultimately can improve the outcome of donation-based crowdfunding.

5.2 Crowdfunding and Behavioural Finance

This section reviews some ideas that incorporate behavioural finance into the analysis and practice of crowdfunding. Behavioural finance is a growing area in finance over the last 20–30 years and intersects with the firm financing strategies and capital structure choice areas (see e.g. Badheka & Pandya, 2022). Behavioural finance-based ideas seem to play a significant role in the theory and practice of crowdfunding as well (see e.g. Miglo, 2021a). In general, behavioural finance assumes that decisions-makers and other participants are not necessarily fully rational individuals and that as human beings they are often biased in setting their objectives or in their valuations and may face constraints that are not considered in traditional models where individuals are assumed to be fully rational and unbiased.

An important area in behavioural finance is decision-maker overconfidence (see e.g. Everett & Fairchild, 2015; Hayward et al., 2006). There are different ideas about how entrepreneurial overconfidence can affect crowdfunding. Some of them predict a negative effect on the outcome of campaigns and some of them suggest that crowdfunding can mitigate inefficiencies created by entrepreneurial overconfidence.[5] For example, an entrepreneur observes the market's reaction to his/her crowdfunding campaign and can make adjustments relatively early in the life of the firm to avoid repeating mistakes in the future. The following example illustrates how this may happen (based on Miglo, 2021b).

An entrepreneurial firm develops its innovative product or service. The firm estimates that if it produces q units, it costscq. The demand for the good is given by the inverse demand function$q = a - p$. Also let's assume $a > c$ (otherwise the firm's profit $qp - cq = q(a - c - q$ cannot be positive). The firm has no initial funds available and plans to raise funds using a reward-based crowdfunding campaign (AON). The firm selects the crowdfunding price p i.e. any backer who invests p will get the firm's product as a reward. The firm also selects the campaign threshold$T$,$T > 0$. If the amount of funds raised during the campaign is less than$T$, funds are returned to the investors/funders. The firm acts in the interest of the founder/entrepreneur and maximizes his/her expected profit. Further,

[5] Lin and Pursiainen (2018) study the importance of overconfidence in experimental setting.

the entrepreneur is biased: he/she can be either overconfident or underconfident.[6] This means that the entrepreneur thinks that the demand for the firm's product equals$q = a + \varepsilon - p$, where ε reflects the extent of the entrepreneur's bias. $\varepsilon > 0$ means that the entrepreneur is overconfident; $\varepsilon < 0$ means that the entrepreneur is underconfident and $\varepsilon = 0$ means that the entrepreneur is unbiased. A positive ε means that the entrepreneur overestimates the expected demand for the firm's product/service.[7] The entrepreneur is assumed to be risk-neutral and the risk-free interest rate is 0.

The timing of events is as follows:

1. Firm selects T.
2. Firm selects p; q is determined.
3. If AON is selected and $pq < T$, the funds are returned to the investors.

The firm maximizes the entrepreneur's expected profit

$$\Pi = pq - cq = (p - c)q = (p - c)(a + \varepsilon - p) \tag{5.2}$$

subject to $p \geq c$ (otherwise the funds raised will not cover the production cost).

Proposition 5.1. An overconfident entrepreneur sets the crowdfunding price higher than an unbiased entrepreneur; an underconfident entrepreneur sets the crowdfunding price lower than an unbiased entrepreneur.

Proof. As follows from (Eq. 5.2), from the entrepreneur's point of view the optimal price is:

$$p = (a + \varepsilon + c)/2 \tag{5.3}$$

[6] For a literature review regarding risk and overconfidence see, for example, Bilgehan (2014). See also Reyes et al. (2019).

[7] Alternatively, one can model the entrepreneurial bias regarding the value of M and not the value of expected return. Our interpretation is more intuitive since it reflects the entrepreneur's bias regarding the firm quality (which is measured by the firm expected return) and risk which is measured by p. This alternative modelling may generate some different results quantitatively but unlikely the major intuitions would change.

(note that $p \geq c$ because $a > c$ and $\varepsilon \geq 0$). The proposition follows from comparing (Eq. 5.3) with the optimal price that would be selected by an unbiased entrepreneur: $p = \frac{a+c}{2}$, which follows from (Eq. 5.3) when $\varepsilon = 0$.

Proposition 5.2. An overconfident entrepreneur fails more often than an unbiased entrepreneur.

Proof. With the price determined by (Eq. 5.3),

$$q = a - p = (a - \varepsilon - c)/2$$

and the firm's expected profit equals:

$$\Pi = pq - cq = ((a + \varepsilon + c)/2 - c)(a - \varepsilon - c)/2 = \frac{(a + \varepsilon - c)(a - \varepsilon - c)}{4} \tag{5.4}$$

The entrepreneur, however, thinks that.

$q = a + \varepsilon - p = (a + \varepsilon - c)/2$ and the optimal threshold (which should not be greater than the expected amount of funds raised, otherwise the firm will have to return the money to the funders) from the entrepreneur's point of view should satisfy

$$T \leq pq = p(a + \varepsilon - p) = \frac{(a + \varepsilon + c)}{2}\frac{(a + \varepsilon - c)}{2} = \frac{(a + \varepsilon + c)(a + \varepsilon - c)}{4} \tag{5.5}$$

Objectively, however, the firm's expected sales, when the price is chosen according to (Eq. 5.3), are:

$$pq = \frac{(a + \varepsilon + c)}{2}\frac{(a - \varepsilon - c)}{2} = \frac{(a + \varepsilon + c)(a - \varepsilon - c)}{4} \tag{5.6}$$

which is less than the RHS of (Eq. 5.3). Two cases are possible. If

$$T \leq \frac{(a + \varepsilon + c)(a - \varepsilon - c)}{4} \tag{5.7}$$

the amount of funds raised during crowdfunding, given by (Eq. 5.6), will reach the campaign threshold, which is determined according to the rule

(Eq. 5.5). The firm's profit then equals:

$$\Pi = pq - cq = ((a + \varepsilon + c)/2 - c)(a - \varepsilon - c)/2 = \frac{(a + \varepsilon - c)(a - \varepsilon - c)}{4}$$

If, however

$$T > \frac{(a + \varepsilon + c)(a - \varepsilon - c)}{4} \tag{5.8}$$

the threshold will not be reached and the money will be returned to the funders.

If it is assumed that the entrepreneur can select any T that satisfies the optimality conditions from his point of view (given by Eq. 5.5), we get Proposition 5.2. It follows from noting that the RHS of (Eq. 5.5) is greater than the right side of (Eq. 5.7) for an overconfident entrepreneur so the entrepreneur will select T such that $\frac{(a+\varepsilon+c)(a-\varepsilon-c)}{4} < T \leq \frac{(a+\varepsilon+c)(a+\varepsilon-c)}{4}$, which leads him to think that the threshold will be reached when in reality it will not be.

One can ask why then does the entrepreneur not try to minimize the campaign threshold as much as possible, or use KIA instead of AON?! This is of course a possibility but as discussed in the previous chapters AON may bring other advantages to the entrepreneur including the opportunity to signal his firm's quality and mitigating potential moral hazard issues. In the above model, you will notice we ignored that the amount of funds raised needs to be greater than the fixed cost to begin production and focused solely on variable costs.

Miglo (2021b) suggests that crowdfunding can mitigate inefficiencies due to entrepreneurial bias. An entrepreneur can observe the market's reaction to the crowdfunding campaign and can make adjustments relatively early in life of the firm to avoid repeating mistakes in the future. The paper considers an entrepreneurial firm that plans a crowdfunding campaign and knows the potential demand for its product. Under reward-based crowdfunding the firm should be able to determine the optimal price and quantity produced because the demand is known. Now suppose that the entrepreneur is overconfident and overestimates the demand. In this case, the entrepreneur will offer a price that is higher than optimal which will not only reduce the demand but also the firm's overall profit. Miglo (2021b) also considers equity-based crowdfunding. During the sale of shares, a rational entrepreneur (i.e. am entrepreneur that is not biased in his/her demand estimation) will expect to raise an amount equal to the amount needed from a rational entrepreneur's point of view in order to produce the optimal quantity of the product. Now suppose that the entrepreneur is overconfident. In this case, during the sale of shares he/she will expect to raise a greater amount. After observing the actual amount raised, the entrepreneur will realize that he/she made a mistake in estimating the product's demand and will be able to make some adjustments during the production stage that follows. The paper finds that equity-based crowdfunding is a more efficient tool for an entrepreneur to learn the market's wisdom, which is consistent with Arkrot et al. (2017).

Fairchild et al. (2017) analyse a model of a choice between venture capital and crowdfunding. Venture capital provides "network benefits", while crowdfunding investors demonstrate emotional excitement when using a crowdfunding platform. In the model, the entrepreneur is overconfident (with regard to the benefits of the venture capital network and the level of the crowd's excitement. Under venture capital financing, there is a moral hazard problem related to both the venture capitalist's and the entrepreneur's choices of effort level. The firm weighs all of these factors when selecting the best strategy. It is shown, for example, that a higher level of overconfidence usually benefits venture capital financing.

Belleflamme et al. (2013)[8] compared for-profit and non-profit firms when conducting a crowdfunding campaign. The manager's objective function in non-profit firms is different from that of managers of for-profit firms and includes a social factor. They argue that crowdfunding campaigns of non-profit firms are usually more successful than those of for-profit firms. This is consistent with the more general idea that non-profit organizations may find it easier to attract money for initiatives that are of interest to the general community due to their reduced focus on profits. Among other papers note Belleflamme et al. (2014), where a firm faces different funders with different demand functions. The behavioural aspect of this paper is that the objective function of funders includes social benefits. The paper predicts that the crowdfunding price should be higher than the spot sale price although no clear evidence exists regarding this point.

[8] Their model is based on Belleflamme et al. (2010).

5.3 Other Aspects of Crowdfunding

In this section, we consider some ideas about crowdfunding that are related to behavioural finance and the network aspects of crowdfunding. The first idea is the connection between geography and crowdfunding. Some research finds that equity crowdfunders are sensitive to distance. Initially it sounds counterintuitive because crowdfunding is an online method of raising funds. So why should distance matter at all?! From classical corporate finance literature, we know that there a home bias problem, which is difficult to explain rationally. It implies that investors are more willing to invest in projects from their own countries. One of the classic explanations for home bias is a behavioural bias (see e.g. Lütje & Menkhoff, 2007). We will see that this same bias can exist with regard to locations in crowdfunding i.e. funders prefer projects that are close to their geographic location. A good example is considered in Guenther et al. (2018). They analyse data from Australian crowdfunding campaigns and find that geographic distance is negatively correlated with investment probability for home country investors. The authors suggest that intuitively there remain advantages for investors to invest in local firms maybe because online information is imperfect and they can visit the store and speak personally with the employees or entrepreneurs behind local crowdfunding campaigns.

Among other papers note Miglo (2022) that analyses technology crowdfunding campaigns in the UK on Kickstarter. The paper compares the performance of campaigns originated in different cities and finds some interesting connections like the influence of the number of bike commuters in a city on the number of crowdfunding campaigns in that city in their performance. Some other research has found that there is local bias in crowdfunding which is consistent with the idea that large cities should have an advantage over smaller cities (see e.g. Agrawal et al., 2015; Hornuf et al., 2022). Further, Mollick (2014) found that the project mix of founders echoes the cultural products of the cities in which they are based (see also Mollick & Robb, 2016). Cumming and Sewaid (2025) suggest that cultural distance from a platform affects the rate of success in crowdfunding. For example, the success rate of culturally distant entrepreneurs improves when they attract backers from a platform's host-country.

The second idea is whether crowdfunding in general contributes to the democratization and improved access to entrepreneurial finance.

We have just discussed one aspect of this namely geography. But also there are some other aspects e.g. age, gender, ethnicity etc. (see e.g. Davis & Davis, 2021). Generally, the literature suggests that crowdfunding helps to improve access to some groups of entrepreneurs and investors but there are still significant frictions. Regarding age, Cumming et al. (2021) suggest an improved access to finance via crowdfunding for young entrepreneurs for example. For an interesting research paper regarding the gender aspect in crowdfunding see e.g. Gafni et al. (2021).

Among other papers note that Brown and Davies (2020) analyse a model of crowdfunding where investors can acquire some information about a project's quality. The entrepreneur gets a signal by observing fundraising amounts and then decides whether or not to undertake a risky project. There is a "non-investment threshold" that creates a "loser's blessing", i.e. the presence of the threshold encourages contributing without information by reducing the risk of investment in bad projects.

Questions and Exercises

1. Entrepreneurial overconfidence may affect the likelihood of crowdfunding campaign success.
2. The data suggests that crowdfunding investors favour short rather than long distances.
3. Some research finds that companies with younger members are more likely to use crowdfunding.
4. Suppose there are two perspective consumers/buyers of a firm's product. Suppose the firm sells the product on the spot market and the price of the product is 5. Each consumer gets an amount 6 of benefits 6 if they purchase the product and an additional benefit 2 only if other consumers also purchase the product.

   a. Consider the game similar to the one discussed in the text. Draw the matrix of payoffs.
   b. Find the possible equilibria.
      a. Now suppose that the price is 7. Draw the payoff matrix and find the equilibrium.
      b. Discuss the results.
5. Consider an entrepreneurial firm that develops a product (the cost is 2 per item) and considers reward-based crowdfunding to raise funds where each participant gets the firm's product as a reward. The firm estimates that the demand is determined by: $q = 100 - p$, where p

is the crowdfunding price. Assume that there is no discounting or waiting costs for potential buyers so in the case of crowdfunding all potential buyers are interested in participating.

a. Suppose the entrepreneur is fully rational and unbiased. What is the optimal crowdfunding price? What is the number of products sold and the firm's profit?
b. Suppose now that the entrepreneur is overconfident and believes that the demand is $q = 150 - p$. What will be the crowdfunding price in this case?
c. Now consider equity-based crowdfunding. Suppose for that the entrepreneur sells 3% of the firm during the campaign. Investors provide funds if the expected values of their holdings cover the investment amount. During the sale of shares, the entrepreneur expects to receive an amount M. Suppose the entrepreneur is fully rational and unbiased. Find M.
d. Now suppose that the entrepreneur is overconfident and believes that the demand is $q = 150 - p$. Find M in this case.
e. Discuss the results.

References

Agrawal, A., Catalini, C., & Goldfarb, A. (2015). Crowdfunding: Geography, social networks, and the timing of investment decisions. *Journal of Economics & Management Strategy, 24*(2), 253–274.

Akin, E. (2016). The iterated prisoner's dilemma: Good strategies and their dynamics ergodic theory. *Advances in Dynamical Systems*, 77–107.

Argo, N., Klinowski, D., Krishnamurti, T., & Smith, S. (2020). The completion effect in charitable crowdfunding. *Journal of Economic Behavior & Organization, 172*(C), 17–32.

Arkrot, W., A. Unger, & Åhlström, E. (2017). *Crowdfunding from a marketing perspective.* Thesis. http://www.diva-portal.org/smash/get/diva2:1106397/FULLTEXT01.pdf

Badheka, G. T., & Pandya, K. (2022). Behavioural capital structure: A systematic literature review on the role of psychological factors in determining the capital structure. *International Journal of Financial Management, 12*(3), 1–9.

Belleflamme, P., Lambert, T., & Schwienbacher, A. (2010). *Crowdfunding: An industrial organization perspective.* Prepared for the Workshop Digital Business Models: Understanding Strategies, Held in Paris on June 2010. http://economix.fr/pdf/workshops/2010_dbm/Be

Belleflamme, P., Lambert, T., & Schwienbacher, A. (2013). Individual crowdfunding practices. *Venture Capital: An International Journal of Entrepreneurial Finance, 15*(4), 313–333.
Belleflamme, P., Lambert, T., & Schwienbacher, A. (2014). Crowdfunding: Tapping the right crowd. *Journal of Business Venturing, 29*(5), 585–609.
Borkovsky, R., Ellickson, P., Gordon, B., Aguirregabiria, V., Gardete, P., Grieco, P., Gureckis, T., Ho, T.-H., Mathevet, L., & Sweeting, A. (2015). Multiplicity of equilibria and information structures in empirical games: Challenges and prospects. *Marketing Letters, 2*, 115–125.
Bilgehan, T. (2014). Psychological biases and the capital structure decisions: A literature review. *Theoretical & Applied Economics, 12*(601), 123–142.
Brown, D. C., & Davies, S. W. (2020). Financing efficiency of securities-based crowdfunding. *The Review of Financial Studies, 33*(9), 3975–4023.
Brown, R., Mawson, S., & Rowe, A. (2019). Start-ups, entrepreneurial networks and equity crowdfunding: A processual perspective. *Industrial Marketing Management, 80*, 115–125.
Cason, T., & Zubrickas, R. (2019). Donation-based crowdfunding with refund bonuses. *European Economic Review, 119*(C), 452–471.
Cumming, D., Meoli, M., & Vismara, S. (2021). Does equity crowdfunding democratize entrepreneurial finance? *Small Business Economics, 56*, 533–552.
Cumming, D. J., & Sewaid, A. (2025). Culture, internationa stakeholders, and crowdfunding. *Global Strategy Journal, 15*(1), 184–216.
Davis, B., & Davis, M. (2021). *Crowdfunding and the democratization of finance*. Bristol University Press.
Deb, J., Oery, A., & Williams, K. R. (2024). Aiming for the goal: Contribution dynamics of crowdfunding. *American Economic Review, 114*(12), 3847–3876.
Everett, C. R., & Fairchild, R. J. (2015). A theory of entrepreneurial overconfidence, effort, and firm outcomes. *The Journal of Entrepreneurial Finance (JEF), 17*(1), 1–26.
Fairchild, R., Liu, W., & Yao, Y. (2017). An Entrepreneur's choice of Crowd-Funding or venture capital financing: The effect of entrepreneurial overconfidence and CF-Investors' Passion. working paper. Available at SSRN: https://ssrn.com/abstract=2926980
Gafni, H., Marom, D., Robb, A., & Sade, O. (2021). Gender dynamics in crowdfunding (kickstarter): Evidence on entrepreneurs, backers, and taste-based discrimination. *Review of Finance, 25*(2), 235–274.
Gerber, E. M., Hui, J. S., & Kuo, P. Y. (2012). Crowdfunding: Why people are motivated to post and fund projects on crowdfunding platforms. *Proceedings of the International Workshop on Design, Influence, and Social Technologies: Techniques, Impacts and Ethics, 2*(11), 10.

Guenther, C., Johan, S., & Schweizer, D. (2018). Is the crowd sensitive to distance?—How investment decisions differ by investor type. *Small Business Economics, 50*(2), 289–305.

Hayward, M., Shepherd, D., & Griffin, D. (2006). A Hubris theory of entrepreneurship. *Management Science, 52*(2), 160–172.

Hornuf, L., Schmitt, M., & Stenzhorn, E. (2022). The local bias in equity crowdfunding: Behavioral anomaly or rational preference? *Journal of Economics & Management Strategy, 31*(3), 693–733.

Kromidha, E., & Robson, P. (2016). Social identity and signalling success factors in online crowdfunding. *Entrepreneurship & Regional Development, 28*(9–10), Article 605629.

Lin, T-C., & Pursiainen, V. (2018). *Gender differences in crowdfunding—Entrepreneur overconfidence and campaign outcomes*. working paper. Available at SSRN: https://ssrn.com/abstract=3045050

Lütje, T., & Menkhoff, L. (2007). What drives home bias? Evidence from fund managers' views. *International Journal of Finance & Economics, 12*(1), 21–35.

Miglo, A. (2020). Crowdfunding in a competitive environment (D. Cumming & S. Johan, Ed.). *Journal of Risk and Financial Management*, Special Issue on Crowdfunding, *13*(3), 39.

Miglo, A. (2021a). STO vs. ICO: A theory of token issues under moral hazard and demand uncertainty. *Journal of Risk and Financial Management, 14*, 232.

Miglo, A. (2021b). Crowdfunding under market feedback, asymmetric information and overconfident entrepreneur. *Entrepreneurship Research Journal, 11*(4), 20190018.

Miglo, A. (2022). Comparing crowdfunding theory and practice: The case of technology industry in England. *Available at SSRN 3818387*.

Mollick, E. R. (2014). The dynamics of crowdfunding: An exploratory study. *Journal of Business Venturing, 29*(1), 1–16.

Mollick, E., & Robb, A. (2016). Democratizing innovation and capital access: The role of crowdfunding. *California Management Review, 58*(2), 72–87.

Mourao, P., Silveira, M., & de Melo, R. (2018). Many are never too many: An analysis of crowdfunding projects in Brazil. *International Journal of Financial Studies, 6*(4), 95.

Reyes, J. A. P., Miranda, M. R., & Vera-Martinez, J. (2019). Capital structure construct: A new approach to behavioral finance. *Investment Management and Financial Innovations, 16*(4), 86–97.

Tomassini, M., & Pestelacci, E. (2010). Coordination Games on Dynamical Networks. *Games, 1*, 242–261.

PART II

Different Topics

This part covers such topics as a firm's choice between crowdfunding and other financing strategies, the role of regulation in crowdfunding, fintech developments related to crowdfunding, the role of discounting cost in crowdfunding and others.

CHAPTER 6

Crowdfunding vs. Other Types of Financing/Investment

6.1 Crowdfunding and Bank Loans

We saw in Chapter 3 that one of the advantages of crowdfunding over traditional financing is to help entrepreneurs learn the market demand. In this section we discuss other differences between crowdfunding and bank loans. The idea of considering crowdfunding along with traditional bank financing has been well recognized among practitioners. Here is a quote from a report by the crowdfundinder.co.uk website: "...Using crowdfunding alongside traditional funding can add an additional layer of sustainability to projects..."[1] Also bank loans remain the main source of financing for small-and medium-size firms. Empirical evidence shows that in practice crowdfunding is still behind bank loans among, for example, small-medium-size enterprises (SMEs).[2] Some papers, including

[1] https://www.crowdfunder.co.uk/uploads/biz_dev/special_report_grants_loans_crowdfunding.pdf.

[2] Example, the total amount of bank loans outstanding is 168 bln in the UK (Fig. A.1 in Small Business Finance report by British Business Bank (2019/20)) and the volume of reward-based crowdfunding is about 6 bln. (based on https://p2pmarketdata.com/crowdfunding-statistics-worldwide/).

Supplementary Information The online version contains supplementary material available at https://doi.org/10.1007/978-3-032-10724-4_6.

© The Author(s), under exclusive license to Springer Nature Switzerland AG 2026
A. Miglo and V. Miglo, *The Theories and Developments of Crowdfunding*, https://doi.org/10.1007/978-3-032-10724-4_6

some relatively recent ones, have even discovered a significant interest in debt financing by small entrepreneurial firms (see, e.g. Ang, 1992; Ang et al., 2010; Berger et al., 1998; Brav, 2009; Cole, 2006, 2013; Robb & Robinson, 2014). It might seem surprising given that SMEs are supposed to have difficulties with obtaining bank loans because they lack experience, credit history, credit rating and assets that can be used as collateral.[3]

One of the ideas discussed in Miglo (2022b) is that firms that use crowdfunding may face a conflict of interest when making the production scale choice as well as in their commitment to select a spot market price as it may affect potential backers' decisions to participate in the crowdfunding campaign. If the firm cannot credibly commit to a spot price that will not be lower than the crowdfunding price, the backers may not be interested in participating in a crowdfunding campaign and instead wait to purchase the product on the spot market. The following model illustrates this point.[4]

Consider a firm with an innovative product or service. It requires an investment I (the variable costs of production are assumed to be negligibly small). The production is q. The expected spot market price is p. The firm can use traditional bank financing or it can use a reward-based crowdfunding campaign where the firm promises to deliver the product to backers as a reward (the crowdfunding price during the campaign is p_c, i.e. any backer who make a contribution p_c will get the firm product as a reward). The inverse demand function is $p = a - q$. Under bank financing the firm gets an amount I and promises to pay it back (the interest rate is assumed to be 0 for simplicity). Under crowdfunding, the firm determines p_c and demand during the crowdfunding stage is $c = a - p_c$. . After finishing the crowdfunding campaign, the firm determines the number of items that should be sold on the spot market (s). Further assume that (1) the spot market price is determined using the same inverse demand function $p = a - q = a - c - s$, , and (2) under crowdfunding the amount of funds that can be raised during the campaign is limited (see, e.g. Bernardino & Santos, 2020; Durkin et al., 2016; Hui et al., 2014). This is because for example not all potential customers have access to the

[3] See, e.g. Stiglitz and Weiss (1981), Jaffee and Russell (1976), Watson (1984), Bhattacharya and Thakor (1993), Parker (2003), Arnold and Riley (2009) and Su and Zhang (2017).

[4] In the spirit of Miglo (2022b).

internet; not all of them like to purchase goods on the internet; not of all of them are comfortable with financing innovations, etc. We model this aspect by assuming that opportunities to raise funds using crowdfunding are limited. Let $\overline{q}$ be the maximum number of orders that can be collected during crowdfunding.

Miglo (2022b) argues that crowdfunding has an advantage compared to bank financing when there is demand uncertainty, e.g. a is not known to the entrepreneur, which is consistent with the ideas we discussed in Chapter 3. When demand is known on the other hand, the two-stage decision-making process in the case of crowdfunding may create a disadvantage for the firm.

Consider the case when the entrepreneur is subject to moral hazard, i.e. the production decision by the entrepreneur is non-contractible. Consider bank financing. Consider the firm's production decision. When selecting s, the firm maximizes its expected profit, which equals $pq - I = q(a - q) - I$. The solution is:

$$q = \frac{a}{2}$$

The firm's expected profit is

$$\frac{a^2}{4} - I \tag{6.1}$$

Now consider crowdfunding. First consider the production decision after the campaign is finished. The entrepreneur chooses s to maximize the firm's profit on the spot market or $sp = s(a - c - s)$. The optimal

$$s = \frac{a - c}{2}$$

so the firm's profit during the production stage is

$$\frac{a - c}{2}\left(a - c - \frac{a - c}{2}\right) = \frac{(a - c)^2}{4}$$

During the crowdfunding stage, the entrepreneur choses c to maximize

$$c(a - c) + \frac{(a - c)^2}{4} - I$$

Here the first term shows the amount received during the crowdfunding campaign (it equals $p_c c = c(a - c)$) and the second term is the profit during the spot market sales stage. So the optimal $c = \frac{a}{3}$, the optimal price is $p_c = 2a/3$ and the spot price is then $a - c - \frac{a-c}{2} = \frac{a}{3}$. The spot price is lower than the crowdfunding price, so the crowdfunding campaign fails since backers are not interested to pay a higher price. The above analysis is for the case when $\overline{q}$ is sufficiently large or when $\frac{a}{3} < \overline{q}$. Consider $\frac{a}{3} \geq \overline{q}$. If the firm uses the same crowdfunding price, i.e. $p_c = 2a/3$ the maximum demand will be reached, i.e. $a - p_c = \frac{a}{3} \geq \overline{q}$ implying $c = \overline{q}$ and the spot price is $p = (a - \overline{q})/2$. If, for example, $p_c = a - \overline{q}$ then the crowdfunding price is greater than the spot market price, so the campaign fails. So is there no way for the entrepreneur to have a successful crowdfunding campaign?!

The only way to conduct a successful crowdfunding campaign is to select a relatively low crowdfunding price so the firm can credibly commit to the spot price not being lower than the crowdfunding price. Two scenarios are possible. First $a - p_c \leq \overline{q}$. In this case one can show that, similarly to the analysis above, the spot price is $a-c-s = a-c-\frac{a-c}{2} = \frac{a-c}{2}$ while the crowdfunding price p_c is $a-c$ by definition so this scenario does not work because the spot price is lower than the crowdfunding price. Now consider

$$a - p_c > \overline{q} \tag{6.2}$$

Then $c = \overline{q}$. The expected spot price is $a - c - s = a - \overline{q} - \frac{a-\overline{q}}{2} = \frac{a-\overline{q}}{2}$. The firm should select the maximal (credible) crowdfunding price which is $\frac{a-\overline{q}}{2}$. . This can work because condition (6.2) works or because $a - \frac{a-\overline{q}}{2} > \overline{q}$. The firm's total profit is $\frac{a-\overline{q}}{2}\left(\overline{q} + \frac{a-\overline{q}}{2}\right) - I$. Unfortunately, this is still less than (Eq. 6.1) so bank financing is optimal.

Of course in a perfect market without limits to the potential size of the crowdfunding market and without moral hazard (assuming for example that the entrepreneur can credibly promise to backers to set the spot price higher than crowdfunding price) the same profit can be achieved as can be achieved under bank financing. The entrepreneur would set $p_c = p = \frac{a}{2}$. Then $c = a - p = \frac{a}{2}$ and $s = a - p - c = 0$. The firm's profit is $c(a - c) - I = \frac{a^2}{4} - I$. A more realistic approach is to assume that markets are imperfect and that such a scenario is unrealistic.

Miglo (2022b) argues that this result holds under different assumptions, e.g. if mixed financing is allowed (crowdfunding and bank financing), if different types of crowdfunding campaigns can be used, or if crowdfunding participants can receive a discount related to waiting costs. To summarize, under crowdfunding the firm collects cash for some part of its future products/services before making production decisions, which may distort incentives in the production stage. This problem does not exist with bank financing where products are sold on the spot market. The disadvantage of bank financing is that it does not provide any information about market demand. Next, we consider a model that combines both factors, i.e. the advantage of crowdfunding in learning market demand and its disadvantage in that it creates a problem in choosing the firm's production scale and crowdfunding price, as discussed previously.

Consider a model similar to the one just discussed with the only change being that the firm faces demand uncertainty: $a = a_h$ with probability μ and $a = 0$ with probability $1 - \mu$, $a_h > 0$.

Under bank financing, when selecting s, the firm maximizes its expected profit from spot sales, which equals $\mu ps + (1 - \mu)0 = \mu(a_h - s)s$. Here $p = a_h - s$ is the price when demand is high (note that there are no sales when there is no demand!). The solution is:

$$s = \frac{a_h}{2}$$

The firm's expected profit is

$$\frac{\mu {a_h}^2}{4} - I \tag{6.3}$$

With crowdfunding, the firm gets to know the demand after the crowdfunding campaign because the firm can observe c, which reflects the true value of a. If after the crowdfunding campaign the firm realizes that $a = a_h$ then the firm selects s to maximize $(a_h - c - s)s$. The solution is:

$$s = \frac{a_h - c}{2}$$

Also

$$p = a_h - c - s_h = \frac{a_h - c}{2}$$

If during crowdfunding the firm realizes that $a = 0$ then no funds will be collected and the investment will not be made. When preparing the crowdfunding campaign, the firm sets the crowdfunding price expecting a high demand (that would happen with probability μ). There is no point for the firm to deviate from this strategy since there are no opportunities to earn any profit in the scenario when the demand is absent. Then similarly to the previous reasoning the firm will set the crowdfunding price to be $\frac{a_h - \overline{q}}{2}$. Then $c = \overline{q}$ and $s = \frac{a_h - c}{2} = \frac{a_h - \overline{q}}{2}$. Then the expected spot price is $a_h - c - s = a_h - \overline{q} - \frac{a_h - \overline{q}}{2} = \frac{a_h - \overline{q}}{2}$. The firm's profit is $\frac{a_h - \overline{q}}{2}\left(\overline{q} + \frac{a_h - \overline{q}}{2}\right) - I$ with probability μ and 0 otherwise, so the firm expected profit is

$$\mu(\frac{a_h - \overline{q}}{2}\left(\overline{q} + \frac{a_h - \overline{q}}{2}\right) - I) \tag{6.4}$$

This can be greater or less than (Eq. 6.3). Note that for crowdfunding to work the amount of funds collected during the campaign should not be less than I in order to cover the investment costs; in other words $\frac{a - \overline{q}}{2}\overline{q} \geq I$.

The difference between (Eq. 6.4) and (Eq. 6.3) can be written as

$$-\frac{\mu\overline{q}^2}{4} + (1 - \mu)I \tag{6.5}$$

If Eq. (6.5) is positive crowdfunding provides a higher payoff to the entrepreneur than bank financing and vice versa. For a given value of I, (Eq. 6.5) is more likely to be positive if $\overline{q}$ and μ are sufficiently small. Small $\overline{q}$ implies a small c, which means that if crowdfunding is chosen, the campaign size is relatively small (which is generally consistent with empirical evidence). Small μ means that the risk of low demand is quite high implying that the project is quite risky, which is consistent with the spirit of the empirical evidence that a lot of crowdfunding campaign fail.

Small $\overline{q}$ can also be interpreted as a small market for crowdfunding investments. Interestingly, the model predicts that the likelihood of using crowdfunding increases when the potential size of the crowdfunding market decreases. If the crowdfunding market size is too big it will be hard for firms to credibly commit to not lowering the spot market price, which disincentivizes potential backers to participate in crowdfunding. In a similar spirit Miglo (2022b) also suggests that mixed financing may be optimal when the crowdfunding market is limited but a large investment size is needed. In this case pure crowdfunding may not deliver sufficient funds to cover investment costs while pure bank financing may imply large investment losses when demand is low. Practical examples of the simultaneous usage of crowdfunding and bank financing include startup Mous, the creator of innovative phone cases, that used a combination of a loan and a crowdfunding campaign on Kickstarter and the cases of Even Gori and Andrew Denham among others.[5] Further, recently a fintech firm Mipise recognized the potential synergies between traditional banking and innovative financing methods as crowdfunding started to offer services to banks to create their own crowdfunding platforms.[6] Similarly the crowdfunding platform Ulule develops partnerships with banks[7] to provide firms with opportunities to use a financing strategy that includes a mix of crowdfunding and traditional bank loans.[8] Also Cole et al. (2019) noted that many entrepreneurs use bank financing to finance some costs of their crowdfunding campaign and many of them use personal or business credit cards etc. Further debts can arise from not necessarily bank loans but, for example, from relationships with suppliers (see, e.g. Cuñat & Garcia-Appendini, 2012; Kohler et al., 2000; Yazdanfar & Öhman, 2017). In the future, one would expect that the problem of the choice between bank loans and crowdfunding will become even more important given reductions in the knowledge gap and also given that more sources of debt financing become available for entrepreneurs (e.g. FinTech loans).[9] Some legal researchers also mention the importance of a mix that includes both crowdfunding and bank financing (see, e.g. Tamburro, 2017).

Another aspect that affects the comparison between crowdfunding and bank loans is asymmetric information between entrepreneurs and

[5] See https://www.entrepreneur.com/article/249069, https://socialmediaweek.org/blog/2012/02/crowdfunding-bicycle-building-an-interview-with-andrew-denham-of-the-bicycle-academy/, https://www.virginstartup.org/how-to/mix-and-match-funding-options-launch-your-business.

[6] https://www.mipise.com/en/menu_item_pages/banques-crowdfunding-marque-blanche.

[7] Including such banks as BNP Paribas. See, e.g. https://lenderkit.com/blog/banks-and-crowdfunding/.

[8] https://www.americanbanker.com/news/french-crowdfunding-platform-courts-bank-partners-to-gain-U-S-foothold.

[9] Fenwick et al. (2017) mentioned supply chain financing related to fintech development.

investors. Two ideas usually emerge when discussing the effect of asymmetric information on bank financing. On the positive side research suggests that debt, and bank financing more specifically, can serve as a signal of a firm's quality when compared to equity financing (see, e.g. Leland & Pyle, 1977; Ross, 1977). Different methods exist for high-quality firms to obtain bank loans including collateral (Bester, 1985) and other types of signals (e.g. Eddleston et al., 2016). Empirical evidence regarding the signalling effect of debt vs. equity is mixed.[10] In addition, signalling models do not usually include crowdfunding, and in particular reward-based crowdfunding. We will provide more discussion in Sect. 6.4.

On the negative side note the credit rationing idea. It argues that firms operating in uncertain environments with imperfect information (e.g. SMEs, innovative firms, start-ups, etc.) should have difficulties with obtaining bank loans due to market failure in an environment with asymmetric information (Stiglitz & Weiss, 1981). Under this view all such firms (including good firms) should look for alternative finance. Blaseg and Koetter (2016), for example, find a substitution effect between equity-based crowdfunding and bank loans, i.e. firms working with distressed banks will more likely seek crowdfunding.

Among other factors that can affect the choice between bank financing and crowdfunding, note that bank financing is often accompanied by different types of moral hazard costs. It includes debt overhang problems, assets substitution and a lack of flexibility (see, e.g. Diamond, 1991; Jensen & Meckling, 1976; Miglo, 2025a). Other costs of bank financing may include direct costs like preparing business plans and other documents and the time and effort spent negotiating with banks. As well as indirect costs such as bankruptcy/liquidation costs in case the firm fails and is not able to continue its operations. Miglo and Miglo (2019) mention bankruptcy costs in their model and compared crowdfunding with bank financing. If a firm takes a bank loan and cannot pay it back then the firm is bankrupt and bankruptcy costs accrue. On the other hand, banks have a better ability to monitor and control entrepreneurs (as, for example, in Diamond, 1984). So optimal financing strategies should trade

[10] The empirical studies typically find a negative relation between profitability and leverage (Fama & French, 2002; Frank & Goyal, 2009; Rajan & Zingales, 1995; Titman & Wessels, 1988). Eckbo (1986) and Antweiler and Frank (2006) find insignificant changes in stock prices in response to straight corporate debt issues.

off these factors. Generally, the costs related to crowdfunding are lower than those related to bank financing.

Finally, Miglo (2022b) finds that firms usually prefer short over long crowdfunding campaigns since they are better able to overcome the moral hazard problem related to the production scale choice. Xu et al. (2020) investigate a firm's choice between crowdfunding and bank financing with both market uncertainty and word-of-mouth (WoM) communication. They find that the firm should adopt intertemporal pricing under crowdfunding, where the exact format is determined by WoM and market uncertainty; under bank financing, however, the firm should always charge a fixed price invariant of those parameters. Another line of literature argues that high-quality firms can use crowdfunding to signal their quality and subsequently seek traditional finance provided by banks or other large investors (Babich et al., 2019; Roma et al., 2017, 2018).[11]

6.2 Crowdfunding and Venture Capital

Venture capital (VC) represents an investment (usually equity-based or convertible equity-based—see, e.g. Kaplan and Stromberg [2003] or Cumming [2005]) into an entrepreneurial firm with the objective to support an innovative idea that has a potential to make a real impact on the market. It is a high-risk investment and is usually done by specialized professional firms, which is in contrast to other types of investments like bank financing and angel investing (the latter has some certain characteristics with venture capital in that both are often equity based and private[12]). VCs are usually actively involved in the management of firms they invest in while angel capitalists are usually less involved and overall less formal. VCs can provide a lot of potential benefits to firms, including management, organization, marketing and commercial advice by bringing their own team members and negotiating seats on the board of directors. VCs can also bring a lot of difficulties to firms by creating additional moral hazard problems since their efforts are difficult to monitor and their interests may not fully align with those of the firms.

[11] See also Tian et al. (2024) that a consider a model of financing that includes crowdfunding and bank financing and where the campaign duration and the product price are exogenous) and Tang et al. (2025).

[12] As opposed to public equity issues for example an IPO (initial public offering).

One of the advantages of venture capital (and angel investment) when compared to crowdfunding is that the opportunity for another firm to steal or mimic a firm's ideas is limited as they are not publicly disclosed like they are in crowdfunding campaigns. As mentioned in the previous paragraph, venture capital often comes with a double moral hazard problem. What this means is that in addition to the potential moral hazard issues related to the entrepreneur that we discussed in Chapter 3, there can be moral hazard problems between the VC and entrepreneur since their interests may not be fully aligned. A double-moral hazard problem can create what is called a free-rider problem (see, e.g. Grossman & Hart, 1980) where each investor relies too much on the effort provided by the other party. This results in a lower level of effort by both parties compared to the socially optimal level.

Below we develop a model that argues that crowdfunding is more suitable for smaller projects while venture capital is better suited for larger projects. A very general intuition is that in the case of crowdfunding moral hazard problems are limited to only one side/one effort, i.e. the entrepreneurial effort itself, and a smaller project means that investors will not require a large ownership stake meaning the entrepreneur will keep a large fraction of equity, which will help mitigate the moral hazard problem. In the case of venture capital, the entrepreneur retaining a large ownership stake (with a small campaign) only helps with the moral hazard issue described above and not the other between the VC and entrepreneur.

Consider a firm that needs to make an investment$I$. The firm is run by an entrepreneur who can either use crowdfunding or venture capital. Under VC the value of the firm V increases with the effort provided by both the entrepreneur and the VC. We assume that $V = e_1 + e_2$, where e_1 is the effort provided by the entrepreneur and e_2 is the effort provided by the VC. The costs of effort are e_1^2 and e_2^2, respectively. Under crowdfunding the firm value depends on the effort provided by the entrepreneur. However, there are also additional crowdfunding benefits B (discussed previously eg. learning demand and network benefits) so the firm value is $V = e + B$, where e is the entrepreneur's effort. Finally, assume that under crowdfunding there is a risk that the firm's idea will be stolen. The probability of that is γ.

Consider the first-best scenario where $\gamma = 0$ and there are no moral hazard problems so any effort can be negotiated directly. The firm value under VC is $e_1 + e_2 - e_1^2 - e_2^2 - I$. Hence, the socially optimal $e_1^* = e_2^* =$

1/2. Under crowdfunding the firm value is $e - e^2 + B - I$. The socially optimal $e^* = 1/2$. The firm value under VC is then $1/2 - I$ and under crowdfunding it is $1/4 + B - I$. To focus on the role of moral hazard assume that in a perfect market both strategies bring the same value to the firm or that $B = 1/4$.

Suppose that moral hazard exists. Consider VC. Under VC, the entrepreneur (E) has a fraction k of the firm's equity. So E will maximize $k(e_1 + e_2) - e_1^2$. Optimal $e_{1'} = k/2$. Similarly, we find $e_{2'} = (1-k)/2$. The VC's payoff equals $(1-k)(e_1 + e_2) - e_2^2 = \frac{1-k}{2} - \frac{(1-k)^2}{4}$. It should be greater than I. So $k < \sqrt{1-4I}$.

E's profit is then $\frac{k}{2} - \frac{k^2}{4}$.

Consider crowdfunding. E will maximize $(1-\gamma)k(e+B) - e^2$. Optimal $e = (1-\gamma)k/2$. The backers' total payoff equals $(1-\gamma)(1-k)(e+B) = (1-\gamma)(1-k)((1-\gamma)k/2 + B)$. It should be greater than I. So $K < \frac{1-\gamma+\sqrt{(1+8(1-\gamma)(1-4\gamma I))}}{4}$.

E's profit is then $(1-\gamma)k\left(\frac{k}{2} + 0.25\right) - \frac{k^2}{4}$. Figure 6.1 illustrates the payoffs under VC and crowdfunding when $\gamma = 0.18$. As one can see, crowdfunding provides a higher payoff for smaller size projects and VC provides a higher profit for larger projects.

Among literature that analyzes crowdfunding and venture capital note the following. Schwienbacher (2018) analyzes the role of entrepreneurial moral hazard in the choice between crowdfunding (AON) and venture

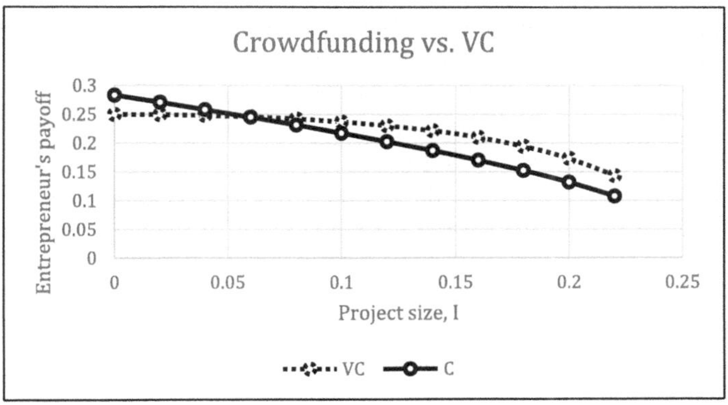

Fig. 6.1 VC vs crowdfunding

capital. The paper finds that the entrepreneur prefers crowdfunding to venture capital if the effort cost is low or when the demand in low-demand scenarios is very small. This is because continuation happens under venture capital more often than it does under AON, however this continuation may be inefficient in a low-demand scenario if the demand is very low. Schwienbacher (2018) also argues that entrepreneurs raise more money to minimize project discontinuation. This effect is exacerbated when there is a risk that the idea can be quickly replicated by others, leading to even higher fundraising goals but overall fewer projects. Conversely, the presence of professional investors (business angels, venture capitalists) reduces the entrepreneurs' incentives in their crowdfunding campaign, which leads to more but, on average, smaller crowdfunding campaigns. The overall impact on crowdfunding volume is unclear. Despite this effect on campaigns, professional investors lower the entrepreneur's risk-taking, supporting the notion that crowdfunding can complement rather than substitute existing financing methods.

Babich et al. (2019) study an optimal financing strategy for a start-up that includes a mix of crowdfunding, venture capital (VC) and bank financing. A moral hazard problem exists between an entrepreneur and a bank, and a double-sided moral hazard problem exists between an entrepreneur and a VC (both sides are affected). The entrepreneur considers opportunities to get VC or bank financing after concluding a crowdfunding campaign. In some cases, crowdfunding is not beneficial when the probability of project success is too high prior to bargaining with a VC or when the amount of funds raised during a campaign is too large (overfunded project), which can create competition from banks and worsen the position of the VC and ultimately the outcome of the bargaining. The finding that a VC can walk away after successful crowdfunding campaign is consistent with Ryu et al. (2019). Babich et al. (2019) also find that projects that projects with relatively low required external capital may not benefit as much from successful crowdfunding campaigns.[13]

[13] Among other papers analyzing the choice between crowdfunding and VC note for example Fairchild et al. (2017).

6.3 Crowdfunding and Security Design

When analyzing the choice between crowdfunding and other forms of financing, existing papers usually take the parameters of contracts/securities as given. In this section we look at this choice from a more general perspective where optimal contract/security types emerge from the model internally. This is analogous to the security design problem compared to the traditional debt/equity choice problem where contracts/securities (e.g. debt and equity) are given. One of the reasons why this general approach can be useful is that crowdfunding campaigns have a lot of interesting yet not very well understood features. Another reason is that crowdfunding regulation, which affects the features of crowdfunding campaigns and their consequences for different participants is still in of its development stage (see, e.g. Sadzius & Sadzius, 2017). Finally, existing theoretical literature on reward-based crowdfunding usually models backer behavior using traditional demand functions, however, as we know the costs and benefits for backers may include different types of financial costs and benefits (see, e.g. Appio et al., 2020; Bakri et al., 2021; Dobrynskaya & Grebennikova, 2023) so their objective function is rather multidimensional.

Consider a model of financing where the choice of financing is affected by moral hazard problems around the production scale choice and the uncertainty around consumer valuation of a firm's product. Financing contracts affect the entrepreneur's incentives selecting the firm production scale and the level of effort so the providers of capital should rationally anticipate these decisions when designing or negotiating financing contracts because these decisions ultimately affect investor payoffs.[14] Consider an entrepreneurial firm that designs a financing campaign for the production of its innovative product or service. The production is denoted by q. The cost of production is $K = cq^2/2$. The firm has no initial resources available. To finance the production cost the firm needs to raise funds from an infinite number of potential investors. Investors are identical. The value of the product to investors equals v. The market price of the product after the campaign's completion is also v. During the campaign, the firm raises an amount F. The firm is owned by an entrepreneur. After the completion of production, the firm's amount of cash equals $C = F - K$ and the total value of the firm's assets equals

[14] Based on Miglo (2022a).

$X = C + v(q - q_0)$, where q_0 is the number of items promised to investors (payments-in-kind or PIK). In contrast to traditional financing/security design models where payments to investors are made in cash here the firm can use two kinds of payments: in cash $(P(X))$ or PIK. Assume for simplicity that everybody is risk-neutral and the risk-free interest rate is zero. Investors provide funds as long as their expected payoff covers their investment cost. The firm's main decision (q) is non-contractible.

Under perfect market conditions an optimal outcome is achievable using different types of traditional contracts which is consistent with the Modigliani and Miller (1958) proposition. Indeed, suppose no moral hazard problems exist, i.e. q can be contracted and v is common knowledge. Investors will provide funds if $vq_0 + P(F - \frac{cq^2}{2} + v(q - q_0)) \geq F$. Here vq_0 is the value of the goods to investors and $P(F - \frac{cq^2}{2} + v(q - q_0))$ is their cash payment. The entrepreneur maximizes $v(q - q_0) - \frac{cq^2}{2} + F - P(v(q - q_0) - \frac{cq^2}{2} + F)$ under the condition that $vq_0 + P(v(q - q_0) - \frac{cq^2}{2} + F) \geq F$ and $F \geq \frac{cq^2}{2}$. The latter condition means that the amount of funds raised needs to cover the cost of production. Ideally a socially optimal q (that maximizes total surplus) maximizes $vq - \frac{cq^2}{2}$. So the optimal $q = v/c$. In a perfect market when q is contractible, is a contract with $q = v/c$ feasible? Consider the following contract written between the entrepreneur and investors: $q = v/c$, $q_0 \leq v/c$, $F = v^2/2c$ and $P\left(v\left(\frac{v}{c} - q_0\right)\right) = \frac{v^2}{2c}$. The entrepreneur's profit in this case equals $v(q - q_0) - \frac{v^2}{2c} + F - P\left(v(q - q_0) - \frac{v^2}{2c} + F\right) = v(q - q_0) - P\left(v\left(\frac{v}{c} - q_0\right)\right) = \frac{v^2}{c} - \frac{v^2}{2c} = \frac{v^2}{2c}$. Investors' payoff equals: $vq_0 + P\left(F - \frac{cq^2}{2} + v(q - q_0)\right) = vq_0 + P(v(q - q_0)) = \frac{v^2}{2c}$ so investors will agree to provide an amount of financing F that equals $\frac{v^2}{2c}$. So in a perfect market, a large variety of financing strategies exist that can be optimal. For example, a contract with $q_0 = 0$ and $P(X) = \frac{v^2}{2c}$, $\forall X \geq 0$ or one with $q_0 = v/c$ and $P(X) = 0, \forall X \geq 0$ can be optimal. More specifically, in a perfect market (i.e. when q is contractible) any contract is optimal such tht: $q = v/c$, $q_0 \leq v/c$, $F = v^2/2c$ and $P\left(v\left(\frac{v}{c} - q_0\right)\right) = \frac{v^2}{2c}$.

Under moral hazard (i.e. when q is non-contractible) but when market valuation (v) is still common knowledge a large variety of contracts still exist (although smaller than in the previous case) that generate an optimal outcome (see Exercise 7). The main difference with the previous case (perfect market) is that the solution should contain a non-decreasing function of payoffs for both the entrepreneur and investors (otherwise the entrepreneur has no incentive to improve his effort). Miglo (2022a) argues that when demand is uncertain, i.e. v is unknown to the entrepreneur, traditional contracts (without PIK) do not achieve a perfect outcome. The paper then argues that if financing is two-staged and financing includes PIK features then a perfect outcome is achievable. Indeed, suppose that financing has 2 stages. In stage 1 the entrepreneur offers a menu of contracts $(F_1(q_{01}), P_1(X))$ and investors can select a contract (i.e. the value of q_{01} and respectively $F_1(q_{01})$) that is most profitable to them. Note that $F_1(q_{01})$ means that the firm promises to deliver q_{01} items to investors in exchange for an investment $F_1(q_{01})$. Also, after production is completed a cash payment to investor $P_1(X)$ is promised. In stage 2 (negotiation about stage 2 are conducted after stage 1 financing is completed) the entrepreneur offers $(q_{02}, F_2, P_2(X))$. Production takes place after both stages of financing are completed.

The timing of events in this situation is in Fig. 6.2. Miglo (2022a) argues that a contract described in Proposition 6.1 provides an optimal outcome for the entrepreneur.

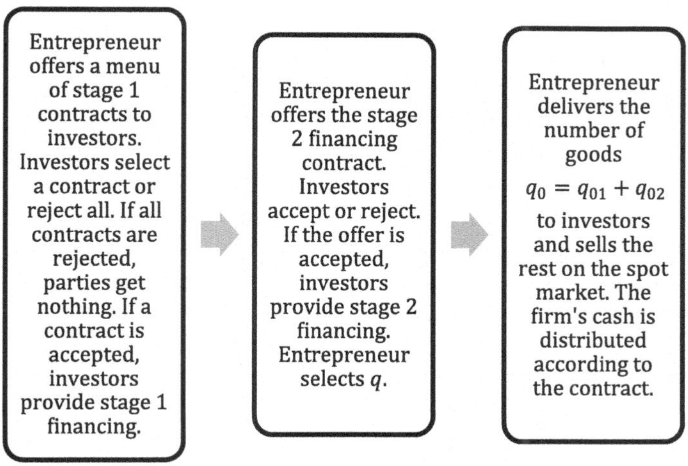

Fig. 6.2 Sequence of events

Proposition 6.1 The following contract is optimal: $P_1(X) = 0$, $F_1(q_{01}) = ncq_{01}{}^2/2$, $q_{02} \leq v/c$, $F_2 = v^2/2c - F_1$, $vq_{02} + P_2(v(q - q_{01} - q_{02})) = v^2/2c$ *and* $0 \leq P\prime_2(X) \leq 1$.

Proof. Consider the contract described in the proposition. First as we will show below, at the end of stage 1 the entrepreneur will learn v because the contract selected by investors in stage 1 depends on v. So during production the entrepreneur maximizes $v(q - q_{01} - q_{02}) - \frac{cq^2}{2} + F_1 + F_2 - P_2(v(q - q_{01} - q_{02})) - \frac{cq^2}{2} + F_1 + F_2$ under the condition that $q \geq q_{01} - q_{02}$. We have $F = F_1 + F_2 = F_1 + \frac{v^2}{2c} - F_1 = \frac{v^2}{2c}$. Since $v^2/2c \geq (\frac{v}{c})^2/2$ the optimal $q = v/c$. Now consider stage 1 financing. After the entrepreneur offers $P_1(X) = 0$, the only possible payoff for investors are goods. The investors will select a contract that maximizes $vq_{01} - F_1$ where $F_1(q_{01}) = ncq_{01}{}^2/2$. So $q_{01} = v/(nc)$ and $F_1 = v^2/2cn$. The investors' (stage 1) payoff equals: $vq_{01} = v^2/cn$, whichis greater than their total investment $v^2/2cn$. So stage 1 financing will be accepted, and the investors will select $q_{01} = v/(nc)$. In stage 2, the investors' payoff equals $vq_{02} + P_2(v(q - q_{01} - q_{02})) = v^2/2c$ so stage 2 financing will be accepted too. The entrepreneur's payoff equals: $v(q - q_{01} - q_{02}) - \frac{cq^2}{2} + F_2 + F_1 - P_2\Big(v(q - q_{01} - q_{02}) - \frac{cq^2}{2} + F_2 + F_1\Big) = \frac{v^2}{2c} - (\frac{v^2}{2cn} + v^2/cn)$, which approaches $v^2/2c$ as n increases.

The interpretation of this result is that optimal financing for the entrepreneur under demand uncertainty is crowdfunding in stage 1 and mixed financing (crowdfunding campaign and traditional financing) in stage 2. Although the model provides an interesting addition to traditional security design literature by injecting PIK payments into the analysis, future research is expected by analyzing, for example, analyzing why not every firm uses a two-stage financing model with the first stage being a crowdfunding campaign.

Finally, Miglo (2022a) argues that when information about firm quality is asymmetric but market valuation is common knowledge, the optimal contract is similar to traditional debt, which is consistent with traditional asymmetric information literature (Leland & Pyle, 1977; Nachman & Noe, 1994 etc.). This is because a debt contract (fixed payments) is naturally less sensitive to informational problems then other contracts. In the case where both information about firm quality is asymmetric and the market valuation of products is unknown, the optimal contract is a two-stage financing where stage 1 is crowdfunding (small size) and stage 2 is debt financing.

Although there are no direct tests of these results in existing literature, some papers provide evidence consistent with these results. For example, the following papers illustrate that crowdfunding followed by subsequent financing is quite popular and seemingly a growing phenomenon (Colombo & Shafi, 2016; Drover et al., 2017; Roma et al., 2017; 2018; Vanacker et al., 2019; Xu, 2018). Some empirical research finds results that are consistent with the spirit of this prediction, e.g. that crowdfunding plays a positive role for subsequent financing. For example, Colombo and Shafi (2016) find that crowdfunding improves subsequent bank financing opportunities. In a similar spirit, the crowdfunding platform Ulule provides good conditions for participating entrepreneurs to obtain bank loans in addition to funds received from crowdfunding.[15,16] For literature related to security design, see, e.g. Nachman and Noe (1994), Brennan and Kraus (1987), Koufopoulos et al. (2019), Malenko and Tsoi (2020) and Miglo (2022a, 2025c). In addition/in contrast to the literature mentioned above, in the model above, the payments to investors can be made in cash as well as using goods produced by the firm (payment-in-kind or PIK).

6.4 New "Pecking Order"

As we discussed previously, asymmetric information plays an important role in studying firm financing decisions (Leland & Pyle, 1977; Myers & Majluff, 1984; Ross, 1977 etc.). The pecking-order theory (POT) (Myers & Majluf, 1984) is often considered to be one of the major theories of financing and is an important tool for analyzing the connections between firm quality and financing choices. One of the main predictions of this theory is that a pecking order exists where firms prefer internal funds (retained earnings, undistributed profits, etc.) to finance their investment projects. Raising funds using external sources is costly because of a lack of information known by potential investors. In these conditions signalling

[15] See, e.g https://lenderkit.com/blog/banks-and-crowdfunding/.

[16] Another example is the UK-based platform Zopa, that created its own bank that allows entrepreneurs to rely both on funds originated directly by online deposits, as well as on other traditional banking sources of funding (Navaretti et al., 2018).

by high-quality firms is usually costly/impossible. Further, debt is better than equity because its value and the investors' payoff are less dependent on firm performance and so is less sensitive to the problems of asymmetric information.

Asymmetric information is recognized as an important factor in crowdfunding as well (Mollick, 2014, etc.). Can the POT be applied to crowdfunding?! As we know there are 4 different types of crowdfunding: debt-based, equity-based, reward-based and donation-based crowdfunding. Elements of POT seem to be consistent with crowdfunding. For example, the amount of debt-based crowdfunding largely exceeds that of equity-based (see, e.g. p2pmarketdata where debt-based crowdfunding volume is $297.64 bn, which represents 97.9% of all crowdfunding funds raised). Reward-based crowdfunding though is a new financing method different from traditional debt and equity. The data on one hand show that the volume of reward-based crowdfunding is smaller than that of debt-based and even equity-based crowdfunding.[17] On the other hand a lot of reward-based crowdfunding firms do not demonstrate high quality. For example, empirical evidence regarding qualities of firms conducting crowdfunding campaigns shows that a very large number of campaigns fail and many firms that successfully completed a reward-based crowdfunding campaign do not deliver promised rewards (see, e.g. Appio et al., 2020; Blaseg et al., 2020; Cumming et al., 2023; Mollick, 2014, 2015). Empirical evidence also shows that in practice crowdfunding is still behind bank loans among small-medium-size enterprises (SMEs).[18]

Below we provide an explanation for the above patterns that relies on asymmetric information. One of the ideas is that reward-based crowdfunding payments to backers (firm products or non-financial rewards) are not directly related to firm value/profit. Crowdfunding sales (pre-sales)/revenues are usually received before the actual investment and production takes place and respectively before the actual quality of product becomes known. It means the entrepreneur's payoff does not depend much on the

[17] In p2pmarketdata for example non-investment crowdfunding methods (i.e reward-based and donation-based) only account for $1.52 bn or 0.5% of the worldwide crowdfunding volumes.

[18] Example, the total amount of bank loans outstanding is 168 bln in the UK (Fig. A.1 in Small Business Finance report by British Business Bank (2019/20)) and the volume of reward-based crowdfunding is about 6 bln. (based on https://p2pmarketdata.com/crowdfunding-statistics-worldwide/).

firm quality. Intuitively this is similar to some of the ideas behind POT in that equity is more sensitive to firm quality (debt is not completely independent but the payment to investors is more "flat" (as a function of firm profit) compared to equity) than debt. So the entrepreneur can fully benefit from the increased performance, ie. sales/revenue, of his/her firm when the firm is financed with debt and the investor's payoff is "flat". This is a result of asymmetric information being related to the quality of the firm's project. This relationship is opposite to the effect of asymmetric information about the cost of production in crowdfunding analyzed in some papers (see, e.g. Ellman & Hurkens, 2019; Miglo & Miglo, 2019; Strausz, 2017). In these papers the high-quality firm would be able to benefit from a lower cost of production after finishing a crowdfunding campaign.

Consider the following model.[19] An entrepreneur has an idea of a new product/service. Before production can start a capital investment I is required. The expected quality of the future product after the project is completed is uncertain and can be high (with probability π) or low. There are two types of entrepreneurs. Type l (low-quality) is characterized by the parameter π_l, type h (high quality) has parameter π_h where $\pi_l < \pi_h$. By definition, h has a higher expected quality of his/her product. π is the entrepreneur's private information while the public is only aware of the distribution of π. Let μ be the proportion of type h entrepreneurs, $0 < \mu < 1$. Let $\pi_m = \mu\pi_h + (1 - \mu)\pi_l$ be the average probability of the high-quality product among the entrepreneurs. The entrepreneur can finance the required investment by issuing equity or using crowdfunding.[20] If the firm uses equity financing, investors offer finance in exchange for a fraction α of the firm's equity. If the quality of the product is high, all consumers/potential backers value the good at v and if the quality of the product is low the value is 0. The total number of potential customers is N but we assume for simplicity that $N = 1$ without loss of generality. If crowdfunding is selected, the entrepreneur determines the crowdfunding price p, i.e. backers who investred p during the campaign can receive one product of the firm after the campaign is completed and the product is produced and delivered to backers who participated in the

[19] Based on Miglo (2023, 2025b).

[20] Debt is not considered because it is well known that debt dominates equity under asymmetric information. Many small firms especially innovative risky firms do not have access to debt however. See Miglo (2025b) for more details.

campaign. Backers who did not participate in the campaign can purchase the product on the spot market. Under equity financing the firm raises funds from investors. After investment is completed, the product quality becomes known and the firm sells the product on the market for price P. The firm (project) is owned by an entrepreneur who maximizes his/her expected earnings. Everybody is risk-neutral and the risk-free interest rate is zero. These assumptions imply that investors provide equity financing as long as their expected earnings cover their investment costs. They also imply that funders participating in a crowdfunding campaign use risk-neutral estimation of the expected quality of the product. Backers make their choice of whether or to participate in a crowdfunding campaign by maximizing their expected surpluses, i.e. the expected value of the product minus the price and compare this option with the option to purchase the product on the spot market. If expected surpluses are equal we assume that the backers participate in the crowdfunding campaign.[21]

There are two types of potential equilibria: a separating one where each type selects a different strategy and a pooling one where both types select the same strategy. If multiple equilibria exist, then we use the minimal mispricing criterion (see, e.g. Nachman & Noe, 1994). We will first show that a separating equilibrium does not exist.

Lemma 6.1 An efficient separating equilibrium where each type's profit is equal to its symmetric information case does not exist.

Proof. Suppose an equilibrium exists where h selects equity. Then $\alpha = \frac{I}{\pi_h v}$. In a signalling equilibrium the firm value is equal to its full information value, i.e. $\pi_h v$. If α is as described above, then the investors' expected payoff equals $\alpha\pi_h v = I$, which is the amount of the investment so the investors' incentive to participate is satisfied. Also, the entrepreneur's payoff is $(1-\alpha)\pi_h v = \pi_h v - I$. Similarly, type l's payoff in a signalling equilibrium equals $\pi_l v - I$. Indeed $p_l = \pi_l v$. The right-hand side shows the expected product value for a crowdfunding campaign participant. The expected value of the product is also $\pi_l v$ (because in a signalling equilibrium potential consumers interpret crowdfunding to be a low-quality signal) all consumers participate in crowdfunding. l makes profit $\pi_l v - I$. l would then mimick h. Indeed if l mimicks h its payoff is $(1-\alpha)\pi_l v = \pi_l \text{v} - \frac{\pi_l v I}{\pi_h v} > \pi_l v - I$ because $\pi_l < \pi_h$. So l would mimick

[21] For different variations of the model see Miglo (2025b).

h and such an equlibrium does not exist. It is consistent with traditional asymmetric information results (see, e.g. Brennan & Kraus, 1987; Nachman & Noe, 1994).

Now suppose an equilibrium exists where h selects crowdfunding. Then $p_h = \pi_h v$. The right-hand side shows the expected product value for a crowdfunding campaign participant. Since $x = 0$, and the expected value of the product is also $\pi_h v$ (because in a signalling equilibrium potential consumers interpret crowdfunding to be a high-quality signal) all consumers participate in crowdfunding. h makes profit $\pi_h v - I$. Also suppose that l selects a different strategy and makes profit $\pi_l v - I$. l would then mimick h. Indeed if l mimicks h its payoff is $\pi_h v - I > \pi_l v - I$.

Now consider pooling. It is well known from traditional finance that debt dominates equity by minimal mispricing (see, e.g. Nachman & Noe, 1994) so we will compare equity and crowdfunding and will argue that pooling with equity dominates pooling with crowdfunding.

Proposition 6.2 Pooling with crowdfunding is less likely than pooling with equity.

Proof. Under pooling with equity $\alpha = \frac{I}{\pi_m v}$. Indeed in this case the investors' expected profit is $\frac{I}{\pi_m v}\pi_m v = I$. h's payoff is $\pi_h v(1 - \frac{I}{\pi_m v})$. Under pooling with crowdfunding $p = \pi_m v$. h's payoff is $\pi_m v - I$. h's payoff under pooling with equity is greater than it is under pooling with crowdfunding. Indeed

$$\frac{(\pi_m v - I)(\pi_h v)}{\pi_m v} \geq \pi_m v - I$$

because $\pi_h > \pi_m$.

Intuitively if a firm uses crowdfunding all cash will be received by the firm in advance and since the fraction of equity sold (in the case of equity financing) is less than 1, a type *h* entrepreneur will do worse under reward-based crowdfunding than he/she would under equity financing (since under equity financing the entrepreneur sells only a fraction of the firm under asymmetric information at the pooling price across *h* and *l* types). Miglo (2025b) considers different variations of this basic idea including a variation where asymmetric information is combined with other types of market imperfections, and argues that the basic result largely holds.

Proposition 6.2 implies the following. If asymmetric information exists about the product quality, the pecking order exists where firms should prefer internal funds followed by debt, followed by equity, which in turn is followed by crowdfunding (reward-based). Empirical evidence is generally consistent with these predictions. For example, according to some sources, the total volume of P2P lending/debt-based crowdfunding exceeds that of equity-based crowdfunding (see, e.g. Alternative Finance 2021 or p2pmarketdata).[22] Walthoff-Borm et al. (2018) find that firms use equity-based crowdfunding when they do not have sufficient internal funds, whichis also consistent with the spirit of the pecking-order described above.

6.5 Rates of Return: Crowdfunding vs. Other Types of Investments

This section discusses the question of risk and return in crowdfunding. This topic is underexplored in existing literature, though from an investor's point of view, it is quite an important question, at least for some types of crowdfunding, e.g. debt-based or equity-based crowdfunding where investors expect a financial return on their investments. In traditional literature related to the risk and return of traditional types of investments, the rate of return is usually discussed in connection to the risk (see, Fig. 6.3) of investments and usually a higher risk is associated with a higher expected rate of return. The way the rate of return, or the level of risk, of an investment is calculated may be different, but usually the same connection (higher risk implies higher return) is observed. Figure 6.3 shows the historical level of risk (measured by the standard deviation of return) and the average rates of return of the two traditional and most important types of investments: stocks and corporate bonds. One can see that bonds (a classical example of a traditional debt-based investment) have lower risk and lower average return than corporate stocks (a classical example of a traditional equity-based investment).

The intuition of why equity usually has a higher risk and a higher return is related to the nature of debt and equity: payments on debt are usually more stable (fixed in many cases) while in the case of equity they

[22] https://www.jbs.cam.ac.uk/wp-content/uploads/2021/06/ccaf-2021-06-report-2nd-global-alternative-.nance-benchmarking-study-report.pdf; https://p2pmarketdata.com/articles/crowdfunding-statistics-worldwide/.

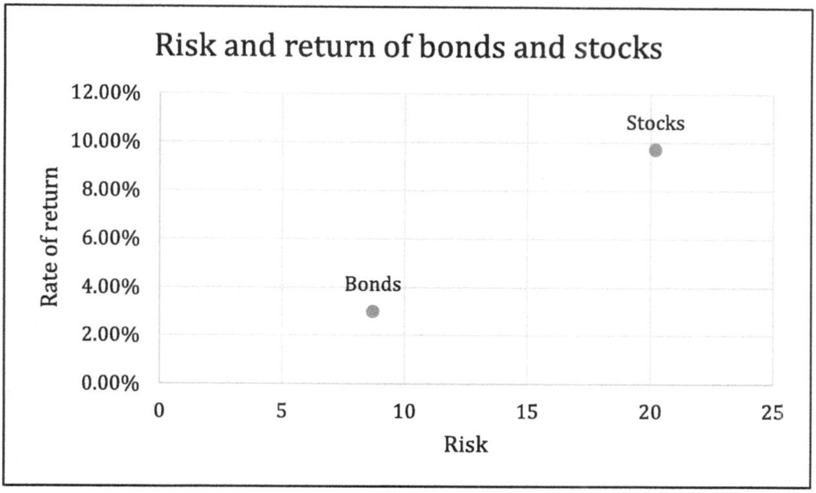

Fig. 6.3 Risk-return of traditional debt and equity[23]

sharply depend on firms profits and are more volatile than debt returns. If we apply the same logic to crowdfunding investments then by analogy, we should expect that returns on equity-based crowdfunding have higher risk and higher rates of return than returns on debt-based crowdfunding (see Fig. 6.4).[24] What about reward-based crowdfunding?

The difficulty here is that there is no promised financial return in the case of reward-based crowdfunding so any measure of return will be indirect and the question is whether it exists at all. The question is not obvious. First off, it is not clear how exactly one can measure the return on reward-based crowdfunding. If, for example, a backer participating in a campaign wants to consume/use the product or service promised by the firm, then can we compare the price for similar products on the market with the price that is paid by the backers? Researchers (see, e.g. Dobrynskaya & Grebennikova, 2023) have recently attempted to indirectly estimate the return on reward-based crowdfunding. Secondly, intuitively the rates of return on reward-based crowdfunding (if it can be

[23] Based on numbers from Brealey and Myers (2003, ch. 7).

[24] Rates of return on Fig. 6.4. are hypothetical. As far as we know there is no research estimated the rates of return on all types of crowdfunding for the same period of time.

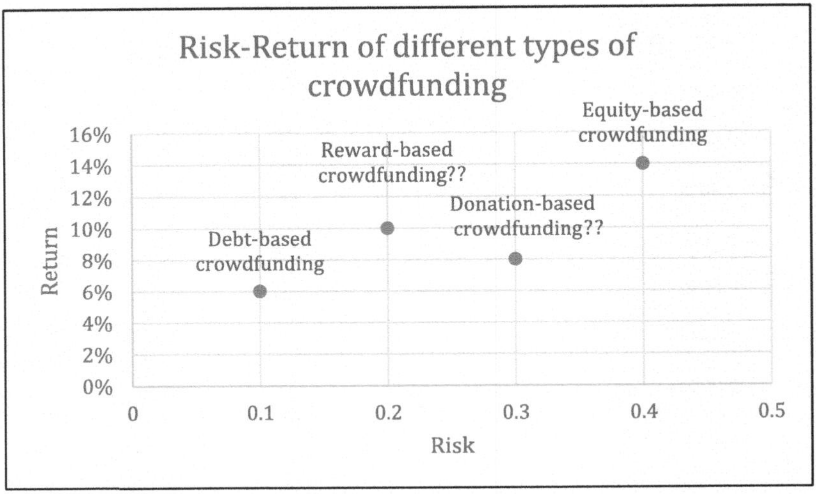

Fig. 6.4 Risk-return of different types of crowdfunding

measured at all) should be somewhere in between debt-based and equity-based crowdfunding. On one hand, reward-based crowdfunding has some elements of debt. As we discussed, there are some promises here, i.e. the entrepreneur promises to provide rewards (usually firm products or services) to backers similar to firms that issue debt promise an interest rate to investors. On the other hand, reward-based crowdfunding results depend a lot on a firm's business risk because as we discussed, it is related to whether demand for a firm's products exists or not, which in turn affects the future profits of the firm and its ability to produce products after finishing the crowdfunding campaign. So there are a lot of factors that are similar to traditional equity in terms of risks. And so intuitively return on reward-based crowdfunding should be somewhere in between debt-based and equity-based crowdfunding.

Where do we put donation-based crowdfunding? Should we try to measure the potential community benefits if the project is implemented and compare the situation to one without this project and try to estimate consumer utility in each scenario, etc.? This is perhaps an area for future investigation. Another interesting question is how do we exactly measure the risk associated with crowdfunding investments? For traditional investment/securities we usually have an active secondary market, so we can, for example, measure the degree of volatility of the return (which depends on changes in the market prices of securities) over time. As we know, generally no active secondary market exists for crowdfunding investments. Further, there are new elements of risk introduced on top of those seen in traditional finance, e.g. the risk of campaign failure, perhaps the risk of platform failure, the risk of ideas being stolen or damaged by competitors.

Among the few papers analysing the rates of return in crowdfunding note the following. Signori and Vismara (2019) analyze equity-based crowdfunding and find that the expected annualized return for an initial crowdfunding investor is 8.8%, implying an overall annual value creation of £25 m. Dobrynskaya and Grebennikova (2023) analyze reward-based crowdfunding and suggest that the average unconditional annualized return is 11.5% and the average return on successful projects is 30%. They also conclude that backing money near the end of a campaign, when the probability of success is already high, is a profitable strategy. Vroomen and Desa (2018) find that the target initial rate of return for an efficient crowdfunding portfolio is at least 28% if the crowdfunding asset class is 10% riskier than angel investments. Adhami et al. (2023) find that returns are inversely related to loan riskiness, suggesting that, on average, crowd-funded loans are mispriced. Yet, Granlund and Hansen (2020) mostly confirm that risk and return are positively related using data from the Danish platform Flex Funding.

Questions and Exercises

1. Usually an advantage of crowdfunding as compared to bank financing is an entrepreneur's ability to get market feedback regarding the demand for future products/services. A possible disadvantage is that during reward-based crowdfunding the firm may face a conflict of interest when choosing the production scale and the sales price on the spot market after the crowdfunding campaign is finished.
2. PIK elements in a security design problem may explain why firms may be interested in using crowdfunding.
3. The new pecking order (including reward-based crowdfunding) implies the following order of preferences:

   (a) internal finds, equity, debt, RBC
   (b) internal funds, debt, equity, RBC

(c) RBC, internal funds, debt, equity

4. Consider a firm with an innovative product or service. It requires an investment 1000 (the variable costs of production are assumed to be negligibly small). The production is q. The expected spot market price is p. The firm can use a reward-based crowdfunding campaign where the firm promises to deliver a product to backers as a reward (the crowdfunding price during the campaign is p_c,i.e. any backer who make a contrinution p_c will get the firm's product as a reward) or use traditional bank financing. The inverse demand function is $p = a - q$. Under bank financing, the firm gets an amount 1000 and promises to pay it back (interest rate is assumed to be equal 0 for simplicity). Under crowdfunding, the firm determines p_c. Respectively, the demand during the crowdfunding stage is $c = a - p_c$. After finishing the crowdfunding campaign, the firm determines the number of items that should be sold on the spot market (s). Further assume that: (1) under crowdfunding the amount of funds that can be raised during the campaign is limited, i.e. the maximum amount of orders that can be collected during crowdfunding is 20; (2) the spot market price is determined using the same inverse demand function $p = a - q = a - c - s$. The firm also faces demand uncertainty: $a = 100$ with probability 50% and otherwise $a = 0$. If the latter is the case no one will participate in crowdfunding or spot sales. What is the best strategy for the firm?
5. Consider a firm that must make an investment I. The firm is run by an entrepreneur who can either use crowdfunding or VC. Under VC the value of the firm is $V = e_1 + e_2$, where e_1 is the effort provided by the entrepreneur and e_2 is the effort provided by VC. The costs of effort are e_1^2 and e_2^2 repectively. Under crowdfunding the firm value depends on the effort provided by the entrepreneur. However, in addition there are additional crowdfunding benefits of 0.1 so the firm value is $V = e + 0.1$, where e is the entrepreneur's effort. Finally, we assume that under crowdfunding there is a risk that the idea will be stolen. The probability of that is 20%. The entrepreneur maximizes the value of his/her expected earnings and the backers provide funds as long as the expected profit covers the cost of investments. Find the best strategy for the firm.
6. Consider the model described in the beginning of Sect. 6.3. Assume that v is common knowledge but a moral hazard problem exists with

regard to the choice of q, i.e. q is non-contractible. Prove that the following contract provides the outcome similar to the case when q is contractible: $q_0 \leq v/c$, $F = v^2/2c$, $v(q_0) + P(v(q - q_0)) = v^2/2c$ and $0 \leq P\prime(X) \leq 1, \forall X \geq 0$.

References

Adhami, S., Gianfrate, G., & Johan, S. (2023). Risks and returns in crowdlending. *Eurasian Business Review, 13*(2), 309–340.

Antweiler, W., & Frank, M. Z. (2006). *Do US stock markets typically overreact to corporate news stories?*. Available at SSRN 878091.

Appio, F. P., Leone, D., Platania, F., & Schiavone, F. (2020). Why are rewards not delivered on time in rewards-based crowdfunding campaigns? An empirical exploration. *Technological Forecasting and Social Change, 157*, Article 120069.

Ang, J. S. (1992). On the theory of finance for privately held firms. *The Journal of Entrepreneurial Finance, 1*(3), 185–203.

Ang, J., Cole, R., & Lawson, D. (2010). The role of owner in capital structure decisions: An analysis of single-owner corporations. *The Journal of Entrepreneurial Finance (JEF), 14*(3), 1–36.

Arnold, L. G., & Riley, J. G. (2009). On the Possibility of Credit Rationing in the Stiglitz-Weiss Model. *American Economic Review, 99*(5), 2012–2021.

Babich, V., Marinesi, S., & Tsoukalas, G. (2019). *Updating the crowdfunding narrative.* https://repository.upenn.edu/server/api/core/bitstreams/cbb04c97-62a5-4810-83d2-7731b099765c/content

Bakri, M. H., Radzai, M. S. M., & Rasid, A. M. M. (2021). Technology acceptance in crowdfunding among retailers. *Studies of Applied Economics, 39*(5).

Bhattacharya, S., & Thakor, A. V. (1993). Contemporary banking theory. *Journal of Financial Intermediation, 3*(1), 2–50.

Bernardino, S., & Santos, J. F. (2020). Crowdfunding: An exploratory study on knowledge, benefits and barriers perceived by young potential entrepreneurs. *Journal of Risk and Financial Management, 13*(4), 81.

Bester, H. (1985). Screening vs. rationing in credit markets with imperfect information. *The American Economic Review, 75*(4), 850–855.

Blaseg, D., & Koetter, M. (2016). Crowdfunding and bank stress. *Banking beyond banks and money: A guide to banking services in the twenty-first century* (pp. 17–54). Springer International Publishing.

Blaseg, D., Schulze, C., & Skiera, B. (2020). Consumer protection on Kickstarter. *Marketing Science, 39*(1), 211–233.

Berger, A. N., Saunders, A., Scalise, J. M., & Udell, G. F. (1998). The effects of bank mergers and acquisitions on small business lending. *Journal of Financial Economics, 50*(2), 187–229.

Brav, O. (2009). Access to capital, capital structure, and the funding of the firm. *The Journal of Finance, 64*(1), 263–308.

Brealey, R., & Myers, S. (2003, January 1). *Principles of corporate finance* (7th ed. Paperback).

Brennan, M., & Kraus, A. (1987). Efficient financing under information asymmetry. *Journal of Finance, 42*(5), 1225–1243.

Cole, R. (2006). Financial services used by small businesses: Evidence from the 2003 Survey of Small Business Finances. *Federal Reserve Bulletin.*

Cole, R. A. (2013). What do we know about the capital structure of privately held US firms? Evidence from the surveys of small business finance. *Financial Management, 42*(4), 777–813.

Cole, R. A., Cumming, D. J., & Taylor, J. (2019). *Does FinTech compete with or complement bank finance?* Available at SSRN 3302975.

Colombo, M. G., & Shafi, K. (2016). The impact of patenting on the size of high-tech firms: The role of venture capital and product market regulation. *Economia e Politica Industriale, 43*(1), 85–103.

Cumming, D. J. (2005). Capital structure in venture finance. *Journal of Corporate Finance, 11*(3), 550–585.

Cuñat, V., & Garcia-Appendini, E. (2012, September 18). Trade credit and its role in entrepreneurial finance. In *The Oxford handbook of entrepreneurial finance.* Oxford Handbooks (2012; online ed., Oxford Academic).

Cumming, D., Hornuf, L., Karami, M., & Schweizer, D. (2023). Disentangling crowdfunding from fraudfunding. *Journal of Business Ethics, 182*(4), 1103–1128.

Diamond, D. W. (1984). Financial intermediation and delegated monitoring. *The Review of Economic Studies, 51*(3), 393–414.

Diamond, D. W. (1991). Debt maturity structure and liquidity risk. *Quarterly Journal of Economics, 106*(3), 709–737.

Dobrynskaya, V., & Grebennikova, J. (2023). Financial returns in reward-based crowdfunding economic analysis letters. *Anse Press, 2*(3), 1–9.

Drover, W., Wood, M. S., & Zacharakis, A. (2017). Attributes of angel and crowdfunded investments as determinants of VC screening decisions. *Entrepreneurship Theory and Practice, 41*(3), 323–347.

Durkin, M., Laffey, D., Gandy, A., & Cummins, D., Fearon, C. (2016). *The sme-bank relationship: Exploring the impact of crowdfunding at start-up.* https://www.ulster.ac.uk/__data/assets/pdf_file/0009/168417/crowdfunding.pdf

Eckbo, B. E. (1986). Valuation effects of corporate debt offerings. *Journal of Financial Economics, 15*(1–2), 119–151.

Eddleston, K. A., Ladge, J. J., Mitteness, C., & Balachandra, L. (2016). Do you see what I see? Signaling effects of gender and firm characteristics on financing entrepreneurial ventures. *Entrepreneurship Theory and Practice, 40*(3), 489–514.

Ellman, M., & Hurkens, S. (2019). Fraud tolerance in optimal crowdfunding. *Economics Letters, 181*, 11–16.

Fama, E. F., & French, K. R. (2002). Testing trade-off and pecking order predictions about dividends and debt. *Review of Financial Studies, 15*(1), 1–33.

Fairchild, R. J., Liu, W., & Yao, Y. (2017). *An Entrepreneur's choice of crowd-funding or venture capital financing: The effect of entrepreneurial overconfidence and CF-investors' passion*. Available at SSRN 2926980.

Fenwick, M., McCahery, J. A., & Vermeulen, E. P. (2017). *Fintech and the financing of entrepreneurs: From crowdfunding to marketplace lending* (TILEC Discussion Paper No. 2017–25, ECGI—Law Working Paper No. 369/2017).

Frank, M. Z., & Goyal, V. K. (2009). Capital structure decisions: Which factors are reliably important? *Financial Management, 38*(1), 1–37.

Granlund, J. A., & Hansen, M. (2020). *Investor risks in crowdfunding*. https://research.cbs.dk/en/studentProjects/investor-risks-in-crowdfunding-a-risk-study-of-the-danish-crowdfu

Grossman, S. J., & Hart, O. D. (1980). Takeover bids, the free-rider problem, and the theory of the corporation. *The Bell Journal of Economics*, 42–64.

Hui, J. S., Gerber, E. M., & Gergle, D. (2014, June). Understanding and leveraging social networks for crowdfunding: opportunities and challenges. In *Proceedings of the 2014 conference on Designing interactive systems* (pp. 677–680).

Jaffee, D. M., & Russell, T. (1976). Imperfect information, uncertainty, and credit rationing. *Quarterly Journal of Economics, 90*(4), 651–666.

Jensen, M. C., & Meckling, W. H. (1976). Theory of the firm: Managerial behavior, agency costs and ownership structure. *Journal of Financial Economics, 3*(4), 305–360.

Kaplan, S. N., & Strömberg, P. (2003). Financial contracting theory meets the real world: An empirical analysis of venture capital contracts. *The Review of Economic Studies, 70*(2), 281–315.

Kohler, M., Britton, E., & Yates, A. (2000). *Trade credit and the monetary transmission mechanism* (The Bank of England Working Paper (115)).

Koufopoulos, K., Kozhan, R., & Trigilia, G. (2019). Optimal security design under asymmetric information and profit manipulation. *Review of Corporate Finance Studies, 8*(1), 146–173.

Leland, H., & Pyle, D. (1977). Information asymmetries, financial structure, and financial intermediation. *Journal of Finance, 32*, 371–378.

Malenko, A., & Tsoy, A. (2020). *Asymmetric information and security design under Knightian uncertainty*. Available at SSRN 3100285.

Miglo, A., & Miglo, V. (2019). Market imperfections and crowdfunding. *Small Business Economics, 53*(1), 51–79.

Miglo. A. (2022a). Backers: Consumers or investors? Crowdfunding vs. traditional financing as an optimal security design problem. In *Handbook on Digital Entrepreneurship* (Ch. 12; Springer; pp 236–255). Edward Elgar Publishing.

Miglo, A. (2022b). Crowdfunding and bank financing: Substitutes or complements? *Small Business Economics, 59*(3), 1115–1142.

Miglo, A. (2023). *A theory of crowdfunding under asymmetric information and discounting cost*. Available at SSRN 4659368.

Miglo, A. (2025a). *Capital structure in the modern world: The fundamentals of capital structure management and financing decisions*. Springer Nature.

Miglo, A. (2025b). Crowdfunding, asymmetric information and pecking order. *Journal of Economic Studies, 52*(6), 1156–1170.

Miglo, A. (2025c). Security Design and Financing Innovations. In: *Capital Structure in the Modern World*. Palgrave Macmillan, Cham.

Modigliani, F., & Miller, M. H. (1958). The cost of capital, corporation finance and the theory of investment. *The American Economic Review, 48*(3), 261–297.

Mollick, E. (2014). The dynamics of crowdfunding: An exploratory study. *Journal of Business Venturing, 29*(1), 1–16.

Mollick, E. R. (2015). *Delivery rates on Kickstarter*. Available at SSRN 2699251.

Myers, S., & Majluf, N. (1984). Corporate financing and investment decisions when firms have information that investors do not have. *Journal of Financial Economics, 13*, 187–221.

Nachman, D. C., & Noe, T. H. (1994). Optimal design of securities under asymmetric information. *The Review of Financial Studies, 7*(1), 1–44.

Navaretti, G. B., Calzolari, G., Mansilla-Fernandez, J. M., & Pozzolo, A. F. (2018). Fintech and banking. Friends or foes? *Friends or Foes*.

Parker, S. (2003). Do banks ration credit to new enterprises? And should governments intervene? *Scottish Journal of Political Economy, 49*(2), 162–195.

Rajan, R., & Zingales, L. (1995). What do we know about capital structure: some evidence from international data. *Journal of Finance, 50*, 1421–1460.

Robb, A. M., & Robinson, D. T. (2014). The capital structure decisions of new firms. *The Review of Financial Studies, 27*(1), 153–179.

Roma, P., Petruzzelli, A. M., & Perrone, G. (2017). From the crowd to the market: The role of reward-based crowdfunding performance in attracting professional investors. *Research Policy, 46*(9), 1606–1628.

Roma, P., Gal-Or, E., & Chen, R. R. (2018). Reward-based crowdfunding campaigns: Informational value and access to venture capital. *Information Systems Research, 29*(3), 679–697.

Ross, S. (1977). The determination of financial structure: The incentive signaling approach. *Bell Journal of Economics, 8*, 23–40.

Ryu, S., Kim, K., & Hahn, J. (2019, July). The effect of crowdfunding success on subsequent financing outcomes of start-ups. In *Academy of management proceedings* (Vol. 2019, No. 1, p. 17486). Academy of Management.

Sadzius, L., & Sadzius, T. (2017). Existing legal issues for crowdfunding regulation in European Union member states. *International Journal of Business, Humanities and Technology, 7*(3), 52–62.

Schwienbacher, A. (2018). Entrepreneurial risk-taking in crowdfunding campaigns. *Small Business Economics, 51*(4), 843–859.

Signori, A., & Vismara, S., (2019). *Returns on investments in equity crowdfunding*. Available at SSRN: https://ssrn.com/abstract=2765488

Stiglitz, J. E., & Weiss, A. (1981). Credit rationing in markets with imperfect information. *American Economic Review, 71*(3), 393–410.

Strausz, R. (2017). A theory of crowdfunding: A mechanism design approach with demand uncertainty and moral hazard. *American Economic Review, 107*(6), 1430–1476.

Su, X., & Zhang, L. (2017). A Re-examination of credit rationing in the stiglitz and Weiss model. *Journal of Money, Credit and Banking, 49*(5), 1059–1072.

Tamburro, A. (2017). Far from the madding crowd: Crowdfunding a small business reorganization. *Emory Bankruptcy developments Journal, 34*, 521.

Titman, S., & Wessels, R. (1988). The determinants of capital structure choice. *The Journal of Finance, 43*(1), 1–19.

Tsoukalas, G., Marinesi, S., & Babich, V. (2019). *Updating the crowdfunding narrative*. https://repository.upenn.edu/server/api/core/bitstreams/cbb04c97-62a5-4810-83d2-7731b099765c/content

Tang, M., You, T.-H., & Cao, B. (2025) Comparative analysis of crowdfunding and bank financing: The effect of market uncertainty. *International Journal of Production Economics, Elsevier, 286*(C).

Tian, J., Wei, J., Fan, W., & Wang, Y. (2024). When crowdfunding meets bank financing: Substitute or supplement? *International Journal of Production Economics, 277*, Article 109374.

Vanacker, T., Vismara, S., & Walthoff-Borm, X. (2019). *What happens after a crowdfunding campaign?* (pp. 227–247). Edward Elgar Publishing.

Vroomen, P., & Desa, S. (2018). Rates of return for crowdfunding portfolios: Theoretical derivation and implications. *Venture Capital, 20*(3), 261–283.

Walthoff-Borm, X., Schwienbacher, A., & Vanacker, T. (2018). Equity crowdfunding: First resort or last resort? *Journal of Business Venturing, 33*(4), 513–533.

Watson, H. (1984). Credit markets and borrower effort. *Southern Economic Journal, 50*(3), 802–813.

Xu, T. (2018). *Learning from the crowd: The feedback value of crowdfunding*. Available at SSRN 2637699.

Xu, F., Guo, X., Xiao, G., & Zhang, F. (2020). *Crowdfunding strategy with word-of-mouth communication*. Available at SSRN 3707839.

Yazdanfar, D., & Öhman, P. (2017). Substitute or complement? The use of trade credit as a financing source among SMEs. *Management Research Review, 40*(1), 10–27.

CHAPTER 7

Crowdfunding, Spot Sales and Discounting Cost

7.1 Advantages and Disadvantages of Crowdfunding vs. Spot Sales

Some papers argue that crowdfunding can be used as a substitute for sales (e.g. Brown et al., 2017). What are the similarities and differences between crowdfunding and advanced sales? When should firms use crowdfunding as opposed to just selling their products or services on the spot market? Can crowdfunding also be used as a tool to demonstrate/signal a firm's quality?! We will discuss these and related questions in this section.

One of the main differences between crowdfunding and sales is that many entrepreneurs use crowdfunding as a funding source for product development. In addition, entrepreneurs who want to use crowdfunding need to be familiar with the basics of online technologies and need to be able to create a good website (or hire specialists who can help them do this). Crowdfunding is usually done before major product development decisions are made. For example, firms can start a campaign before deciding whether they will even develop their product; they will often wait

---

Supplementary Information The online version contains supplementary material available at https://doi.org/10.1007/978-3-032-10724-4_7.

© The Author(s), under exclusive license to Springer Nature Switzerland AG 2026

A. Miglo and V. Miglo, *The Theories and Developments of Crowdfunding*, https://doi.org/10.1007/978-3-032-10724-4_7

for market validation (crowd wisdom). of the size of the crowdfunding market is also limited compared to that of advanced sales. Finally, note that the crowdfunding is well observed publicly since firms use public websites (platforms), which is different from other pre-sale forms like forward sales. Although there is literature that argues that the disclosure of these pre-sale contracts would be desirable (see, among others, Allaz, 1992; Hughes & Kao, 1997), this issue remains quite ambiguous.

Practitioners recognize that product sales and crowdfunding (in particular reward-based crowdfunding) have a lot of common features and that their connection can bring benefits to firms. One of the largest reward-based crowdfunding platforms Indiegogo introduced Indiegogo Marketplace/InDemand in 2017–2018 where firms who used crowdfunding sell their products or services and compete against other firms that may not have used crowdfunding to launch their products. Both Kickstarter and Indiegogo have teamed up to create the Amazon Launchpad project. The program offers a number of services to entrepreneurs who start new businesses. Both Marketplace and Amazon Launchpad help create an environment where firms that have used crowdfunding compete against firms that have not. Among other examples note that Australian farmers seem to have started using crowdfunding to improve prevalent traditional market structures like duopolies (Askew, 2016).

Launching a crowdfunding campaign prior to spot sales has become part of the strategy for not only start-up firms but also for established, reputable firms. David Mandelbrot, CEO of Indiegogo, for example, mentions examples of Procter and Gamble, Honeywell and Bose.[1] It should be noted that many firms that used Kickstarter go on to use Amazon Launchpad, which features products that are available for purchase on Amazon.com. "…Working with Kickstarter is a great way for us to hear directly from customers what products they care about, since they truly hold the power to bring these products to life…", said Jim Adkins, Vice President of Amazon.[2] Examples include Piper, Zivix, MudWatt and Prynt. Most of these companies are very successful. Note for example Piper's award-winning product "The Piper Computer Kit".[3]

[1] See, e.g. Takahashi (2018).

[2] https://financialpost.com/technology/amazon-com-inc-launches-dedicated-section-for-kickstarter-products-in-u-s-as-part-of-launchpad-initiative.

[3] https://www.playpiper.com/.

There are two lines in advanced pricing literature related to this topic. One line analyzes the advantages of advanced sales in the presence of consumer heterogeneity regarding discount rates (see, e.g. Schaaf & Skiera, 2014) and another line analyzes advanced sales in the presence of asymmetric information about firm quality (see, e.g. de Meza & Reito, 2020; Prescott & Lucas, 1972). Both lines find that advanced sales can be used as an optimal strategy. Crowdfunding to some extent has characteristics of both lines of research. Potential backers (for example in the case of reward-based crowdfunding) can differ in their time preferences, which may affect their decision to participate in a crowdfunding campaign (or wait until the product appears on the spot market).[4] Crowdfunding is usually also done by start-up firms in an environment with a high degree of asymmetric information about firm quality. Note that although these papers have many ideas related to crowdfunding (directly and indirectly) they do not usually consider any specific features of crowdfunding.

Below we analyze some models that include both crowdfunding and spot sales that are related to the questions we discussed above. Consider a firm that can choose between a reward-based crowdfunding campaign where the firm promises to deliver a product to backers as a reward (the crowdfunding price during the campaign is p_c, i.e. any backer who made a contrinution p_c will get the firm's product as a reward) or just use spot sales. The production is q. The expected spot market price is p (costs of production are assumed to be negligibly small). The inverse demand function is $p = a - q$. Under crowdfunding, the firm determines p_c. Respectively, the demand during crowdfunding stage is $c = a - p_c$. After finishing the crowdfunding campaign, the firm together with the spot market price determines the number of items that should be sold on the spot market (s). Assume that: (1) under crowdfunding the amount of funds that can be raised during the campaign is limited. Let $\overline{q}$ be the maximal number of orders that can be collected during crowdfunding; (2) the spot market price is determined using the same inverse demand function $p = a - q = a - c - s$. The firm faces demand uncertainty: $a = a_h$ with probability μ and otherwise $a = a_l$, $a_h > a_l > 0$. The cost of conducting a crowdfunding campaign is F.

Without crowdfunding, when selecting p, the firm maximizes its expected profit from spot sales, which equals $\mu p(a_h - p) +$

[4] We will discuss the role of discounting in Sect. 7.3.

$(1-\mu)p(a_l - p)$. Here $s = a_h - p$ is the number of items sold on the spot market if demand is high and $s = a_l - p$ is the number of items sold on the spot market if demand is low. The solution is:

$$p = \frac{\mu a_h + (1-\mu)a_l}{2}$$

The firm's expected profit is

$$\frac{(\mu a_h + (1-\mu)a_l)^2}{4} \tag{7.1}$$

With crowdfunding, the firm gets to know the demand after the crowdfunding campaign because the firm can observe c, which reflects the true value of a. If after crowdfunding the firm realizes that $a = a_h$ then the firm selects p to maximize $(a_h - c - p)p$. The solution is:

$$p = \frac{a_h - c}{2}$$

Also

$$s = a_h - c - p = \frac{a_h - c}{2}$$

If during crowdfunding the firm realizes that $a = a_l$ then the optimal

$$p = \frac{a_l - c}{2}$$

Also

$$s = a_l - c - p = \frac{a_l - c}{2}$$

The trade-off for a firm that considers crowdfunding is that can learn about the market demand (discussed in Chapter 3), which can help with optimizing the spot market price, but they have to credibly commit to not lowering the spot market price below the crowdfunding price destroying any potential backer's incentive to participate in crowdfunding (discussed in Chapter 6). Several cases are possible. It can be shown that if $\overline{q}$ is too large, eg. greater than a_h, then c will be not be limited by $\overline{q}$ and will therefore be equal to $a - p_c$ and the spot price will be lower than crowdfunding price (i.e. $p_c = a - c$ while $p = (a - c)/2$) making it impossible to run a successful crowdfunding campaign. On the other hand, if $\overline{q}$ is too small then $c = \overline{q}$ regardless of the demand for the product, which implies that no signal about total demand can be received by the firm during the crowdfunding campaign making crowdfunding less profitable than spot sales. Crowdfunding can be feasible and desirable if $\overline{q}$ is moderate. Firms can receive a signal about market demand if the demand is either high $c = \overline{q}$ or low $c < \overline{q}$. This can be the case when $p_c = \frac{a_h - \overline{q}}{2}$ and $c = a_h - p_c \geq \overline{q}$ (which holds because $a_h > \overline{q}$) and $c = a_l - p_c < \overline{q}$. In this case the campaign is successful when demand is high and fails otherwise. Indeed $c = \overline{q}$ when demand is high and $c = 0$ otherwise. No one would be interested to pay p_c when demand is low since $c = a_l - p_c$ and $p = \frac{a_l - c}{2} = \frac{p_c}{2} < p_c$.

So when demand is high $c = \overline{q}$ and $s = \frac{a_h - c}{2} = \frac{a_h - \overline{q}}{2}$. The expected spot price is $a_h - c - s = a_h - \overline{q} - \frac{a_h - \overline{q}}{2} = \frac{a_h - \overline{q}}{2}$. When demand is high $c = 0$ and $s = \frac{a_l - c}{2} = \frac{a_l}{2}$. The expected spot price is $a_l - c - s = a_l - \frac{a_l}{2} = \frac{a_l}{2}$. The firm's profit is $\frac{a_h - \overline{q}}{2}\left(\overline{q} + \frac{a_h - \overline{q}}{2}\right) - F$ with probability μ and $\frac{a_l^2}{4} - F$ otherwise so the firm's expected profit is

$$\mu\left(\frac{a_h - \overline{q}}{2}\left(\overline{q} + \frac{a_h - \overline{q}}{2}\right)\right) + (1 - \mu)\frac{a_l^2}{4} - F \tag{7.2}$$

The difference between (7.2) and (7.1) can be written as

$$D = -\frac{\mu\overline{q}^2}{4} - \frac{\mu a_h(1 - \mu)a_l}{2} + \mu(1 - \mu)\frac{a_h^2}{4} + \mu(1 - \mu)\frac{a_l^2}{4} - F =$$

$$= -\frac{\mu\overline{q}^2}{4} - +\mu(1 - \mu)\frac{(a_h - a_l)^2}{4} - F \tag{7.3}$$

Several observations can be made from (7.3). Probably the most interesting one for us is that $\frac{\partial^2 D}{\partial \mu^2} = -\frac{(a_h - a_l)^2}{2} < 0$. This has a nice interpretation in terms of information quantity: when μ is either very small or very large the amount of information (about market demand) that can be received from crowdfunding is not very large. For example, in the extreme case when $\mu = 0$, the demand is clearly low and vice versa if $\mu = 1$, the demand is clearly high, so crowdfunding does not add too much information. Crowdffunding is most valuable when μ is in the middle range or when the amount of information learning is highest.

Another implication of (7.3) is that it increases with a_h and decreases with a_l, which can to some extent be interpreted as the risk of demand which is also quite intuitive. Also (7.3) is decreasing in $\overline{q}$ (similar to some points in Chapter 6) and decreasing in F.

In terms of signalling quality using crowdfunding consider the following model that is close to the spirit of what we considered in Chapter 5. Consider the case with two firms with similar products/services that can choose between selling their product on the spot market (the product value is v) and via reward-based crowdfunding. Note that crowdfunding can help with developing not only highly technological (say Apple-esque[5]) products but also traditional physical products as well (see, for example, Kumar et al., 2020). In the latter case firms retain monopoly power during the development stage and sale of the project, which may change the outcome of decision-making compared to more competitive environments or more traditional products. Examples include products and services like handbags, perfumes, toys etc.[6] In our model, backers who invest v will receive the firm's future product as a reward. Further assume that the cost of conducting a crowdfunding campaign is F. For simplicity suppose that the total number of potential consumers/backers is 8. Suppose that if two firms are on the spot market, buyers are split 50-50 between the firms. Further, if an opportunity to pre-order the product during crowdfunding exists potential investors/backers will also be split 50-50. The following situations can occur: both firms select spot sales (denote this strategy S); both firms select crowdfunding followed by spot sales (denote this strategy CF); Firm 1 selects CF and Firm 2 selects S; Firm 2 selects CF and Firm 1 selects S. If both firms select S, in equilibrium the firms' profits are $\pi_1 = \pi_2 = 4v$. If both firms select CF, the equilibrium firms' profits are $\pi_1 = \pi_2 = 4v - F$. Indeed, in this case each firm gets four buyers: two of them pre-order the product during crowdfunding. Now consider the case when one firm, say Firm 1, selects CF and Firm 2 selects S. During crowdfunding Firm 1 pre-sells four goods on the

[5] https://artofthekickstart.com/kickstarter-vs-indiegogo-and-how-to-decide-for-your-crowdfunding-campaign/.

[6] https://www.indiegogo.com/projects/public-goods-revolutionizing-household-products--3#/.

https://www.indiegogo.com/projects/kantala-handbags-inspired-by-traditional-artisans-vegan#/.

spot market with the 4 remaining buyers split 50–50 between firms. So Firm 1's profit equals $6v - F$ and Firm 2's profit equals $2v$.

The matrix of payoffs is then (Table 7.1).

Table 7.1 The matrix of payoffs in a game with two firms

Firm 1/Firm 2	*S*	*CF*
S	$4v, 4v$	$2v, 6v - F$
CF	$6v - F, 2v$	$4v - F, 4v - F$

If $2v > F$, the only equilibrium is one where both firms use crowdfunding. Indeed, consider a situation where both firms select the spot market strategy. Consider Firm 1. Its payoff is $4v$. If it deviates to CF then its payoff is $6v - F$, which is greater than $4v$ so Firm 1 would deviate and situation (S,S) is not an equilibrium. Similarly, the situation where one firm selects S and one selects CF is not equilibrium because the former would deviate to CF. The only equilibrium is (CF, CF) where no firm has an incentive to deviate.

Now suppose that Firm 2's product is of lower quality. More specifically, assume that the product quality is impossible/hard to discover during the product sale or during crowdfunding, but the common knowledge is that the product of one the firm fails in 50% of cases and the consumer loses the product's value in this case. Further suppose that the buyers are risk neutral so if buyers believe that there is 50% chance that the product is good quality they will be ready to pay $v/2$.

If both firms select S, the equilibrium firms' profits are $3v$. Indeed, the probability of having a high-quality product is 6 out of 8 (4 of one firm and 50%, i.e. 2 out of 4 from the other firm) so the buyers are ready to pay $3v/4$. And each firm's profit is $4 * \frac{3v}{4} = 3v$. If both firms select CF, the equilibrium firms' profits are $4v - F$. The reason behind this is similar except that each firm receives 2 orders during the crowdfunding campaign and makes 2 sales on the spot market. The buyers are ready to pay $\frac{3v}{4}$ for each item and there is also a platform fee F. Now consider the case when one firm (suppose Firm 1) selects CF and Firm 2 selects S. During crowdfunding Firm 1 pre-sells four goods and on the spot market the 4 remaining buyers are split 50-50 between the firms. This time buyers can rationally believe that the firm that conducts crowdfunding has high quality and vice versa. Then, Firm 1 can get $6v$ for its products and its profit equals $6v - F$. Also, buyers will be ready to pay $v/2$ for the products of Firm 2 so Firm 2's profit equals $2 * \frac{v}{2} = v$.

Then the matrix of payoffs is (Table 7.2):

Table 7.2 The matrix of payoffs in a game with two firms under imperfect information

Firm 1/Firm 2	*S*	*CF*
S	$3v, 3v$	$2v, 3v - F$
CF	$6v - F, v$	$3v - F, 3v - F$

A signalling equilibrium is one where firms select different strategies. It is easy to see that an equilibrium where Firm 1 selects spot sales and Firm 2 selects crowdfunding does not exist since Firm 2 will deviate to strategy S as it increases its payoff from $3v - F$ to $3v$. The situation where Firm 1 chooses CF and Firm 2 selects S can be an equilibrium under some conditions. In particular if $3v > F > 2v$.

Miglo (2020) analyzes a firm's choice between crowdfunding and spot sales and suggests that crowdfunding can be used as a signal of firm quality. The paper considers a competitive environment where firms considering crowdfunding develop similar products. When information between firms is asymmetric, Miglo (2020) suggests that the only signalling equilibrium that exists is where high-quality (high demand) firms choose reward-based crowdfunding strategically as a signal of quality. Low-quality firms are unlikely to mimick high-quality firms by choosing crowdfunding as this would imply an additional cost related to rewards, and prefer spot sales exclusively instead. On the other hand, an equilibrium where low-quality firms select crowdfunding and high-quality firms do not, does not exist. If the uninformed competitor perceives the firm that uses crowdfunding as a low-quality/low-demand firm, it will be pessimistic about the price and will concede the market. A high-quality firm can benefit from this situation by mimicking the strategy of the low-quality firm during the crowdfunding stage.

Xu et al. (2023) analyze a firm's choice between crowdfunding and traditional selling and suggest that crowdfunding dominates traditional selling when an entrepreneur's initial funding is low or the unit (variable) production cost is high.

7.2 Crowdfunding as an Optimal Mechanism Design

The difference between mechanism design and security design is that the former can be applied to not only financing problems.[7] In general, mechanism design focuses on creating optimal rules (and/or) institutions to achieve desired outcomes. This is opposite to the traditional game theory approach that studies the performance of an existing system and institutions (existing mechanism). Sometimes it is called "reverse game theory", starting with a desired outcome and then working backward to design the rules that will incentivize individuals to act in a way that achieves that outcome (see, e.g. Hurwicz & Reiter, 2006 or Penna & Ventre, 2014).

Strausz (2017) created a model where crowdfunding emerges as an optimal mechanism in the presence of demand uncertainty. To illustrate the idea, consider an entrepreneurial firm that designs a financing campaign for the production of its innovative product or service. Consumers value the good at either $v = 1$ or $v = 0$. Operating cost is c, $c < 1$. Investment cost is I. Suppose that there is a total of N consumers in the economy and N' consumers value the good at $v = 1$, $N' \leq N$. The entrepreneur needs to decide how many goods to produce. If demand is observable then the entrepreneur starts production only if N' is sufficiently high, i.e. even though the operating cost c is smaller then the value (or the price that is equal to 1), the entrepreneur needs to cover the fixed cost I. The critical minimum number of items that the entrepreneur will produce is given by the following equation:

$$N'' = I + cN' \tag{7.4}$$

The LHS shows the total value of the goods produced $N'' * 1$ and the RHS shows their total cost. For $N > N''$ the LHS of (7.4) is greater than the RHS because the LHS increases faster than the RHS ($c < 1$). If on the other hand demand is unknown (i.e. the entrepreneur does not know N') the entrepreneur can use the probability distribution of demand to make a decision such that the expected profit is positive. In this case, however, the profit will be lower than the profit under perfect conditions, ie when demand is certain. How can the entrepreneur improve

[7] For more information about mechanism design see, e.g. Fudenberg and Tirole (1991, Ch. 7).

the outcome? It is impossible to ask all consumers directly if they are going to buy the product. However, the entrepreneur can offer a contract (p, T) to consumers where p is the price of the product and T is the total amount of pledges required. The entrepreneur commits to delivering his/her product to consumers who pay p and the money will not be charged if the total amount of pledges is less than T. It is easy to see that the contract $(1, N')$ provides the same surplus to the entrepreneur as the case of perfect information about demand. The interpretation of this contract (mechanism design) is crowdfunding (reward-based AON)!

Strausz (2017) further develops the basic insight and analyzes situations where entrepreneurs have private information about their investment size and consumers' product valuations are not observable and argues that crowdfunding can be an optimal mechanism under two conditions: entrepreneurs do not get excess funds until products are delivered and entrepreneurs do not have full information about the total volume of funds raised during the campaign. Although some elements of these suggestions are observed in practice, they do not have ultimate empirical support. Ellman and Hurkens (2017, 2019) counterargue with Strausz (2017) that in some cases a cross-subsidy (a pooling equilibrium) can exist, which can be better than the outcome described in Strausz (2017). They further argue that in general crowdfunding may not necessarily be optimal but a mechanism where prices are not observed (unlike crowdfunding) and some entrepreneurs are paid (ex-post) for not producing good. This argument also does not have ultimate practical support. Other papers that have some elements of mechanism design are Belavina et al. (2020), that discusses the deferred payment feature of crowdfunding and Miglo (2022) that discusses the PIK feature of crowdfunding. See also Chemla and Tinn (2021).

7.3 Role of Discounting Cost

Time discounting and waiting costs are mentioned in Miglo (2020) as a factor that may be important for crowdfunding. It is related mostly to reward-based crowdfunding because reward-based crowdfunding is closely connected to spot sales. Backers who like the product may want to support the development of the product. Or they can wait until the product development is completed and purchase the product on the spot market. Although for many backers this choice is obvious based on individual preferences, for many of them this choice depends on several factors including the crowdfunding price, the expected spot price of the product and the waiting cost since participating in a crowdfunding campaign does not give them immediate access to the product. The waiting cost in turn may depend on several factors including the level of inflation, etc. There are two main effects here. First, if the rate of inflation increases, the discounting cost increases. So, people would have less incentive to participate in crowdfunding. On the other hand, an inflation rate increase can also signal negative economic conditions, which can negatively affect the firm's performance in the crowdfunding and spot sales stages.

The following model illustrates some of the above points.[8] An entrepreneur requires capital input I to develop a new product, $I > 0$. Development succeeds with probability π. The entrepreneur considers raising funds for developing the product using crowdfunding. Consumers/backers have to wait until the product is delivered if they participate in crowdfunding. They value the good at v on the spot market and apply a discount rate r for waiting if they participate in crowdfunding. The total number of potential backers/customers is normalized to unity and r is uniform on [1; 2]. Let the spot price be P and the crowdfunding price p and also let C denote the amount raised during crowdfunding and S the value of spot sales. The amount of funds raised during crowdfunding should cover the project development cost I, $C \geq I$. Backers/consumers are rational and will participate in crowdfunding if $p \leq v/r$, otherwise they will purchase the product on the spot market if $P \leq v$. The entrepreneur has a discount rate d, $d \in [1; 2]$. The entrepreneur is responsible for determining p and P.

Note that risk-neutrality of backers implies a risk-neutral probability estimation of project success. The entrepreneur maximizes the present value of expected earnings minus investment cost $C - I + \frac{\pi}{d}S$ subject to $C \geq I$.

The sequence of events is illustrated in Fig. 7.1.

On the spot market the optimal price is $P = v$, which extracts the full surplus from the potential customers. If the crowdfunding price is p and if

$$1 \leq \frac{\pi v}{p} \leq 2 \tag{7.5}$$

[8] Based on Miglo (2023).

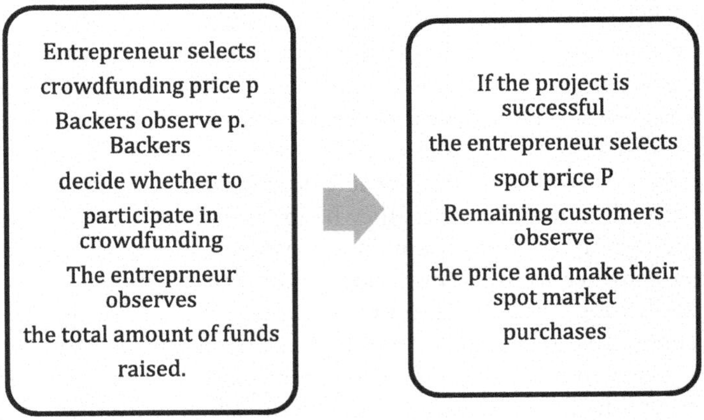

Fig. 7.1 Sequence of events

the discount cutoff is $r = \frac{\pi v}{p}$; i.e. backers with discount rate $r < \frac{\pi v}{p}$ will participate in crowdfunding because it gives them a positive surplus since the cost of the product in this case (p) is smaller than the expected present value of the product $(\frac{\pi v}{r})$. So the total number of backers participating in crowdfunding is $\frac{\pi v}{p} - 1$. This implies $C = p\left(\frac{\pi v}{p} - 1\right) = \pi v - p$. The expected spot revenue for the entrepreneur is $\pi v\left(2 - \frac{\pi v}{p}\right)$. The entrepreneur's total expected profit is

$$\Pi = \pi v - p - I + \frac{\pi v}{d}\left(2 - \frac{\pi v}{p}\right) \tag{7.6}$$

The firm maximizes (7.6) under condition

$$\frac{\pi v}{2} \leq p \leq \pi v - I \tag{7.7}$$

The first inequality of (7.7) follows from (7.5) and if $p > \pi v - I$ the amount raised will not be sufficient to cover the required amount of investment. Before solving the entrepreneur's problem let us return to the condition (7.5). If $\frac{\pi v}{p} < 1$, no backers will participate in crowdfunding and therefore the project will not be undertaken since the firm will have no funds to finance its investment needs. If $\frac{\pi v}{p} \geq 2$ or $\frac{\pi v}{2} \geq p$ then all backers participate in crowdfunding; the firm's profit is then $p - I$ if

$p \geq I$ and 0 otherwise. Note that the latter will always be the case if $I > \frac{\pi v}{2}$ because $\frac{\pi v}{2} \geq p$. The same holds if we look back at condition (7.7). It may not hold if $I > \frac{\pi v}{2}$ so the project will not be undertaken. Note also that $\frac{\pi v}{2} > p$ is never optimal since the profit is less than it is when $\frac{\pi v}{2} = p$. Profit equals $\frac{\pi v}{2} - I$ when $\frac{\pi v}{2} = p$, which is the same amount as in (7.6) so we can focus on conditions (7.6) and (7.7) to find the optimal strategy for the firm. From (7.6):

$$\frac{\partial \Pi}{\partial p} = \frac{\pi^2 v^2}{dp^2}$$

$$\frac{\partial^2 \Pi}{\partial p^2} = -\frac{2\pi^2 v^2}{dp^3}$$

Two cases are possible. 1.

$$\pi v - \frac{\pi v}{\sqrt{d}} \geq I \tag{7.8}$$

Then we have an interior solution since (7.7) holds when p is the global maximand of (7.6) so p is determined from (7.8) by solving $\frac{\partial \Pi}{\partial p} = 0$ taking into account that $\frac{\partial^2 \Pi}{\partial p^2} \leq 0$. So the optimal

$$p = \frac{\pi v}{\sqrt{d}} \tag{7.9}$$

The entrepreneur's profit is

$$\pi v - \frac{2\pi v}{\sqrt{d}} - \frac{2\pi v}{d} - I \tag{7.10}$$

2. $\pi v - \frac{\pi v}{\sqrt{d}} < I \leq \frac{\pi v}{2}$. Then we have a corner solution with $p = \pi v - I$. In this case the entrepreneur's expected profit is

$$\frac{\pi v}{d}\left(2 - \frac{\pi v}{\pi v - I}\right) = \frac{\pi v(\pi v - 2I)}{d(\pi v - I)} \tag{7.11}$$

This leads to the following proposition.

Proposition 7.1 *When information between entrepreneurs and backers is symmetric then: (1) if* $\pi v - \frac{\pi v}{\sqrt{d}} \geq I$*, the optimal* $p = \frac{\pi v}{\sqrt{d}}$*,* $C = \pi v - \frac{\pi v}{\sqrt{d}}$ *and* *the entrepreneur's expected profit is* $\pi v - \frac{2\pi v}{\sqrt{d}} - \frac{2\pi v}{d} - I$; *(2) if* $\pi v - \frac{\pi v}{\sqrt{d}} < I \leq \frac{\pi v}{2}$, *the optimal* $p = \pi v - I$, $C = I$ *and the entrepreneur's expected profit is* $\frac{\pi v(\pi v - 2I)}{d(\pi v - I)}$; *(3) if* $I > \frac{\pi v}{2}$, *the project will not be undertaken.*

Proof Follows from above.

Corollary 1 *C and p increase with* π; *C and p do not depend on I if I is sufficiently small; C increases with I and p decreases with I otherwise; the firm's overall profit decreases with d and I.*

Proof Follows from above.

The amount of funds raised during the crowdfunding campaign and the crowdfunding price both increase in π. If backers are more optimistic about the firm's prospects they are willing to pay a higher price. Also, when I is sufficiently large then the entrepreneur may find it optimal to reduce the price, which will lead to an increase in the amount of funds raised in order to cover the investment requirements.

Note also that crowdfunding should not be used when $d = 1$ (i.e. there is no discounting cost for the entrepreneur) and $I = 0$ (Proposition 7.1 implies that $C = 0$ in either case so no funds raised if crowdfunding is used). The entrepreneur's discount rate along with backer heterogeneity in discount rates (which is consistent with research on discount rates in other areas, e.g. Frederick et al., 2002; Hausman, 1979) is crucial in the model and creates an incentive for crowdfunding. The overall interpretation of these results is based on one hand on time value of money and on the other hand is influenced by the firm's optimal combination of crowdfunding vs/expected spot market revenues i.e. expected marginal benefits from spot sales equals the firm's discount factor. Now we will look at the impact of ex-ante asymmetric information.

Miglo (2023) further extends the model by considering different factors including asymmetric information and moral hazard.

Questions and Exercises

1. One of the advantages of crowdfunding as compared to spot sales is the learning market demand idea. Crowdfunding is more likely to be used for small-sized projects.
2. Some research suggests that in a competitive environment crowdfunding can be used as a signal of firm quality.

3. Consider a firm with an innovative product or service. The production is q. The firm trades on the spot market (the price is p) and (prior to that) it can use a crowdfunding campaign (the crowdfunding or pre-sale price is denoted by p_c). Let c and s denote crowdfunding pre-sales and spot sales respectively: $q = c + s$. The firm makes its decision about c and s. Price determination is driven by the following rule: $p = a - q = a - c - s$. We assume a no-arbitrage environment, i.e. in equilibrium $p_c = p$. However, if a firm uses crowdfunding, the funders (those who pre-order the product during the pre-sale/crowdfunding stage) expect to receive an extra-benefit (reward) β from the firm that reflects the cost of waiting. Also, the firm faces demand uncertainty: $a = a_h$ with probability μ and otherwise $a = a_l$, $a_h > a_l$.

   a. Find the firm's profit if it does not use crowdfunding and only uses spot sales.
   b. Find the firm's profit (as a function of c) if it uses crowdfunding
   c. Find the difference between questions a and b if c is negligeably small. Provide an interpretation. Analyze this difference as a function of μ. Prove that this difference is maximized when $\mu = 1/2$. Provide an interpretation.

4. An entrepreneur requires capital input I to develop a new product, $I > 0$. Development succeeds with probability π. The entrepreneur considers raising funds for developing the product using crowdfunding. Consumers/backers have to wait until the product is delivered if they participate in crowdfunding. They all value the good at v on the spot market but the discount rates r they apply for waiting if they participate in crowdfunding are different. The total number of potential backers/customers is normalized to unity and r is uniform on $[1; 3]$. Let the spot price be P and let the crowdfunding price be p.Let C denote the amount raised during crowdfunding and let S be the value of spot sales. The amount of funds raised by crowdfunding should cover the project development costs I, $C \geq I$. Backers/consumers are rational and will participate in crowdfunding if $p \leq v/r$ and if not they will purchase the product on the spot market if $P \leq v$. The entrepreneur has a discount rate d, $d \in [1; 3]$. The entrepreneur is responsible for determining p and P. Find the optimal p and P.

References

Allaz, B. (1992). Oligopoly, uncertainty and strategic forward transactions. *International Journal of Industrial Organization, 10*(2), 297–308.

Askew, P. (2016). https://readyfundgrow.com.au/crowdfunding-startup-aussie-food/

Belavina, E., Marinesi, S., & Tsoukalas, G. (2020). Rethinking crowdfunding platform design: Mechanisms to deter misconduct and improve efficiency. *Management Science, 66*(11), 4980–4997.

Brown, T. E., Boon, E., & Pitt, L. F. (2017). Seeking funding in order to sell: Crowdfunding as a marketing tool. *Business Horizons, 60*(2), 189–195.

Chemla, G., & Tinn, K. (2021). How wise are crowds on crowdfunding platforms? *The Palgrave Handbook of Technological Finance*, 397–406.

De Meza, D., & Reito, F. (2020). Too much waste, not enough rationing: The failure of stochastic, competitive markets. *Journal of Economic Theory, 188*, Article 105067.

Ellman, M., & Hurkens, S. (2017). *A theory of crowdfunding—A mechanism design approach with demand uncertainty and moral hazard: Comment*. Available at SSRN 3094034.

Ellman, M., & Hurkens, S. (2019). Optimal crowdfunding design. *Journal of Economic Theory, 184*, Article 104939.

Frederick, S., Loewenstein, G., & O'donoghue, T. (2002). Time discounting and time preference: A critical review. *Journal of Economic Literature, 40*(2), 351–401.

Fudenberg, D., & Tirole, J. (1991). *Game theory*. MIT Press.

Hausman, J. A. (1979). Individual discount rates and the purchase and utilization of energy-using durables. *The Bell Journal of Economics*, 33–54.

Hughes, J. S., & Kao, J. L. (1997). Strategic forward contracting and observability. *International Journal of Industrial Organization, 16*(1), 121–133.

Hurwicz, L., & Reiter, S. (2006). *Designing economic mechanisms*. Cambridge University Press.

Kumar, P., Langberg, N., & Zvilichovsky, D. (2020). Crowdfunding, financing constraints, and real effects. *Management Science, 66*(8), 3561–3580.

Miglo, A. (2020). Crowdfunding in a competitive environment. *Journal of Risk and Financial Management, 13*(3), 39.

Miglo, A. (2022). Backers: Consumers or investors? Crowdfunding vs. traditional financing as an optimal security design problem. In *Handbook of digital entrepreneurship* (pp. 236–255). Edward Elgar Publishing.

Miglo, A. (2023). *A theory of crowdfunding under asymmetric information and discounting cost*. Available at SSRN 4659368.

Penna, P., & Ventre, C. (2014). Optimal collusion-resistant mechanisms with verification. *Games and Economic Behavior., 86*, 491–509.

Prescott, E. C., & Lucas, R. E. (1972). A note on price systems in infinite dimensional space. *International Economic Review, 13*(2), 416–422.

Schaaf, R., & Skiera, B. (2014). Effect of time preferences on optimal prices and profitability of advance selling. *Customer Needs and Solutions, 1*(2), 131–142.

Strausz, R. (2017). A theory of crowdfunding: A mechanism design approach with demand uncertainty and moral hazard. *American Economic Review, 107*(6), 1430–1476.

Takahashi, D. (2018, June). *Indiegogo moves beyond crowdfunding to help startups with manufacturing*. https://venturebeat.com/entrepreneur/indiegogo-moves-beyond-crowdfunding-to-help-startups-with-manufacturing

Xu, S., Ling, L., Du, S., & Liu, L. (2023). Crowdfunding or traditional mode? Strategy choices in product selling. *Transportation Research Part E: Logistics and Transportation Review, 172*, Article 103011.

CHAPTER 8

Crowdfunding Regulation and Bankruptcy

8.1 Why Is Crowdfunding Regulation Often Soft?!

As we mentioned previously, the JOBS Act 2012 is considered to be one of the cornerstones of crowdfunding regulation as it created and incorporated many basic ideas of raising funds by entrepreneurial firms, including limiting the bureaucracy that usually accompanies traditional debt and equity. This section discusses why tightening crowdfunding regulation is not necessarily optimal even if the cost of the regulatory change is relatively low, which is consistent with a variety of approaches to crowdfunding regulation that are observed in different countries, and why in many cases these regulations seem to be relatively soft.

The following illustrates the point.[1] An entrepreneur requires capital input I to develop a new product, $I > 0$. Development succeeds with probability π. The entrepreneur considers raising funds for developing the product using crowdfunding. Potential consumers/project backers can purchase the product on the spot market or can participate in crowdfunding. They value the good at v on the spot market. The total number

[1] Based on Miglo (2023).

Supplementary Information The online version contains supplementary material available at https://doi.org/10.1007/978-3-032-10724-4_8.

© The Author(s), under exclusive license to Springer Nature Switzerland AG 2026

A. Miglo and V. Miglo, *The Theories and Developments of Crowdfunding*, https://doi.org/10.1007/978-3-032-10724-4_8

of potential backers/customers is normalized to unity without loss of generality. Let the spot market price be p, the crowdfunding price be p_c and denote the amount raised during crowdfunding by C. The amount of funds raised by crowdfunding should cover the project development costs I, $C \geq I$. There are two types of information asymmetries between the entrepreneur and the potential backers/consumers. Ex-ante asymmetric information is related to the probability of project success. Prior to starting the campaign, the entrepreneur gets to know π. . There are two types of entrepreneurs. Type l (low-quality project) is characterized by the parameter π_l, , type h (high-quality project) has parameter π_h where $\pi_l < \pi_h$. By definition, h has a higher probability of success. π is the entrepreneur's private information while the public is aware about the distribution of π. Let μ be the proportion of type h entrepreneurs, $0 < \mu < 1$. Let $\pi_m = \mu\pi_h + (1 - \mu)\pi_l$ be the average probability of project success among the entrepreneurs. Ex-post asymmetric information is related to the inability of the crowd to directly observe and control the usage of funds raised by the entrepreneur during the campaign. More specifically we assume that after raising funds the entrepreneur can decide to cash in and run away with the cash (similar ideas were discussed in Chapter 4). The expected utility of the entrepreneur in this case is $C(1 - \gamma)$, where γ is the probability of being caught. γ is related to the strength of regulation development.

Also, there is a social planner or the government agency that is responsible for crowdfunding regulation. In the model, the social planner selects γ. The social planner is interested in maximizing firm expected earnings plus consumer surplus. Suppose that the planner's objective is

$$G = a\Pi + bCS - cF(\gamma) \tag{8.1}$$

Here Π is the entrepreneurs' expected profit, CS is the consumer surplus and $F(\gamma)$ is the cost of the regulation system (assume that $F'(\gamma) > 0$, i.e., a stricter regulation is costlier although this assumption is not crucial for the results) and a, b, c are the weights of each component in the objective function, $a, b, c > 0$.

The entrepreneur wants to finance the required investment by using reward-based crowdfunding. The entrepreneur determines the crowdfunding price p_c, i.e., backers who investred p_c during the campaign can receive the product of the firm after the campaign is completed and the product is produced and delivered. Those who did not participate in crowdfunding can purchase the product on the spot market if the project is successful for the price p. . The firm (project) is owned by an entrepreneur who maximizes his expected earnings. Everybody is risk-neutral and the risk-free interest rate is zero. These assumptions imply a risk-neutral probability estimation of expected project success by funders participating in the crowdfunding campaign. Backers make their choice of whether to participate in the crowdfunding campaign by maximizing their expected surpluses. A backer's expected surplus during crowdfunding equals the expected value of the product ($vE\pi$, where $E\pi$ is the expected probability of project success) minus the price p_c. For those who purchase the product on the spot market the surplus equals $v - p$. Backers can purchase the product on the spot market or participate in crowdfunding if the estimated surplus is not negative. Further if the surplus from participating in the crowdfunding campaign and from purchasing the product on the spot market are equal, we assume that customers are split 50-50 between crowdfunding and the spot market.

The sequence of events is illustrated in Fig. 8.1.

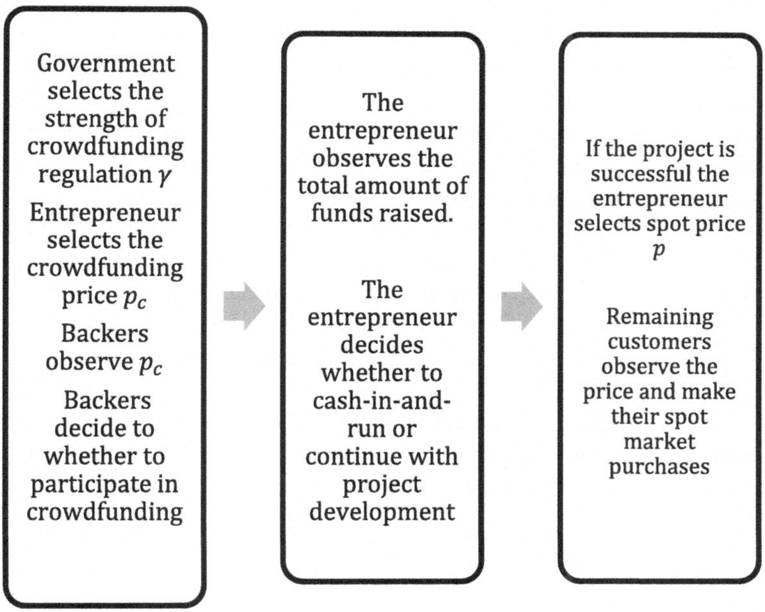

Fig. 8.1 Sequence of Events

On the spot market the firm charges the price $p = v$ and extracts full surplus from customers. What is the optimal crowdfunding price? If information about π is symmetric then h makes $p_c = \pi_h v$. A backer's expected surplus in this case is $vE\pi - p_c = \pi_h v - \pi_h v = 0$ so backers agree to participate. Similarly for type l $p_c = \pi_l v$. Under asymmetric information there are two types of potential equilibria: a separating one where each type selects a different strategy and a pooling one where both types select the same strategy. Similarly to Chapter 6 one can show that a separating equilibrium does not exist since the low-quality firm mimicks the high-quality firm.

Now consider pooling. Under pooling $p_c = \pi_m v$. It means that the backers evaluate the expected probability of project success at π_m and are ready to make an investment $\pi_m v$. In this case their expected surplus is $\pi_m v - p_c = \pi_m v - \pi_m v = 0$ so they are interested in participating. Also, backers anticipate that the spot market price of the product will be $p = v$ and respectively their expected surplus from purchasing the product on the spot market is $\pi_m v - p_c = \pi_m v - \pi_m v = 0$ so they are indifferent between participating in crowdfunding or waiting and purchasing the product on the spot market. In this case as we assume potential backers are split 50-50 between participating in crowdfunding and purchasing the product on the spot market; since the total number of potential buyers/backers is equal to one, the number of backers participating in crowdfunding equals ½ and the number of buyers purchasing the product on the spot market equals ½ as well.

After completing the crowdfunding campaign, the entrepreneur can either run away with the collected funds (in this case the entrepreneur's payoff is $(1-\gamma)\frac{\pi_m v}{2}$) or continue with the project. If the latter then h's payoff is $\frac{\pi_h v}{2} + \frac{\pi_m v}{2} - I$. This is because the firm collects an amount $C = \frac{1}{2}p_c = \frac{\pi_m v}{2}$ during the crowdfunding campaign and the firm's revenue on the spot market is $\frac{v}{2}$ while type h's expected revenue is $\frac{\pi_h v}{2}$ because the probability of project success is π_h and, respectively, type l's expected revenue on the spot market is $\frac{\pi_l v}{2}$. So h's total payoff is $\frac{\pi_h v}{2} + \frac{\pi_m v}{2} - I$. Respectively l's payoff is $\frac{\pi_l v}{2} + \frac{\pi_m v}{2} - I$. If

$$\frac{\pi_l v}{2} + \frac{\pi_m v}{2} - I \geq (1-\gamma)\frac{\pi_m v}{2} \tag{8.2}$$

then no firm type would steal funds in equilibrium because, for each type, developing the product brings a higher profit than running away with the cash. Now consider the case

$$\frac{\pi_l v}{2} + \frac{\pi_m v}{2} - I < (1-\gamma)\frac{\pi_m v}{2} \leq \frac{\pi_h v}{2} + \frac{\pi_m v}{2} - I \tag{8.3}$$

Then h is interested in continuing with the project while l has an incentive to cash-in-and-run. h makes $\frac{\pi_h v}{2} + \frac{\pi_m v}{2} - I$ in total and l makes $(1-\gamma)\frac{\pi_m v}{2}$. So Π, or the expected entrepreneur's profit, equals $\mu\left(\frac{\pi_h v}{2} + \frac{\pi_m v}{2} - I\right) + (1-\mu)(1-\gamma)\frac{\pi_m v}{2}$.

In this model a pooling equilibrium is possible where the low-quality entrepreneur successfully raises funds using crowdfunding and then diverts them. So, what is the optimal crowdfunding regulation?! In the model the regulator selects γ. In general, γ affects several things. A higher γ increases the government's costs related to regulation as discussed above. On the other hand, it reduces the expected payoff of the type l entrepreneur.

Then as follows from (8.1), the total social surplus is

$$G = a\left(\mu\left(\frac{\pi_h v}{2} + \frac{\pi_m v}{2} - I\right) + (1-\mu)(1-\gamma)\frac{\pi_m v}{2}\right) - cF(\gamma) \tag{8.4}$$

This is because the consumer surplus is zero.

Proposition 8.1 Soft *crowdfunding regulation may be better than strict regulation.*

Proof Follows from (8.4) noting that $\frac{\partial G}{\partial \gamma} = -a(1-\mu)\frac{\pi_m v}{2} - cF'(\gamma) < 0$.

The model suggests that in some cases tightening crowdfunding regulation, i.e., increasing γ (and potentially reducing/eliminating any moral hazard problems) may not necessarily be optimal. The model predicts that in the context of crowdfunding a pooling equilibrium (with some value loss for the high-quality type) may dominate. The high frequency of reward non-delivery observed in practice (according to Hauge and Chimahusky [2016] 60% of firms had issues with rewards delivery) is determined by the assumption of the projects' probabilistic outcome (that can be related to the production process issues in the spirit of Mollick and Kuppuswamy [2014]) but also by the existence of pooling ("with funds diversion") which can explain not only a high degree of rewards non-delivery but also non-delivery via fraud (consistent with Cumming et al., 2023).

Further, the existence of pooling equilibria is consistent with the excessive entry of low-quality firms into the crowdfunding market, as follows: from the evidence of many cases of crowdfunding conditions violations (as in, e.g., Blaseg et al., 2020) and, in general, with the high fraction of firms that fail to deliver rewards because of fraud cases, etc. Also, as follows: from (8.2) and (8.3), l is more likely to divert funds in pooling equilibria with higher I (condition [8.3]) than in pooling with lower I, which is consistent with the spirit of the evidence that campaigns with lower targets have higher chances of success. Tightening regulation is not necessarily optimal even if the cost of regulation change is relatively low (but not zero), which is consistent with a variety of approaches to crowdfunding regulation observed in different countries and why in many cases they seem to be relatively soft.

Note the following ideas related to the above. Gutiérrez-Urtiaga and Sáez-Lacave (2018) argue that standard measures of consumer or investor protection may be counterproductive. They also suggest that the implicit no-penalty (for entrepreneurs; in the case of non-delivery) reward-based crowdfunding contract is a contractual innovation specifically designed for talent discovery. Moores (2015) suggests that the legal obligations between the project creator and backers in reward-based crowdfunding remain undetermined. The paper also suggests that the contract between the entrepreneur and backers is difficult to enforce because of the disparity in the ability to initiate a lawsuit, due to the high cost, and the reality that most backers only pledge a small amount to the project. In a similar spirit, Hornuf and Schwienbacher (2017) argue that investor protection that is too strong may harm small firms and entrepreneurial initiatives, which contrasts with the traditional "law and finance" view that stronger investor protection is better. They mostly focus on equity-based crowdfunding.[2]

Among other papers that have some elements related to entrepreneurial fraud and crowdfunding regulation, Ellman and Hurkens (2017) provide a simple example of a crowdfunding design that tolerates some fraud risk. Strausz (2017) suggests that entrepreneurs should not receive funds until products are produced and should not receive information about how much funding is raised during the campaign; Belavina et al. (2020) suggest forbidding campaigns from raising funds above

[2] See also Wojahn and Wilms (2020).

targets; and Ellman and Hurkens (2019) suggest restricting campaigns with high investment costs, etc. Note that the area is heavily debated and many different ideas are competing for empirical and political support.

8.2 Regulation of Equity-Based and Debt-Based Crowdfunding

There are three large areas of crowdfunding regulation that are under the close scrutiny of researchers and practitioners. One is the aspects of crowdfunding regulation related to requirements for registering a crowdfunding campaign. One area of interest is what exactly was changed/invented that helped crowdfunding grow successfully in recent years. A second area of interest relates to firm bankruptcy. Traditional bankruptcy regulations (mostly related to debt financing) differ significantly across countries. So, it is interesting to understand what exactly is the difference between regulations related to traditional bankruptcies and bankruptcies related to crowdfunding. A third area relates to the differences between countries (this question will be discussed in Sect. 8.4). We start with the first one, namely, the aspects of regulation related to crowdfunding campaign registration.

A good example is the USA (it is probably one of the earliest examples of crowdfunding related regulation from a formal regulation point of view). As was previously mentioned, the Jumpstart Our Business Start-ups (JOBS) act of 2012 determined the major differences between traditional equity registration and crowdfunding. Since the 1930s, the U.S. Securities and Exchange Commission (SEC) has imposed severe restrictions on an entrepreneur's ability to raise capital using public advertising. The idea is that firms should know their investors. The origins of this tradition are related to the greatest financial crisis in modern history, i.e., the crisis of 1929, and subsequent economic struggles in many countries around the world. One of the reasons behind this crisis was attributed to the lack of financial regulation (see, e.g., Barton & Waymire, 2004). On March 27, 2012, US Congress passed the JOBS Act in order to simplify the procedures related to equity issues for smaller companies and facilitate capital formation. It was signed into law by President Obama on April 5, 2012. It had two interesting sections: Title II and Title III. Title II allowed for "crowdfunding" by "accredited investors" (a restrictive form of crowdfunding). An accredited investor means an investor that satisfies a set of conditions.[3] At the time accredited investors were those who made over $200,000 in annual salary for the previous two years or made over $300,000 in joint annual salary (for spouses) over the previous two years; or had over $1M in net worth, excluding their primary residence.

Title III allowed for "crowdfunding" by all investors (i.e., accredited and non-accredited). An issuer may sell up to $1,000,000 of its securities every 12 months and, depending on their net worth and income, investors are permitted to invest up to $100,000 in crowdfunding issues every 12 months. The proposed equity-crowdfunding rules under Title III were issued by the SEC in October 2013. The final equity-crowdfunding rules under Title III were issued by the SEC in October 2015, and the rules became effective in May 2016.

Further, firms can also select Title IV or Regulation A+ where the registration process requires submitting documents to the SEC. The company is then allowed to raise a larger amount of capital (up to $75 million every 12 months); the whole process is simpler and less bureaucratic than a traditional equity offering. For example, the company can start to look for investor interest and support before even filing an offering statement.[4] Regulation A+, or Reg A, went into effect on June 19, 2015. The company can use crowdfunding under Title 4 as well. The first Regulation A+ offering, Elio Motors, used StartEngine's platform. Elio Motors raised $17M using crowdfunding.[5]

In August 2020, the SEC expanded the definition of accredited investors to add new eligibility criteria, which included holders of certain professional licenses as well as limited liability companies with at least $5M in assets and "family offices" with at least $5M in assets under management. The definition of "accredited investors", even after this expansion, is still quite limited and only applies to a small subset of the population.

This example is quite typical for many developed countries where the issues of traditional securities by businesses is quite costly and time consuming. We will discuss more examples in Sect. 8.4. The challenge here is to achieve and balance the following 3 objectives: (1) to make

[3] See, e.g., https://www.cato.org/policy-analysis/walk-through-jobs-act-2012-deregulation-wake-financial-crisis.

[4] See, e.g., https://koreconx.com/what-is-the-difference-between-title-ii-iii-and-iv-crowdfunding/.

[5] https://www.startengine.com/offering/elio-motors /https://blogstartenginecom.kinsta.cloud/blog/regulation-a-what-entrepreneurs-need-to-know/.

crowdfunding legally possible, (2) ensure that regulation is efficient and able to effectively support the development of crowdfunding and eliminate major roadblocks it faces and (3) ensure crowdfunding is accessible to small and risk-taking firms who do not pose significant resources (in-line with the general Fintech objectives of lowering barriers of entry and transaction costs).

The next question of this section is about the connections between crowdfunding and bankruptcy. The topic of regulation of debt-based and equity-based crowdfunding is to some extent related to the regulation of traditional debt and equity, which in turn is closely related to the concept of bankruptcy and bankruptcy regulation (for more information, see, e.g., Claessens & Klapper, 2005). For example, the topic is related to such issues as what happens when a firm becomes bankrupt and what the penalties are for violating or delaying payments. Crowdfunding is an interesting area in this sense because it involves different types of potential failures in addition to classical business failure, such as campaign failure and failure or delay in delivering rewards (the latter will be discussed in the next section). With regard to business failure, there are two possible connections between the topics of business failure and crowdfunding. The first is, of course, the traditional link: if the firm has debt and is not able to make payments related to this debt, the firm can be forced into bankruptcy. In the case of crowdfunding, a firm can be declared bankrupt if it uses debt-based crowdfunding and fails to make payment to crowdloanholders. The second interesting link between these topics is that, as practice shows, firms can use crowdfunding to raise funds when they are in a situation of financial distress or are close to bankruptcy. We start our discussion with the first link, namely, that firms that use debt-based crowdfunding and are not able to make payments can be declared bankrupt.

An important issue is the priority of claims when a firm is bankrupt. This is because the resources and assets of a bankrupt firm are often not able to satisfy 100% of all its debts/claims outstanding, so creditor priority becomes important. The rules can vary between countries, but generally, in developed countries, the main rules are (1) first, secured or preferred debts or claims are paid before unsecured debts, and (2) equityholders are paid last. Secured debt is usually debt with collateral, i.e., an asset is pledged that can be seized by debtholders in the case of bankruptcy (see, e.g., Bester, 1987). Preferred debts or claims are, for example, outstanding wages, bankruptcy proceedings, fees, etc.[6] The order of priorities between secured and preferred claims can vary.[7] Debt received during a debt-based crowdfunding campaign is usually unsecured,[8] so usually crowdloanholders have low priority. Combined with the fact that these investments are usually small and that they involve coordination problems among a large number of small creditors, legal action by crowdloanholders is generally difficult and does not yield preferred results. Of course, any debtholder usually has a higher priority than an equityholder, including backers who become equityholders during equity-based crowdfunding campaigns.

As we mentioned, debt created during debt-based crowdfunding campaigns or P2P campaigns is usually unsecured. This means that compared to secured debt, it is a higher risk and potentially higher reward type of debt. In line with this, Wang and Overby (2022) analysed data from Lending Club and found that the ease of receiving a loan causes some borrowers to borrow too much, which often leads to bankruptcy. Dömötör et al. (2023) find debt-based crowdfunding to be high risk as well. Another line of research investigates how borrowers manage to be successful in obtaining these high-risk loans during debt-based crowdfunding campaigns. It was suggested that important aspects of these types of loans are social collateral and soft information. Social collateral includes things like trust, network, group pressure and training (see, e.g., Hadi & Kamaluddin, 2015). Soft information (see, e.g., Iyer et al., 2016; Lui et al., 2023) means that crowdfunding firms often voluntarily provide information about their businesses that is usually not part of the traditional bank lending process, which can be effective in the age of artificial intelligence that can be used to analyse this kind of information.

The second point related to the connections between bankruptcy and crowdfunding is that firms in financial distress can and often use crowdfunding. For example, Wang and Overby (2022) find that the objective of debt used by firms who are considering bankruptcy is often to restructure their debt and/or to withdraw some earnings before they file for

[6] https://www.investopedia.com/terms/p/preferred-creditor.asp.

[7] See, e.g., https://publications.gc.ca/Collection-R/LoPBdP/BP/prb0134-e.htm#A.%C2%A0Status%20of%20Unpaid%20Wages%20under%20the%20Current%20Canadian%20Bankruptcy%20Regime(txt).

[8] See, e.g., https://www.ibanet.org/article/a29ff266-ce4a-44f2-b623-f3d49dfa4432.

bankruptcy. Another example is taken from the platform Gofundme.[9] This is a campaign to support KW Symphony musicians. Located in the Kitchener-Waterloo region of Canada. It is an interesting case because it is regarding a pretty solid and experienced organization, like a Symphony orchestra, using crowdfunding to help them overcome their financial issues. There are a couple of aspects here. First, crowdfunding is an alternative financing source that you can use like any other source to help you when you are in financial distress or close to bankruptcy. The idea is that in many cases, it is not easy to find a good financing source when a firm is in financial distress as investors are skeptical its ability to satisfy its previous obligations. Reward-based (and even donation-based) crowdfunding can work better than traditional financing sources as backers might put less weight on a firm's financial position and more on the specific product idea (and/or the entrepreneurial team itself). So, firms can use a situation of being in financial distress to try out a new creative idea to help them out of the distress. The spirit of this idea is to some extent similar to the idea of using a debtor-in-possession claim or project financing in traditional finance (see, e.g., Dahiya et al., 2003). In this case, a firm is trying to issue new debt that will not go directly to all the creditors and try to revive the firm.

Another important aspect of bankruptcy related to crowdfunding is the potential bankruptcy risk of the crowdfunding platform itself, which would affect every company that uses the platform even though the campaigns themselves might be successful. So, it is important for entrepreneurs to make good choices when selecting platforms for their campaigns. China is an interesting example. By the numbers, China is one of the leading, if not the leading, countries in developing P2P platforms that facilitate loans to a variety of potential borrowers such as small businesses and private individuals.[10] Several big bankruptcies (including Ezuabo and Tuandai) (see, e.g., He & Li, 2021) on these platforms took place between 2016 and 2020, leading to what many experts said was a P2P platform crisis. A related line of research analyses the factors behind the failure of these platforms. For example, He and Li (2021) analyse the influence of financial and political factors on P2P platforms in China.

[9] See, e.g., https://www.gofundme.com/f/support-your-kwsymphony-musicians.

[10] See, e.g., https://en.wikipedia.org/wiki/Peer-to-peer_lending.

They find that large platforms, platforms with large/listed firms as shareholders, and platforms with better disclosure practices were less likely to be bankrupt or be involved in malpractice. Gu et al. (2024) develop a theoretical model of platform competition and argue that one of the main reasons behind platform failure is that many platforms offer unsustainable principal guarantees. They suggest that there is a need for moderate entry barriers, enhanced investor education and a balanced regulatory approach that can reduce platform misconduct without stifling competition.

As mentioned above, one suggestion of the above literature is that platforms with better information disclosure are less likely to fail. This is consistent with asymmetric information problems in crowdfunding as well as traditional debt and equity investments (as discussed in previous chapters). The disclosure requirements are affected by regulations. Many countries are making efforts to create environments with better transparency, etc. For example, in Europe, note such documents/ideas as the Regulation on European Crowdfunding Service Providers for Business (ECSP) and the Key Investment Information Sheet (KIIS), which states that business decisions should be understood by investors in their native language.[11] Yet, the topic remains debated among academics. As mentioned previously, Hornuf and Schwienbacher (2017), for example, suggest that overly strict disclosure requirements for equity-based crowdfunding may not be optimal.

The last point is related to taxes. As we know one of the major theories in debt-equity choice literature is the trade-off theory that is based on the idea that when choosing between debt and equity, firms should trade off the benefits of debt financing related to its tax advantages and the disadvantage of the higher risk and cost of bankruptcy (see, e.g., Kraus & Litzenberg, 1973 or Miglo, 2025). This idea can be applied to some extent to crowdfunding. Note that the tax advantage of debt usually means that firms can use interest payments on debt to reduce their profit for the purpose of corporate tax reporting. The latter is usually applicable to corporations, large firms and firms with limited liability. Therefore, this tax-shield idea becomes relevant when a large public company decides

[11] See, e.g., https://eur-lex.europa.eu/legal-content/EN/TXT/HTML/?uri=CELEX:32020R1503&from=EN.

https://fin-law.de/en/capital-markets-law/key-investment-information-sheet-kiis/#:~:text=A%20key%20investment%20information%20sheet%20under%20the%20ECSP%20Regulation%20must,authorized%20under%20the%20ECSP%20Regulation.

to use crowdfunding. The applicability depends also on whether or not debt-based crowdfunding has more bankruptcy risk and cost than equity-based crowdfunding.[12] For more ideas about the connections between crowdfunding and taxes see, e.g., Beebe (2020).[13]

8.3 Regulation of Reward-Based Crowdfunding

The two most interesting areas of regulation related to reward-based crowdfunding are first regulation related to information disclosure and second regulation related to the penalties for the non-delivery of rewards or bankruptcy. With regard to the former the issue is two-fold. On one hand the problems of information disclosure are related to the asymmetric information problems in crowdfunding discussed previously. Requirements related to information disclosure would help with direct signalling as discussed previously in Chapter 3. Yet, in general creating very strict regulations with a lot of requirements would make crowdfunding similar to the traditional issues of securities by undermining the basic ideas of crowdfunding. It may also come with other costs as discussed in Sect. 8.1. Macchiavello and Valenti (2022) discussed different regulations related to reward-based crowdfunding and come to similar conclusions.

With regard to the second area, note that, on one hand, as mentioned in Heminway (2021), consumption interest crowdfunding or reward-based crowdfunding in the United States is regulated through general federal and state consumer protection and unfair trade practices laws. On the other hand, as some authors suggest (e.g., Moores, 2015), the legal obligations between the project creator and backers in reward-based crowdfunding and the legal consequences in different scenarios are not entirely clear. For example, there is an opinion that a crowdfunding platform is not a "store" in the classical meaning of the word, and so the legal exposure of crowdfunding organizations should be limited.[14]

Some platforms recognize this problem and make efforts to enhance the legal responsibilities of entrepreneurs for the non-delivery of rewards. Cascino et al. (2019) discuss the case of Kickstarter, which in September

[12] For more discussions see, e.g., https://bold-awards.com/crowdfunding-risks-and-returns/.

[13] https://www.bakerinstitute.org/research/tax-considerations-crowdfunding.

[14] See, e.g., https://www.kickstarter.com/blog/kickstarter-is-not-a-store.

2014 announced that it would change its terms of use to clarify the nature of the contract between backers and creators. This change was aimed at minimizing moral hazard problems by trying to strengthen the backers' position. In general, the legal settlements of the cases related to reward delivery are not simple.[15] Furthermore, a theoretical debate exists about how strong the penalties should be to the entrepreneur in case of reward non-delivery or in case of reward delivery delays (see, e.g., Broere & Christmann, 2024; Gutiérrez-Urtiaga & Sáez-Lacave, 2018; Miglo, 2023).

An interesting and growing area of research is to analyse the features of campaigns that are in danger of potential reward non-delivery problems and, respectively, potential bankruptcy. It is an interesting area because the frequency of reward non-delivery remains pretty high and, as mentioned above, regulation may not be the ultimate solution to these problems. For example, Lee et al. (2022) found that creator-related features such as whether there is a link to a Facebook ID, the number of external links and websites, the number of projects the creator has backed and the number of projects done by the creator are quite significant. Cumming et al. (2023) find that fraudsters typically only use crowdfunding once, they are less likely to be on Facebook, Twitter and LinkedIn, they are less likely to have photos or videos, and they are more likely to have poorly worded campaigns.[16]

8.4 Comparing Crowdfunding Regulation in Different countries

We will first discuss different aspects of the financial systems around the world, which should help us understand some ideas and principles of crowdfunding regulation in different countries. A financial system is a system that allows for the exchange of funds between different parties involved, in particular, investors, lenders, issuers of securities and borrowers. A financial system usually consists of complex, closely related services, markets and institutions. The objective of a financial system is to create efficient links between different parties. Different types of financial

[15] See, e.g., Heminway (2021) for some examples including the cases of The Forking Path Co, Asylum Playing Cards and Hanfree, etc.

[16] See also Appio et al. (2020).

systems exist around the world. Modern financial systems usually include traditional institutions such as banks or stock exchanges but also some innovative elements such as fintech companies and crypto exchanges. The type of system depends on many factors, including the history of the country, the type of the economy, the political system, culture, etc. First, consider a capital market or simply a market-based system (also sometimes called the Anglo-Saxon financial system; examples include the USA and the UK; see, e.g., Schmidt & Hryckiewicz, 2006). It has a lot of advantages, such as the availability of many different funding strategies for entrepreneurs, including venture capital, angel financing, etc. It is called a market-based system because firms get most of their funds from capital markets (see, e.g., Levine, 2002). Another type of financial system is a bank-based system (sometimes called the German or corporatist system; examples include Germany and Japan; see, e.g., Schmidt & Hryckiewicz, 2006). In this system, banks are the dominant source of funds for businesses. In a market-based system, businesses are largely owned by households, while under a bank-based system, business ownership is less dispersed and banks often have a lot of ownership in firms.[17] Further, uncertainty avoidance is likely to play a role in a society's preference for a market- or bank-oriented financial system. When societies are more accepting of risk and ambiguity, market-based financing is preferred to bank financing and vice versa. Some research shows that people in a capital-based system are more risk-tolerant than people in a bank-based system (see, e.g., Aggarwal & Goodell, 2016).

The US in the 1990s is a good illustration of the advantages of the market-based system. The entrepreneurial risk taken by Silicon Valley companies, like Google, Microsoft and Apple, was supported by the risk tolerance of the market-based system. Banks are more conservative by nature, and if they were the primary sources of capital, it can be argued that not as many firms would have flourished as they did.

too

If one applies similar logic to the development of crowdfunding (which is by definition a risky investment type), one should assume that it would be more likely to succeed in a capital-market-based financial system. The

[17] These two types of financial systems are considered dominant among developed countries although a variety of different systems is often discussed in literature in particular a variety of systems in developing countries and the Islamic financial system. See, e.g., Salman and Nawaz (2018) and Schmidt and Winkler (1999).

trade-off here, though, is that, as we know, the financial system is one of the most regulated sectors of the economy. It has been argued, and we have discussed many times, that the finance industry is by nature dominated by market imperfections, asymmetric information, agency problems and other issues. The objective of financial regulation is to reduce the extent of these imperfections. In general, only large, well-established corporations have easy access to securities markets. Presumably, in more developed countries, regulation should be more developed, but, as we discussed before, this can be costly for industries that require a lower level of bureaucracy. Small companies cannot afford to pay higher fees to overcome high barriers to entry caused by strict regulation. This is why innovative, small entrepreneurial firms always seek new ways of raising funds, like crowdfunding.

Consider the capital-market-based system. In general, this system has very good results in crowdfunding development. The USA has the two largest reward-based crowdfunding platforms in the world (Kickstarter and Indiegogo); Kiva is also headquartered in the USA and is one of the leading debt-based crowdfunding platforms. The UK is recognized as the leading country in Europe in terms of fintech development and is also strong in crowdfunding,[18] in particular equity-based crowdfunding (note the well-known platforms CrowdCube and Republic Europe). What about the crowdfunding regulations in these countries? The USA was where the JOBS Act was created. The UK generally has good regulations; it was one of the first to start developing crowdfunding regulation according to a significant standard. In general, in the UK, the Financial Conduct Authority ("FCA") plays a crucial role in crowdfunding regulation. The first FCA-regulated crowdfunding platform launched in the UK was Abundance Investment, approved in July 2011 and launched to the public in the spring of 2012. Abundance Investment provides debt-based finance. Further, note that the UK is well-known for providing tax benefits to start-up firms, including investors investing in these firms, etc.[19] The Abundance platform is a good example. On their website they announced that they offer tax-free investing with an Innovative Finance

[18] See, e.g., Chervyakov and Rocholl (2019).

[19] See, e.g., https://www8.cao.go.jp/cstp/tyousakai/innovation_ecosystem/4kai/siryo4.pdf.

ISA (IFISA). This allows individuals to invest tax-free into peer-to-peer lending platforms and other debt-based investments.[20]

The FCA regulates investment-based crowdfunding platforms (i.e., debt-based and equity-based crowdfunding). Firms operating such platforms require FCA authorisation where they conduct regulated activity. The FCA does not regulate firms that only operate donations-based, prepayment or rewards-based crowdfunding platforms. The FCA however issued specific warnings concerning online platforms, namely, misleading information and the deletion of negative comments. The FCA stated that they will continue to monitor the market and will take appropriate actions if market risks require it to do so or if there are changes to EU regulations. Even though there are no specific authorities regulating reward-based crowdfunding there are lawyers advising firms preparing such campaigns on intellectual property rights protection (because under crowdfunding the risk of losing is very high as was mentioned previously), consumer protection rights in terms of potential reward non-delivery liability, and different taxes.[21]

Consider the bank-based system. For example, in Japan, crowdfunding development was slower than it was in the US, and it also followed a different path. It started out primarily as a way to raise money for charitable causes and at some point seemed to have a more significant impact on corporate Japan than on smaller Japanese ventures (consistent with the spirit of a bank-based or corporatist system).[22] According to Kato (2021), in Japan, good comprehensive crowdfunding regulation does not exist (at least in the early stages of development), while a later paper by Honjo and Kurihara (2024) suggest that overall procedures for platforms and businesses interested in crowdfunding are more stringent than they are in the UK, for example, which is consistent with the spirit of the differences between market-based and bank-based financial systems.

[20] https://www.pensionbee.com/uk/savings-and-investments/isas/what-is-an-innovative-finance-isa.

[21] See, e.g., https://legalfoundations.org.uk/blog/crowdfunding-in-the-uk-legal-considerations-and-best-practices/.

https://sprintlaw.co.uk/articles/legal-considerations-for-uk-crowdfunding-platforms-what-startups-need-to-know/#:~:text=Crowdfunding%20platforms%20in%20the%20UK%20are%20subject%20to%20key%20laws,raise%20capital%20from%20the%20crowd.

[22] See, e.g., https://www.disruptingjapan.com/crowdfunding-in-japan-is-not-about-startups-ryotaro-nakayama/.

They point to different limits for investors and firms using equity-based crowdfunding, for example. Platforms planning on using investment-type crowdfunding in Japan (similar to traditional equity-based or debt-based crowdfunding but also including so-called fund-based crowdfunding[23]) need to register according to the rules in the Financial Instruments and Exchange Act (FIEA). Further, they need to comply with various reporting, disclosure and investor protection requirements. Firms that want to use investment-type crowdfunding in Japan must satisfy several criteria, including a minimum amount of capital. They also have to submit financial reports and disclose key information about the company and the investment opportunity. Donation-based and reward-type crowdfunding in Japan is subject to the Payment Services Act (PSA), which regulates payment services and electronic money. Platforms have to register as Payment Service Providers and comply with various consumer protection and disclosure requirements. If a firm wants to raise funds through donation/reward-based crowdfunding, it has to comply with certain regulations, such as setting clear funding goals and targets, disclosing information about the product and rewards, and ensuring timely delivery of the rewards to backers.[24]

An interesting area is the development of crowdfunding in countries with Islamic finance principles. On the one hand, as we know, the approach to debt and, in particular, the rejection of interest on debt,[25] at least without risk sharing or other arrangements, may create difficulty for the development of certain kinds of crowdfunding, like debt-based crowdfunding. On the other hand, the idea of project-based finance and risk-sharing finance, where the issuer needs to carefully describe the project, describe the risk involved, and explain the risk-sharing principles, is consistent with some principles of crowdfunding, especially for small firms and entrepreneurial firms. We think the regulation of crowdfunding under the Islamic finance system is an interesting and growing area.[26]

[23] Fund-based crowdfunding is a mechanism where the crowdfunding platform forms a fund for each company that needs to raise funds, and the investor purchases a share of the fund and receives dividends, etc. from the fund. https://monolith.law/en/general-corporate/crowd-funding-law-point.

[24] https://scalingyourcompany.com/crowdfunding-in-japan/.

[25] See, e.g., https://www.oxera.com/wp-content/uploads/2018/03/Islamic-finance.pdf.

[26] For more discussion see, e.g., Noor et al. (2022).

An interesting example is Indonesia. Crowdfunding shows good rates of growth in the country. In terms of regulation, in 2018, the Indonesian Services Authority (OJK) issued the crowdfunding regulation POJK.04/ 2018. This regulation is mostly focused on equity-based crowdfunding. For example, all crowdfunding platforms operating in Indonesia have to register and report their operations to OJK (see, e.g., Mustafida et al., 2021).

To conclude this chapter, note that crowdfunding regulation is a growing area of interest in theory and practice (see, among others, Alhammad et al., 2021; Cascino et al., 2019; Farris, 2016; Lazzaro & Noonan, 2021; Rau, 2020; Sadzius & Sadzius, 2017; Tamburro, 2017, etc.). One area that does not seem to be sufficiently covered is whether regulation should be more investor or entrepreneur-friendly. The enforcement of reward delivery and the exact strength and depth of regulation are difficult areas, and any solution/regulation would come with its own costs and benefits. We know that in terms of traditional debt and equity, there are shareholder-friendly types of regulation, e.g., US (for example, equity has more perks in bankruptcy procedures than debt in some cases, like Chapter 7 bankruptcy), and some are creditor-friendly, e.g., Germany or UK.[27] It would be interesting to see what approach is adopted for crowdfunding in different countries.

Questions and Exercises

1. In the US Title V of the JOBS act of 2012 allows for "crowdfunding" by all investors (i.e., accredited and non-accredited).
2. In the UK, the FCA does not regulate firms that only operate donation-based or reward-based crowdfunding platforms.
3. Bankruptcy resulting from the inability to pay debt and the failure of reward delivery are usually regulated by different types of regulations.
4. The following factors usually do not describe crowdfunding fraud well:

    a. Fraudsters typically only use crowdfunding twice.
    b. Fraudsters are less likely to be present on Facebook, Twitter and LinkedIn

[27] See, e.g., Schoenherr and Starmans (2022).

c. Fraudsters are less likely to have photos or videos on their campaign website.
d. Fraudsters usually have poorly worded campaigns

5. Failure to deliver rewards after a reward-based crowdfunding campaign does not fall under financial default regulation but rather under contractual failure under current regulation.
6. Equity-based crowdfunding is usually associated with a higher level of bureaucracy than traditional equity and a higher level of liquidity of issued shares.
7. Consider a firm that plans to use crowdfunding. In a world without any market imperfections except where bankruptcy or contract failure is costly, the optimal strategy for the firm is:

   a. firm uses as much debt-based crowdfunding as possible
   b. firm uses as much equity-based crowdfunding as possible
   c. firm uses a debt-equity ratio of 1.0
   d. firm uses as much reward-based crowdfunding as possible.

8. An entrepreneur requires capital input 4 to develop a new product.

Development succeeds with probability π. The entrepreneur considers raising funds to develop the product using crowdfunding. Potential consumers/project backers can purchase the product on the spot market or can participate in crowdfunding. They value the good at $v = 1$ on the spot market. The total number of potential backers/customers is 20. Prior to starting the campaign, the entrepreneur gets to know π. There are two types of entrepreneurs. Type l (low-quality project) is characterized by the parameter $\pi_l = 0$, type h (high-quality project) has parameter $\pi_h = 1$. π is the entrepreneur's private information while the public is aware of the distribution of π. Let 0.5 be the proportion of type h entrepreneurs. After raising funds, the entrepreneur can decide to cash-in-and-run without investments. The expected utility of the entrepreneur in this case is $C(1 - \gamma)$, where $\gamma = 0.5$ is the probability of being caught. There is also a social planner or the government agency that is responsible for crowdfunding regulation. In the model, the social planner selects γ. The planner's objective function is $G = 0.5\Pi + 0.3CS - 0.2F(\gamma)$. Here Π is the entrepreneurs' expected profit, CS is the consumer surplus, $F(\gamma) = 0.1\gamma$ is the cost of the regulation system. The timing of events is as described in Fig. 8.1 in the text.

The entrepreneur wants to finance the required investment by using reward-based crowdfunding. The entrepreneur determines the crowdfunding price p_c, i.e., backers who investred p_c during the campaign can receive the product of the firm after the campaign is completed and the product is produced and delivered to backers who participated in the campaign. Those who did not participate in crowdfunding can purchase the product on the spot market if the project is successful for the price p. The firm (project) is owned by an entrepreneur who maximizes his/her expected earnings. Everybody is risk-neutral and the risk-free interest rate is zero. These assumptions imply a risk-neutral probability estimation of the expected project success by the funders participating in the crowdfunding campaign. Backers make their choice of whether or to participate in the crowdfunding campaign by maximizing their expected surpluses. The backers' expected surplus during crowdfunding equals the expected value of the product ($vE\pi$, where $E\pi$ is the expected probability of project success) minus the price p_c. For those who purchases the product on the spot market the surplus equals $v - p$. Backers can purchase the product on the spot market or participate in crowdfunding if the estimated surplus is not negative. Further, if the surplus from participating in the crowdfunding campaign and from purchasing the product on the spot market are equal, we assume that customers are split 50-50 between crowdfunding and the spot market.

a. Describe the crowdfunding prices and spot prices if information about π is symmetric. Would both types of firms be able to develop their businesses?!
b. Now analyse the equilibria if information is asymmetric. Find the values of γ when a pooling equilibrium may exist. Interpret the found conditions.

References

Aggarwal, R., & Goodell, J. W. (2016). National preferences for bank or market financing. *Economic Commentary* (2016-04).

Alhammad, M. M., Alothman, R., & Tan, C. (2021). Review of crowdfunding regulations across countries: A systematic review study. *Journal of Information Systems Engineering and Management, 6*(4), 1–13.

Appio, F. P., Leone, D., Platania, F., & Schiavone, F. (2020). Why are rewards not delivered on time in rewards-based crowdfunding campaigns? An empirical exploration. *Technological Forecasting and Social Change, 157*, Article 120069.

Barton, J., & Waymire, G. (2004). Investor protection under unregulated financial reporting. *Journal of Accounting and Economics, 38*, 65–116.

Beebe, J. (2020). *Tax considerations of crowdfunding*. https://www.bakerinstitute.org/research/tax-considerations-crowdfunding

Belavina, E., Marinesi, S., & Tsoukalas, G. (2020). Rethinking crowdfunding platform design: Mechanisms to deter misconduct and improve efficiency. *Management Science, 66*(11), 4980–4997.

Bester, H. (1987). The role of collateral in credit markets with imperfect information. *European Economic Review, 31*(4), 887–899.

Blaseg, D., Schulze, C., & Skiera, B. (2020). Consumer protection on Kickstarter. *Marketing Science, 39*(1), 211–233.

Broere, M., & Christmann, R. (2024). *Signaling and fraud when crowdfunding campaigns compete for pledges* (MPRA Paper 121784). University Library of Munich, Germany.

Cascino, S., Correia, M., & Tamayo, A. M. (2019). Does consumer protection enhance disclosure credibility in reward crowdfunding? *Journal of Accounting Research, 57*(5), 1247–1302.

Chervyakov, D., & Rocholl, J. (2019). *How to make crowdfunding work in Europe* (No. 2019/6). Bruegel Policy Contribution.

Claessens, S., & Klapper, L. (2005). Bankruptcy around the world: Explanations of its relative use. *American Law and Economics Review, 7*(1), 253–283.

Cumming, D., Hornuf, L., Karami, M., & Schweizer, D. (2023). Disentan gling crowdfunding from fraudfunding. *Journal of Business Ethics, 182*(4), 1103–1128.

Dahiya, S., John, K., Puri, M., & Ramírez, G. (2003). Debtor-in-possession financing and bankruptcy resolution: Empirical evidence. *Journal of Financial Economics, 69*(1), 259–280.

Dömötör, B., Illés, F., & Ölvedi, T. (2023). Peer-to-peer lending: Legal loan sharking or altruistic investment? Analyzing platform investments from a credit risk perspective. *Journal of International Financial Markets, Institutions and Money, 86*, Article 101801.

Ellman, M., & Hurkens, S. (2017). *A theory of crowdfunding—A mechanism design approach with demand uncertainty and moral hazard: Comment*. Available at SSRN 3094034.

Ellman, M., & Hurkens, S. (2019). Optimal crowdfunding design. *Journal of Economic Theory, 184*, Article 104939.

Farris, A. H. (2016). Strict in the wrong places: State crowdfunding exemptions' failure to effectively balance investor protection and capital raising. *Campbell Law Review, 38*, 267.

Gu, D., Gui, Z., & Huang, Y. (2024, October 23). *Fintech market and regulation: Lessons from China's peer-to-peer lending platforms*. HKUST Business School Research Paper No. 2022-065

Gutiérrez-Urtiaga, M., & Sáez-Lacave, M. I. (2018). The promise of reward crowdfunding. *Corporate Governance: An International Review, 26*(5), 355–373.

Hadi, N. A., & Kamaluddin, A. (2015). Social collateral, repayment rates, and the creation of capital among the clients of microfinance. *Procedia Economics and Finance, 31*, 823–828.

Hauge, J. A., & Chimahusky, S. (2016). Are promises meaningless in an uncertain crowdfunding environment? *Economic Inquiry, 54*(3), 1621–1630.

He, Q., & Li, X. (2021). The failure of Chinese peer-to-peer lending platforms: Finance and politics. *Journal of Corporate Finance, 66*, Article 101852.

Heminway, J. M. (2021). The legal regulation of U.S. crowdfunding: An organically evolving patchwork. In C. Kleiner (Ed.), *Legal aspects of crowdfunding. Ius Comparatum—Global studies in comparative law* (Vol. 55). Springer.

Honjo, Y., & Kurihara, K. (2024). Target for campaign success: An empirical analysis of equity crowdfunding in Japan. *The Journal of Technology Transfer, 49*, 926–958.

Hornuf, L., & Schwienbacher, A. (2017). Should securities regulation promote equity crowdfunding? *Small Business Economics, 49*, 579–593.

Iyer, R., Khwaja, A. I., Luttmer, E., & Shue, K. (2016). Screening peers softly: Inferring the quality of small borrowers. *Management Science, 62*(6), 1554–1577.

Kato, T. (2021). The legal regulation of crowdfunding in Japan. In *Legal aspects of crowdfunding* (Vol. 55, pp. 343–362). Springer International Publishing.

Kraus, A., & Litzenberger, R. H. (1973). A state-preference model of optimal financial leverage. *The Journal of Finance, 28*(4), 911–922.

Lazzaro, E., & Noonan, D. (2021). A comparative analysis of US and EU regulatory frameworks of crowdfunding for the cultural and creative industries. *International Journal of Cultural Policy, 27*(5), 590–606.

Lee, S., Shafqat, W., & Kim, H.-C. (2022). Backers beware: Characteristics and detection of fraudulent crowdfunding campaigns. *Sensors, 22*, 7677.

Levine, R. (2002). Bank-based or market-based financial systems: Which is better? *Journal of Financial Intermediation, 11*(4), 398–428.

Lui, S. S., Zhu, Z., & Liu, J. (2023). Success of crowdfunding: A trustworthiness perspective. *Asia Pacific Journal of Management, 40*(2), 681–706.

Macchiavello, E., & Valenti, C. (2022). Beyond the ECSPR and financial return: The regulation of donation and reward-based crowdfunding in the EU. In E.

Macchiavello (Ed.), *Regulation on European crowdfunding service providers for business: A commentary*. Edward Elgar.

Miglo, A. (2023). *A theory of crowdfunding under asymmetric information and discounting cost*. Available at SSRN 4659368.

Miglo, A. (2025). *Capital structure in the modern world: The fundamentals of capital structure management and financing decisions*. Springer Nature.

Mollick, E., & Kuppuswamy, V. (2014). *After the campaign: Outcomes of crowdfunding*. SSRN. https://papers.ssrn.com/sol3/papers.cfm?abstract_id=2376997

Moores, C. (2015). Kickstart my lawsuit: Fraud and justice in rewards-based crowdfunding, UC Davis. *Law Review, 49*(1), 383–424.

Mustafida, R., Fauziah, N. N., & Kurnia, Z. N. (2021). The development of Islamic crowdfunding in Indonesia and its impact towards SMEs. *Hasanuddin Economics and Business Review, 4*(3), 20–29.

Noor, A., Ahamat, H., Marzuki, I., Wulandari, D., Junaidi, A. A., Lisdiyono, E., & Trisnawati, B. (2022). Regulation and consumer protection of fintech in Indonesia: The case of Islamic fintech lending. *Linguistics and Culture Review, 6*(on), 49–63.

Rau, P. R. (2020, July 1). Law, trust, and the development of crowdfunding. *Trust, and the Development of Crowdfunding*.

Sadzius, L., & Sadzius, T. (2017). Existing legal issues for crowdfunding regulation in European Union member states. *International Journal of Business, Humanities and Technology, 7*(3), 52–62.

Salman, A., & Nawaz, H. (2018). Islamic financial system and conventional banking: A comparison. *Arab Economic and Business Journal, 13*(2), 155–167.

Schmidt, R. H., & Hryckiewicz, A. (2006). *Financial systems—Importance, differences and convergence* (IMFS Working Paper Series, No. 4). Goethe University Frankfurt, Institute for Monetary and Financial Stability (IMFS), Frankfurt am Main.

Schmidt, R. H., & Winkler, A. (1999). Building *Financial institutions in developing countries* (Working Paper Series: Finance & Accounting, No. 45). Johann Wolfgang Goethe-Universität Frankfurt am Main, Fachbereich Wirtschaftswissenschaften, Frankfurt am Main.

Schoenherr, D., & Starmans, J. (2022). When should bankruptcy law be creditor- or debtor-friendly? Theory and evidence. *The Journal of Finance, 77*(5), 2669–2717.

Strausz, R. (2017). A theory of crowdfunding: A mechanism design approach with demand uncertainty and moral hazard. *American Economic Review, 107*(6), 1430–1476.

Tamburro, A. (2017). Far from the madding crowd: Crowdfunding a small business reorganization. *Emory Bankruptcy Developments Journal, 34*, 521.

Wang, H., & Overby, E. M. (2022). How does online lending influence bankruptcy filings?. *Management Science, 68*(5), 3309–3329.

Wojahn, O. W., & Wilms, J. F. (2020). The bankruptcy risk of equity crowdfunded companies in Germany. In M. Bilgin, H. Danis, E. Demir, & M. Ucal (Eds.), *Eurasian business perspectives. Eurasian studies in business and economics* (Vol. 12/2). Springer.

CHAPTER 9

Crowdfunding and Fintech Developments

9.1 Reward-Based Crowdfunding Vs Utility Tokens

As we previously mentioned, crowdfunding is a part of FinTech, which represents a newly developing sector of finance. Token issues and their connection to crowdfunding are the focus of this chapter. Tokens represent an important part of fintech and they have a lot of common features with crowdfunding.[1] Similar to the crowdfunding methods studied previously, tokens are a modern way of raising funds from a large number of investors (crowd) for a new project/start-up business. In a sense, token issues represent an advanced form of crowdfunding as we will discuss in this chapter.

Let us look at a typical webpage that shows a list of ICOs (initial coin offerings).[2] Tokens is a term used to describe digital assets; someone who purchases a token receive some rights that depend on the type of tokens

[1] Chen et al. (2021), Bellavitis et al. (2021), Miglo (2022a), Howell et al. (2020) and Adhami and Giudici (2019) provide good reviews of the literature in this field.

[2] See, e.g., https://cryptototem.com/ico-list/.

Supplementary Information The online version contains supplementary material available at https://doi.org/10.1007/978-3-032-10724-4_9.

© The Author(s), under exclusive license to Springer Nature Switzerland AG 2026

A. Miglo and V. Miglo, *The Theories and Developments of Crowdfunding*, https://doi.org/10.1007/978-3-032-10724-4_9

issued. There exists, for example, utility tokens and the issue of utility tokens is called an ICO but there also exist other types of tokens that we will later in this chapter. Utility tokens give the right to their holders the use of products/services offered by the digital platform/firm that issued the tokens.

To some extent the information available about ICOs on the webpages mentioned above is similar to about the information on crowdfunding campaign pages. It includes, for example, information like the total amount raised, the campaign category/industry and the starting date. If we look at the page of a campaign (take FirePepe for example[3]) we will see things like a softcap and a hardcap,[4] which are similar to the campaign target in crowdfunding. There are some differences as well. For example, if we select one of the campaigns (take Tapzi for example) and look at the campaign page[5] we can see information like the type of token being issued (utility token in this case), the token price, token distribution and the token standard. Some of this information is on the more technical side of tokens or is related to one of the most important technologies in fintech, namely blockchain.[6] In the case of Tapzi, for example, the token standard is BEP-20.[7] In general any standard represents a set of rules that allows for good integration with digital wallets, cryptoexchanges and other parts of the network. The most important part for our purposes is the token type, which in this case is a utility token. As was previously mentioned, a utility token usually means that a purchaser of the token gets some rights to use the issuing firm's product or service. In this case we can find on the campaign website: "…On Tapzi, users take TAPZI tokens to compete in live multiplayer games like Chess, Checkers,

[3] https://cryptototem.com/firepepe-afpep/.

[4] Softcap refers to the minimum defined limit for the collection of funds specified by a project's team for its fund-raising. A hard cap, which is the maximum possible funding that a team is looking to collect. Similar to crowdfunding ideas soft caps for example are often used as a signal.

[5] https://cryptototem.com/tapzi/.

[6] More about blockchain see, e.g., Goncharov and Nechesov (2023).

[7] Many firms that issue tokens use Ethereum, which is one of the largest crypto platforms. In this case the standard is for example ERC20. Note also that cryptoexchanges are used because potential buyers may not necessarily pay in regular (fiat) currency when purchasing tokens but can also use cryptocurrencies.

Tic Tac Toe and Rock-Paper-Scissors…"[8] Also, a part of the information is "Whitelist". We have not seen this term in traditional crowdfunding. Roughly speaking it is analogous to the term "prospectus" for traditional financing, which means a document that describes the terms of issuing.

The most important feature of tokens is their type; in the case of Tapzi, it is a utility token. As was previously mentioned, similarly to reward-based crowdfunding, utility tokens give the right to the owner or holder to redeem them in exchange for the service or product offered by the company that issued the tokens. Many companies that use tokens are related to the internet, to the blockchain or to fintech in general. For example, some of them offer the exchange of free memory space. This idea was used by Filecoin, for example, which provides decentralized data storage services using a global network of computers with available space. Customers pay for storage. Storage nodes bid to host files and earn tokens. The Filecoin token is the only means of payment. Miners earn tokens by validating files. The term miner is similar to the old profession in the natural resource industry. In fintech the term miners refers to cryptominers or miners working with digital assets. When a company creates a token, it is quite technical as we discussed previously so they need to hire or employ specialists to get it done. The work includes writing the technical procedures and codes, designing digital contracts, etc. Miners verify all these processes and they also connect the firm with the cryptocurrency environment. The latter is important because investors can pay for tokens using cryptocurrencies like Bitcoin.[9]

Unlike conventional crowdfunding, tokens are usually tradable via online exchanges on the secondary market. This liquidity helps to attract investors. From traditional finance we know the difference between the primary market for securities and the secondary market. The primary market deals with new securities that are offered to the public for the first time. The secondary market is a market for "old" securities that have already been issued on the primary market. So the primary market is for firms to raise capital, i.e., for the issuers of securities. The primary market connects entrepreneurs/firms and investors while the secondary market is a market where transactions between investors take place. Similarly on the primary market for tokens, firms issue new tokens for the first

[8] https://tapzi.gitbook.io/whitepaper/welcome-to-tapzi.

[9] For more information about Bitcoin see, e.g., Velde (2013).

time and on the secondary market investors trade previously issued tokens with each other. This all implies that tokens have a market price, which in most cases marks a big difference with reward-based crowdfunding. As was mentioned previously, some crowdfunding platforms are working on developing secondary markets; for tokens secondary markets exist by definition all the time.

Investors who purchase tokens can decide what to do with these tokens. Unlike reward-based crowdfunding where the only option backers have is just to wait to receive their rewards. With tokens investors can decide whether they want to keep their tokens and for how long they want to keep them. Investors can choose to trade them on the secondary market on a cryptoexchange or they can choose to redeem them.

In terms of the history of utility tokens and their connection to similar ideas in practice one can note for example seatholders at Royal Albert Hall, a famous concert hall in London, UK. The seatholders own a large percentage of the available seats, which creates an opportunity to create a market for these seats where people can buy and sell them freely[10] A similar idea applies to tokens except that the market for seatholders does not have the same audience (say financial investor types) and is not connected to blockchain so they will likely mostly get local buyers/ consumers. Note the Bristol pound (£B) that was a local community currency launched in Bristol, UK on 19 September 2012. Its objective was to encourage people to spend their money at local, independent businesses in Bristol. Unlike traditional utility tokens this was more of a local currency[11] (at some point it had a digital currency format as well).[12]

The first ICO was conducted by Mastercoin (now known as Omnicoin) in 2013 (see, e.g., Tao et al. (2023)). Between 2013–2017, the number of projects grew very quickly, with over 820 billion raised by December 2018 (Coinschedule, 2018). These volumes are greater than the volume of reward-based crowdfunding. The main reason behind this is likely that tokens have secondary markets as they can attract investors larger than those who just want to buy products/services from a company. Tokens can also attract traditional (financial) investors, because there is

[10] www.royalalberthall.com.

[11] https://en.wikipedia.org/wiki/Bristol_pound.

[12] Digital currencies is a big growing area of interests around the world (see eg..). The major difference between tokens and digital currencies is that the former are issued by a business.

the potential to create a capital gain by trading tokens on the secondary market. One can also see a geographical diversity of countries actively involved in trading tokens for example countries like Estonia and Slovenia (see, e.g., Huang et al. (2020, Table 1)). By 2018 however, ICO markets were having a hard time[13] due to moral hazard problems as we discuss later and to imperfections in ICO regulations. In response to the latter some countries have tried to improve ICO regulations. Note for example the 2019 PACTE law in France[14] (Action Plan for Business Growth and Transformation) that includes laws related to crypto-assets regulation.

One of the latest ideas is cryptoairdrops. This is a promotional strategy used to distribute free tokens to potential users.[15] In general, airdrop is a method of distributing tokens or coins to numerous wallet addresses, typically for free. Airdrops can be used for example to reward loyal community members and to promote networks. They are often used by new projects as a marketing strategy to attract users. They can also serve as a compliment to traditional methods of token issues like ICOs to ensure a wider distribution among users. In terms of the theory of airdrops note Allen (2024) that suggests that coevolutionary theory can help us to understand the unique phenomenon of the airdrop design, where participants (projects and users) strategically adapt over time and across different blockchain ecosystems.

Similarly to crowdfunding, market imperfections play a crucial role in token issues. Going back to the Modigliani and Miller (1958) proposition that states that when markets are perfect entrepreneurs or finance managers do not care what type of financing the firm uses. But markets are imperfect. The same applies to tokens. What are the imperfections that affect token issues?! Many of them are similar to the ones related to crowdfunding that we discussed previously. For example, network community benefits. The idea is that investors communicate with each other during token issues. Further, there is a secondary market for tokens, which creates an additional layer of connectedness among investors. To confirm the network benefits of tokens Shakhnov and Zaccaria (2023)

[13] See, e.g., https://www.axios.com/2025/07/31/ico-initial-coin-offering-sec-atkins-trump-crypto.

[14] https://www.amf-france.org/en/news-publications/news/crypto-actifs-lamf-clarifie-sa-doctrine-applicable-aux-psan-autorises-dans-le-cadre-de-la-loi-pacte.

[15] See, e.g., https://www.osl.com/hk-en/academy/article/what-is-a-cryptocurrency-airdrop-and-how-does-it-differ-from-an-ico.

find that ICOs are more common among firms that benefit from network effects, in the sense that customers are attracted to the size of the existing network of a project.

Next, we have transaction costs. The analysis usually shows that in general token issues have a lower cost compared to traditional financing but a higher cost than crowdfunding. Regarding the latter it is related mainly to the overall cost to prepare an ICO versus a crowdfunding campaign and not so much on the specific platform fees.[16] In terms of the former note that in general there is a lower level of bureaucracy compared to public issues of traditional securities, which is consistent with the general the idea in fintech of lower transaction costs, i.e., the "No middleman" idea. Also, with ICOs, unlike STOs that are discussed in the next section, there are no costs related to the formalities of dealing with shareholders.

Next is demand uncertainty and respectively the idea of learning market demand using utility tokens. Since they give the right to use future firm products and services, the demand for tokens is connected to the demand for firm products and services like for example the demand for online storage space in the case of Filecoin. This is similar to the "crowd wisdom" idea related to reward-based crowdfunding (Chapter 3). Further, market uncertainty in fintech is related to some extent to the increasing market sizes and quickly growing amounts of market data. Tokens can help entrepreneurs learn market demand by observing the token price. As was mentioned previously, unlike reward-based crowdfunding, tokens have a secondary market. This helps to implement learning for a longer period of time while under crowdfunding learning is limited to the initial stage of firm development. For more information about learning market demand using tokens see Amsden and Schweizer (2018) and Catalini and Gans (2018). Theoretical papers on ICOs include, among others, Canidio (2018), Catalini and Gans (2018), Li and Mann (2018), Bakos and Halaburda (2022), Cong et al. (2020), Lee and Parlour (2022), Garratt and Van Oordt (2022), Chod and Lyandres (2021), Holden and Malani (2019) and Miglo (2021).

Moral hazard also plays an important role in ICOs. For example, there are a lot of cases of campaign failure including fraud (see, e.g.,

[16] $40,000–200,000 for an ICO see, e.g., https://vlinkinfo.com/blog/cost-of-launching-ico; €5000–25,000 for a crowdfunding campaign see, e.g., https://www.marketing-faktor.de/en/crowdfunding-costs/.

Liebau and Schueffel (2019); Hornuf et al. (2022)). Firm success in an ICO depends on the incentives and efforts of not only the firm itself but on the many participants involved including miners and platforms. In fact, the very nature of fintech platforms is based on the effort and trust existing between the platform participants (sometimes called the distributed ledger emphasizing that the efforts and costs are distributed among many participants). For more analysis on token issues that include moral hazard issues see, e.g., Chod and Lyandres (2021) Gan et al. (2021) and Miglo (2021).

Asymmetric information also plays an important role in ICOs. Among direct methods of mitigating asymmetric information note the previously mentioned whitepaper. In general, it is difficult to completely eliminate asymmetric information directly (the complex nature of ICOs surrounding advanced technology developments (more in Sect. 9.3) contributes to asymmetric information problems as well) so firms can use indirect methods by selecting specific token types or the size of issue, etc. (see, e.g., Momtaz (2021), Chod and Lyandres (2021), Miglo (2023), Sadeh and Ofir (2023)). Philippi et al. (2021) show that ICOs can raise funds more successfully by signalling their quality by releasing their source code to investors.

Among other factors that can be considered note the liquidity of token markets (see, e.g., Gupta et al. (2023)) and behavioural factors. Behavioural factors such as entrepreneurial or investor overconfidence and momentum chasing seem to be important given for example the ICO bubble of 2018, which resembles the dotcom bubble of 1999 Behavioural factors have been argued to be behind these phenomena (see, e.g., Stanley, 2019). Further, tokens represent an area where financing strategy is connected to some extent to monetary economics. This is analogous to the point in the development of financing theory where financing decisions were connected to production decisions (e.g., Brander and Lewis (1986)). The area of financing is currently making a new step. This is closely related to the fintech development in that a firm financing strategy becomes closely related to monetary economics. Tokens are in many ways similar to traditional fiat money since they can be used to buy firm products and services. Financial managers dealing with tokens need to understand concepts like token circulation, their exchange rate (i.e., their secondary market price), token velocity, etc. which requires the knowledge of ideas from monetary economics.[17] This is an up-and-coming area of interest.

Finally, note that the risk and return of investments in tokens is an interesting area for theorists and practitioners. Research can be difficult in the area as it is limited by the short period of time of token existence. Nevertheless, there are some interesting papers that have begun to make contributions here. Note for example Nowak et al. (2025). The authors conclude that tokens on average underperform traditional assets however there is group of tokens that can be recommended to include in a financial portfolio.

9.2 Equity and Debt-Based Crowdfunding Vs. Security Tokens

This section discusses security token offerings (STO). As was mentioned in previous sections ICO or utility token offerings have a lot in common with reward-based crowdfunding. STOs on the other hand are more related to equity-based crowdfunding and debt-based crowdfunding because investors expect a financial reward. Sometimes they are called tokenized securities, i.e., tokenized equity or debt. The registration procedure for security tokens is slightly more complicated than it is for utility tokens. For example, in the USA there exists the Howey test. It defines of "security" of any contract, transaction, or scheme where a person invests money or anything else of value into a firm and is led to expect payout from the efforts of others.[18] So as soon as something issued by the company passes this test it will be classified as a security. There are also some additional requirements in order to assure that the public interests are protected.

There are also other layers of regulation here. For example, AML (anti-money laundering regulations) and KYC (know-your-customer requirements). They are usually separate from securities regulations (for example in the USA they are governed by FinCen and also must comply with

[17] See, e.g., https://www.bis.org/cpmi/publ/d225.pdf.

[18] See, e.g., Devnani (2023).

the Bank Secrecy Act[19]; similar regulations exist in other countries). In general, KYC checks refer to due diligence activities companies must perform to get certain information from potential investors and ensure that the identities of new and existing token purchasers are verified to a reasonable level of certainty. AML checks are designed to prevent money laundering and to mitigate the risk that the company is being used to facilitate financial crime. So one can see that on one hand dealing with tokens (both on the firm side and the regulator side) requires a very high level of education and skills on all levels and on the other hand some basic ideas of fintech like the no-middle mean idea creates a new approach to risk control because in the past a large portion of it was done by financial intermediaries like banks.

So, what factors affect the use of security tokens? Similar to ICOs, STOs are characterized by environments with high uncertainty. A lot of campaigns fail or turn out to be low quality or even fraud in some cases. In addition, there are uncertainties in the market for tokens because the performance of these markets affects the potential returns of token-holders. Research usually finds that the market for tokens has a very high degree of volatility and uncertainty (see, e.g., Moncada et al. (2024)).

Next are moral hazard issues. Same as with utility tokens there are several layers of the problem here that include moral hazard problems faced by entrepreneurs, miners and platforms. An important difference between utility and equity tokens for example is that when the firm uses the latter they dilute the ownership rights of the firm's founders. This may have a negative effect on their incentive, but it also may increase the incentive of the new tokenholders.

Asymmetric information and signalling also play an important role in STOs (see, e.g., Kreppmeier and Laschinger (2023)). It will be discussed more in the next section.

Miglo (2021) considers a model where an entrepreneur with an innovative idea considers launching a web-based platform and chooses between having an ICO and an STO. The success of the platform also crucially depends on the effort provided by the entrepreneurs and the blockchain participants (miners) during the development stage. The paper

[19] https://www.pryorcashman.com/publications/fincen-head-suggests-all-icos-are-money-transmissions-subject-to-regulation.

https://investmentbank.com/insights/bsa-icos#:~:text=Returning%20to%20the%20letter%20previously,with%20BSA%20requirements%5B2%5D.

analyses the trade-off between learning market demand and moral hazard issues.[20]

9.3 Crowdfunding, Fintech and Information Complexities

This section analyses the role of information for token issues and fintech in general. The reasons why this topic is interesting and important are threefold. First, as was previously discussed imperfect information is an important issue for firms raising funds for their investment projects. An example is the pecking-order theory of capital structure (Myers and Majluf (1984)). This theory can be applied to the public issues of securities as well as to other forms of financing such as entrepreneurial finance including venture capital finance (see, for example, Cumming (2006) or Cosh et al. (2009)). Imperfect information is also very important for newly created ways of raising funds such as initial coin offerings (ICOs) (see, for example, Ofir and Sadeh (2019)). It would be interesting to understand the role of information for tokens and perhaps find new angles of information applications. Interestingly, some papers on token issues find differences between the empirical evidence surrounding traditional financing and token issues. An interesting question is for example the initial underpricing of tokens. A similar question exists with traditional public issues of equity. It is known that because of asymmetric information, among other reasons, IPOs (initial public offerings) are underpriced (see, e.g., Ritter and Ivo Welch (2002)). This is to say that firm owners leave money on the table when equity is used and there is a significant higher than average return for investors. A similar question exists regarding tokens especially regarding ICOs and STOs. Naturally many of the factors that affect the issues of traditional equities, like asymmetric information, affect the issues of tokens. For example, in the case of an ICO buyers of tokens enjoy on average higher rates of return after issues (Benedetti and Kostovetsky (2021))[21] than they do in IPOs (initial public offering). Another phenomenon is related to the long-term performance of tokens. In equity issues there is long-term underperformance of firms

[20] See also Gan et al. (2021), Adhami et al. (2018), Ante and Fiedler (2020) and Lambert et al. (2022)).

[21] See also Lyandres et al. (2020, 2022) that focuses on the connections between token returns and volatility.

issuing equity as compared to other types of financing (see, e.g., Jain and Kini (1994)). There seems to be no evidence of long-term underperformance of ICO firms as compared to firms that use other methods. More research is expected in these areas.

Second, information related to token issues seems to be relatively more complex than information in other types of security issues or even crowdfunding. As we discussed previously a typical page about a token issue has a lot of information which is on one hand very technical in nature but also requires a lot of knowledge in new areas of finance and fintech including cryptocurrencies and blockchain. The issue of ICO complexities is discussed for example in Belitski and Boreiko (2022) who mentioned that an ICO is a complex phenomena.[22] First, the ICO is a much more recent phenomenon than traditional equity financing so most investors are less familiar with it; second, an ICO requires that the .firm is connected to a Blockchain (which is often argued to be one of the most sophisticated business innovations of twenty-first century). Further, the industries / sectors that raise the most funds using ICOs are related to fintech/ hightech and are known for employing/developing the most progressive and innovative products and services (for example in Cape et al. (2018) the top 4 sectors are Blockchain Platform and Services, Finance, Trading and Investing, Data, AI and Machine Learning and Payments, Wallets and Cryptocurrencies). Third and finally, from a pure financial theory point of view, an ICO is not only a new way of financing but is also quite different from traditional ways of financing in some of its core features for example the right to use tokens for both creating capital gains and purchasing firm future products and services. Recent work by Schückes and Gutmann (2021) conduct surveys of entrepreneurs considering an ICO and in their opinion investors indeed lack an understanding of modern technologies related to ICOs: "..Simply because they [VC-venture capitalists] lack the understanding of how blockchain technology works. Even today, still, they do not understand it.."(Schückes and Gutmann (2021, p. 1047)). Furthermore, Samieifar and Baur (2021) measure the degree of ICO complexity and find that complexity does indeed matter for ICOs and affects their outcomes.

Third, information ambiguity and information complexities are in general growing areas of interest in other areas e.g., in economics see,

[22] See also https://www.iosco.org/library/ico-statements/Netherlands%20-%20AFM%20-%20Initial%20Coin%20Offerings%20Serious%20Risks.pdf.

e.g., Pich et al. (2002), Banerjee and Montúfar (2021) or Bao et al. (2024).[23]

Can the concept of information complexity be helpful in analysing an entrepreneur's choice of financing?! Miglo (2023) considers a model based on imperfect, asymmetric and complex information. Miglo (2023) suggests that the choice between ICO and equity financing depends on the trade-off between the degree of demand uncertainty, the extent of asymmetric information between the entrepreneur and investors and the message complexity. The paper suggests that unlike traditional equity financing ICOs can be used by high-quality firms as a signal of quality. Message complexity can be beneficial for firms conducting ICOs and can help to support a separating equilibrium.

9.4 The Role of Digital Platforms

This section discusses the role of digital platforms in developing the area of tokens. We will consider digital platforms dealing with tokens. We will also discuss a new type of tokens and the role of platforms in dealing with these. A platform that hosts an issue of tokens (also known as an ICO launchpad), usually offers various services to both project teams and investors, including project vetting, marketing services, investor access, etc. We will consider two questions. Table 9.1 shows some examples of platforms dealing with tokens.

Many platforms conduct due diligence on tokens, i.e., they review the campaign whitepapers and other reports including auditing reports and they can also analyse the firm's potential performance before hosting their token issue.

Table 9.1 Digital platforms dealing with tokens

Platform	*Website*
Binance launchpad	https://launchpad.binance.com/enexchange
CoinList	https://coinlaunch.space/launchpads/coinlist/
KuCoin launchpad	https://www.kucoin.com/

[23] See also https://www.mrg.com/wp-content/uploads/2018/09/Best-Practice-Report-Complexity-and-Ambiguity.pdf.

One of the relatively recent innovations that are based on the active involvement of a digital platform is the IEO (initial exchange offering). In a traditional ICO, the marketing effort is mostly the responsibility of the company. In an IEO, the company has an agreement with a major platform/exchange that gives it access to information on the traders who trade on this exchange. The issue can be done very quickly. When a company chooses between an ICO and an IEO, it needs to evaluate the benefits of this marketing advantage and liquidity advantage against the cost. Examples of IEO analysis include e.g., Myalo (2019), Miglo (2022b) and Magnusson and Renhage (2022).

Non-fungible tokens (NFTs) represent another interesting innovation in the area of tokens. The idea is that traditional tokens (utility tokens and security tokens) are fungible because similar tokens can be issued (perhaps diluting the rewards of the previously issued tokens). In contrast, NFTs cannot be split because each token represents a unique asset, often a digital asset. It can be an image or another piece of art, a piece of music, or a recording of a sporting event, etc. In terms of the differences between fungible and non-fungible tokens, note that because fungible tokens are all the same, they often have an active, liquid secondary market. NFTs, however, are unique. It is a very complex area that depends on many other complicated areas on their own, such as intellectual property rights and creative arts property rights. Often, investors do not get ownership rights to the original product but to the digital copy. In general, NFT platforms like OpenSea and Rarible connect artists with collectors worldwide, increasing the reach of their work and the potential value.[24] The first known NFT (Quantum) was created in May 2014.[25] Quantum is a piece of art that was created by digital artists Kevin McCoy and his wife, Jennifer.[26] After creating Quantum, McCoy wanted to sell the piece in its digital form. After its creation, Quantum was turned into an NFT by McCoy. For more information about non-fungible tokens, see, e.g., Ali et al. (2023), Houser and Holden (2022).

Hybrid tokens are another interesting token type. They can combine the features of utility and security tokens (other combinations are also

[24] https://rebusfarm.net/blog/from-pixels-to-profits-a-deep-dive-into-the-nfts-history.

[25] https://www.mccoyspace.com/project/125/.

[26] https://nftnow.com/art/quantum-the-first-piece-of-nft-art-ever-created/.

possible).[27] Miglo (2022b) considers a model where an innovative firm can consider financing its business by issuing either utility or security tokens. Utility tokens are more beneficial than security tokens in terms of given the entrepreneur information about future demand for firm products or services (similar to reward-based crowdfunding). On the other hand, security tokens do a better job of incentivizing miners during the development stage. When all factors are taken into consideration, issuing hybrid tokens (utility tokens with profit rights) is a better option for the firm. There exists a good level of competition among platforms that host issues of hybrid tokens. Entrepreneurs consider many factors when selecting a platform including the potential scalability of the project, fees, the platform experience, the platform's maturity and also if there exist specific support services for hybrid functions. In general, Ethereum, Binance Smart Chain and Polkadot are popular platforms for hosting hybrid tokens because of their extensibility and established developer communities.[28]

Finally, consider real estate tokens. They represent fractional ownership of a real estate object.[29] There are many interesting features in these tokens, e.g., the opportunity for small investors to participate in large, innovative real estate projects, including projects like smart cities, etc.[30] Interestingly, these types of tokens often have features of other types of tokens, including NFT, utility, security and hybrid tokens. The platforms dealing with real estate tokens often enable a very high level of market liquidity for real estate projects.[31] An example is RedSwan,[32] which places a high priority on liquidity, allowing investors to quickly enter or leave the platform.[33]

[27] See, e.g., https://digitalcurrencytraders.com/hybrid-token-development-insights-and-opportunities-for-2025-808b9fa2c32f.

[28] https://digitalcurrencytraders.com/hybrid-token-development-insights-and-opportunities-for-2025-808b9fa2c32f.

[29] See, e.g., https://www.solulab.com/real-estate-tokenization/.

[30] See, e.g., Waher et al. (2022).

[31] https://www.fciq.ca/blockchain-and-cryptocurrency/real-estate-tokenization-platforms-how-digital-shares-are-revolutionizing-property-investment/.

[32] https://redswan.io/.

[33] For more about digital platforms see, e.g., Brunnermeier and Payne (2022).

Questions and Exercises

1. Utility tokens resemble debt in that an interest rate is almost always paid to backers.

2. Utility tokens are sold during an ICO (initial coin offering)

3. The first ICO was conducted in 2013.

4. A common similarity among all ICOs is the issuance of new tokens in exchange for money or another cryptocurrency (such as Bitcoin).

5. People always buy tokens with cryptocurrencies.
6. The Howey Test determines whether certain transactions qualify as securities.

7. An IEO is a type of ICO where token sales are handled by a renowned cryptoexchange/platform.

8. One of the advantages of an ICO as compared to reward-based crowdfunding is that tokens have a secondary market.

9. Some tokens are hybrid; i.e., they may have similarities with utility tokens (e.g., offer the right to be exchanged for a firm's product/service) and with security tokens (e.g., can offer a financial reward).

10. Which token issue has more chances to succeed in your opinion?

Factor	*Token 1*	*Token 2*
Professional background	Yes	No
Softcap	$10,000,000	No
Whitepaper	Yes	No
Backup by VC	Yes	No
Media	Yes	Yes
Type of assets	Utility token	Utility token

11. Does an ICO/STO Require a Firm to Be Connected to the Blockchain?

References

Adhami, S., & Giudici, G. (2019). Initial coin offerings: Tokens as innovative financial assets. In *Blockchain economics and financial market innovation: Financial innovations in the digital age* (pp. 61–81). Springer International Publishing.

Adhami, S., Giudici, G., & Martinazzi, S. (2018). Why do businesses go crypto? An empirical analysis of initial coin offerings. *Journal of Economics and Business, 100*, 64–75.

Ali, O., Momin, M., Shrestha, A., Das, R., Alhajj, F., & Dwivedi, Y. K. (2023). A review of the key challenges of non-fungible tokens. *Technological Forecasting and Social Change, 187*, 122248.

Allen, D. W. E. (2024). Crypto airdrops: An evolutionary approach. *Journal of Evolutionary Economics, 34*, 849–872.

Amsden, R., Schweizer, D. (2018). Are blockchain crowdsales the new'gold rush'? Success determinants of initial coin offerings. *Success determinants of initial coin offerings (April 16, 2018).*

Ante, L., & Fiedler, I. (2020). Cheap signals in security token offerings (STOs). *Quantitative Finance and Economics, 4*(4), 608–639.

Bakos, Y., & Halaburda, H. (2022). Overcoming the coordination problem in new marketplaces via cryptographic tokens. *Information Systems Research, 33*(4), 1368–1385.

Banerjee, P. K., & Montúfar, G. (2021). Information complexity and generalization bounds. In *2021 IEEE international symposium on information theory (ISIT)* (pp. 676–681). Melbourne.

Bao, T., Duffy, J., & Zhu, J. (2024). Information ambiguity, market institutions, and asset prices: Experimental evidence. *Management Science, 71*(4), 3232–3252.

Belitski, M., & Boreiko, D. (2022). Success factors of initial coin offerings. *The Journal of Technology Transfer, 47*(6), 1690–1706.

Bellavitis, C., Fisch, C., & Wiklund, J. (2021). A comprehensive review of the global development of initial coin offerings (ICOs) and their regulation. *Journal of Business Venturing Insights, 15*, e00213.

Benedetti, H., & Kostovetsky, L. (2021). Digital tulips? Returns to investors in initial coin offerings. *Journal of Corporate Finance, 66*, 101786.

Brander, J. A., & Lewis, T. R. (1986). Oligopoly and financial structure: The limited liability effect. *The American Economic Review, 76*(5), 956–970.

Brunnermeier, M., & Payne, J. (2022). *Platforms, tokens, and interoperability, working papers 2022-8*. Princeton University. Economics Department.

Canidio, A. (2018). *Financial incentives for open source development: The case of blockchain*. MPRA Paper 85352,. University Library of Munich.

Cape, F., Pierluigi, M., & Ripamonti, F. (2018). An empirical study of the efficiency of initial coin offerings adopting a two-stage DEA model. https://www.politesi.polimi.it/retrieve/a81cb05d-4176-616b-e053-1605fe0a889a/2019_07_Cap%C3%A8_Ripamonti.pdf.

Catalini, C., & Gans, J. S. (2018). *Initial coin offerings and the value of crypto tokens* (Vol. No. w24418). National Bureau of Economic Research.

Chen, L., Cong, L. W., Xiao, Y. (2021). A brief introduction to blockchain economics. In *information for efficient decision making: Big data, blockchain and relevance* (pp. 1–40).

Chod, J., & Lyandres, E. (2021). A theory of ICOs: Diversification, agency, and information asymmetry. *Management Science, 67*(10), 5969–5989.

Cong, L. W., Li, Y., & Wang, N. (2020). *Token-based platform finance* (Vol. No. w27810). National Bureau of Economic Research.

Cosh, A., Cumming, D., & Hughes, A. (2009). Outside entrepreneurial capital. *The Economic Journal, 119*(540), 1494–1533.

Cumming, D. (2006). Adverse selection and capital structure: Evidence from venture capital. *Entrepreneurship Theory and Practice, 30*(2), 155–183.

Devnani, GD. (2023). *Creating a Path to Regulation—Digital Assets, Howey and the Regulatory Dilemma*, 27 N.C. Banking Inst. 399.

Gan, J., Tsoukalas, G., & Netessine, S. (2021). Initial coin offerings, speculation, and asset tokenization. *Management Science, 67*(2), 914–931.

Garratt, R. J., & Van Oordt, M. R. (2022). Entrepreneurial incentives and the role of initial coin offerings. *Journal of Economic Dynamics and Control, 142*, 104171.

Goncharov, S., & Nechesov, A. (2023). Axiomatization of blockchain theory. *Mathematics, 11*, 2966.

Gupta, R., Gupta, M., & Gupta, D. (2023). Role of liquidity Pool in stabilizing value of token. *Scientific Journal of Metaverse and Blockchain Technologies, 1*(1), 9–17.

Holden, R. T., & Malani, A. (2019). *Can blockchain solve the hold-up problem in contracts?* (Vol. No. w25833). National Bureau of Economic Research.

Hornuf, L., Kück, T., & Schwienbacher, A. (2022). Initial coin offerings, information disclosure, and fraud. *Small Business Economics, 58*, 1741–1759.

Houser, K. A., & Holden, J. T. (2022). Navigating the non-fungible token, 2022 Utah L. *Rev., 891.*

Howell, S. T., Niessner, M., & Yermack, D. (2020). Initial coin offerings: Financing growth with cryptocurrency token sales. *The Review of Financial Studies, 33*(9), 3925–3974.

Huang, W., Meoli, M., & Vismara, S. (2020). The geography of initial coin offerings. *Small Business Economics, 55*, 77–102.

Jain, B. A., & Kini, O. (1994). The post-issue operating performance of IPO firms. *The Journal of Finance, 49*(5), 1699–1726.

Kreppmeier, J., & Laschinger, R. (2023). Signaling in the market for security tokens. *Journal of Business Economics, 93*, 1515–1552.

Lambert, T., Liebau, D., & Roosenboom, P. (2022). Security token offerings. *Small Business Economics, 59*(1), 299–325.

Lee, J., & Parlour, C. A. (2022). Consumers as financiers: Consumer Sur plus, crowdfunding, and initial coin offerings. *The Review of Financial Studies, 35*(3), 1105–1140.

Li, J., & Mann, W. (2018). *Initial coin offering and platform building*. SSRN.

Liebau, D., & Schueffel, P. (2019). Cryptocurrencies & initial coin offerings: Are they scams—An empirical study. *The Journal of the British Block chain Association, 2*(1), 1–7.

Lyandres, E., Matveyev, E., & Zhdanov, A. (2020). Does the market correctly value investment options? *Review of Finance, 24*(6), 1159–1201.

Lyandres, E., Palazzo, B., & Rabetti, D. (2022). Initial coin offering (ICO) success and post-ICO performance. *Management Science, 68*(12), 8658–8679.

Magnusson, S., & Renhage, D. (2022). Initial exchange offerings (IEOs) and initial DEX offerings (IDOs) a new Hope for blockchain fundraising?. https://research-api.cbs.dk/ws/portalfiles/portal/92145916/1542446_Master_s_thesis_Magnusson_Renhage.pdf.

Miglo, A. (2021). STO vs. ICO: A theory of token issues under moral hazard and demand uncertainty. *Journal of Risk and Financial Management, 14*(6), 232.

Miglo, A. (2022a). Theories of crowdfunding and token issues: A review. *Journal of Risk and Financial Management, 15*(5), 218.

Miglo, A. (2022b). Choice between IEO and ICO: Speed vs. liquidity vs. risk. *FinTech, 1*, 276–293.

Miglo, A. (2023). ICO vs. equity financing under imperfect, complex and asymmetric information. *FinTech, 3*(1), 17–39.

Modigliani, F., & Miller, M. H. (1958). The cost of capital, corporation finance and the theory of investment. *The American Economic Review, 48*(3), 261–297.

Momtaz, P. P. (2021). Initial coin offerings, asymmetric information, and loyal CEOs. *Small Business Economics, 57*, 975–997.

Moncada, R., Ferro, E., Fiaschetti, M., & Medda, F. (2024). Blockchain tokens, Price volatility, and active User Base: An empirical analysis based on Tokenomics. *International Journal of Financial Studies., 12*, 107.

Myalo, A. S. (2019). Comparative analysis of ICO, DAOICO, IEO and STO. Case study. *Finance: Theory and Practice., 23*(6), 6–25.

Myers, S., & Majluf, N. (1984). Corporate financing and investment decisions when firms have information that investors do not have. *Journal of Financial Economics, 13*, 187–221.

Nowak, K. A., Wiśniewski, M., & Litwiński, M. (2025). Is it worth investing in tokens? Investment performance of digital tokens in financial and axiological contexts. *Journal of the Knowledge Economy, 16*, 663–690.

Ofir, M., & Sadeh, I. (2019). A revolution in progress: Regulating P2P lending platforms. *NYUJL & Bus., 16*, 683.

Philippi, S., Schuhmacher, M. C., & Bastian, N. (2021). Attracting Investors in Initial Coin Offerings: The relevance of specific technological capabilities for fundraising success. *Review of Corporate Finance., 1*(3–4), 455–485.

Pich, M. T., Loch, C. H., & Meyer, A. D. (2002). On uncertainty, ambiguity, and complexity in project management. *Management Science, 48*(8), 1008–1023.

Ritter, J. R., & Welch, I. (2002). A review of IPO activity, pricing, and allocations. *The Journal of Finance, 57*(4), 1795–1828.

Sadeh, I., & Ofir, M. (2023). *Asymmetric Information in Blockchain-Based Fundraising: From ICOs to INOs. Available at SSRN*, 4567304.

Samieifar, S., & Baur, D. G. (2021). Read me if you can! An analysis of ICO white papers. *Finance Research Letters, 38*, 101427.

Schückes, M., & Gutmann, T. (2021). Why do startups pursue initial coin offerings (ICOs)? The role of economic drivers and social identity on funding choice. *Small Business Economics, 57*(2), 1027–1052.

Shakhnov, K., & Zaccaria, L. (2023). Utility tokens, network effects, and pricing power. *Management Science, 69*(11), 6417–7150.

Stanley, M. (2019). The application of behavioural heuristics to initial coin offerings valuation and investment. *The Journal of The British Blockchain Association, 2*(1).

Tao, Z., Peng, B., & Ma, L. (2023). Optimal initial coin offering under speculative token trading. *European Journal of Operational Research, 306*(2), 632–644.

Velde, F. (2013). Bitcoin: A primer. https://www.cs.princeton.edu/courses/archive/fall14/cos109/bitcoin.primer.pdf.

Waher, P., Araoz, K., Moström, D., & Pablo Puglar, R. (2022). Tokenization of sustainable real estate in Smart Cities: Monetization as basis for construction, authorization and carbon neutralization. In *CPS, IECON 2022—48th Annual Conference of the IEEE Industrial Electronics Society* (pp. 1–6).

CHAPTER 10

Crowdfunding Examples Analysis

10.1 Crowdfunding of Creative Arts Area

This chapter focuses on the analysis of crowdfunding in two sectors: creative art and technology. Section 10.1 analyses crowdfunding campaigns of art firms. It will be mostly based on the review of existing research as well as practical examples in the area with a particular focus on comparing research findings and examples with theories discussed in the previous chapters. Section 10.2 will analyse crowdfunding by technology firms. It will contain a part of the authors' own empirical analysis.

Crowdfunding of the creative arts area includes crowdfunding campaigns related to theater, movies, images/paintings but also sectors that are more and more recognized as part of the art industry or closely related to it e.g., video games. The history of art crowdfunding is in fact very rich. For example, Garber (2013) suggests that early examples include the 1713 translation of Homer's Illiad into English and Mozart's attempt to fund the performance of his concertos in 1783. Research is continuing to find more examples in this area. Nowadays many media/art/creative industry firms/projects have been actively using

Supplementary Information The online version contains supplementary material available at https://doi.org/10.1007/978-3-032-10724-4_10.

© The Author(s), under exclusive license to Springer Nature Switzerland AG 2026

A. Miglo and V. Miglo, *The Theories and Developments of Crowdfunding*, https://doi.org/10.1007/978-3-032-10724-4_10

crowdfunding to raise funds for their projects incl. The “Veronica Mars” movie/TV show, Fresh Glass Season 2, Media News Network, KWSymphony Musicians, For Freedoms and We The People, etc. Further, creative arts industry projects are the largest sector of firms that use crowdfunding on Kickstarter, which is the largest platform in world. This section will discuss why art firms like Kickstarter, why they prefer reward-based crowdfunding and other questions.

De Voldere and Zeqo (2017) analyse arts related crowdfunding campaigns among European firms. They find that firms prefer Kickstarter and Indiegogo, which are the two largest platforms in the world. It suggests that these firms mostly use reward-based crowdfunding, which is what is used by both Kickstarter and Indiegogo. Further the authors suggest that crowdfunding is not only used for financing purposes but also for learning audience development, community engagement, skills development, promotion and market research. This is consistent with the learning market demand and network benefits ideas that were discussed previously. They also find that crowdfunding is also actively used by public firms in the cultural sector.

Cha (2017) analyses crowdfunding among video games developers. The research finds that an entrepreneur’s experience as well as the quality of materials, i.e., the quality and number of images on the campaign website positively affects the likelihood of success. This is consistent with the asymmetric information and signalling ideas of crowdfunding. Further, some geographical biases were found like for example campaigns from cities where video games developers are prevalent (e.g., San Francisco) have more chances to succeed.

Boeuf et al. (2014) consider theater crowdfunding and focus on the factors of campaign success. They find for example that mutual support of entrepreneurs can be beneficial, i.e., if an entrepreneur supports another entrepreneur, it increases the chances to be supported in return by that entrepreneur. This is consistent with the network benefits idea. They find that donation-based crowdfunding is popular in the theater industry. Further non-significant rewards such as e.g., mentioning the donors on the project webpage can play a role but mostly when there are no other “significant” rewards.

Rykkja et al. (2020) analyse crowdfunding of cultural projects using reward-based crowdfunding campaigns and focus on analysing the entrepreneur’s choice of platform. They find that cultural productions with a high degree of cultural affinity, i.e., projects that are more closely related to local cultural traditions are more likely to use a local platform, while cultural productions with a higher degree of complexity in production or with composite motives are more likely to use an international platform. These findings are consistent with the network benefits of crowdfunding, i.e., high complexity projects benefit from large platforms with a large number of participants, as well as with well-known behavioural biases like the home (cultural) bias because projects that are more connected to local culture are more likely to choose a local platform.

Keyhani et al. (2020) analyse the crowdfunding of theater projects in Canada. They find that these projects are relatively small reflecting probably a smaller market size for Canadian theaters in terms of popularity and audience. The effect of the local market size on crowdfunding project parameters and performance is consistent with behavioural/geographical biases.

Guimarães and Maehle (2025) focus on the analysis of crowdfunding cases in the cultural industry. They suggest that crowdfunding can play a role as an entry door to a new professional path in the sector. They also find that some project creators take into account the cost of crowdfunding campaigns in their decision-making. Overall, this is consistent with some elements of moral hazard related ideas when effort choice is part of the decision-making during crowdfunding campaigns. Dalla Chiesa and Dekker (2021) focus on the non-financial aspects of crowdfunding for artists. They suggest that many artists consider crowdfunding as a step towards building a reputation for their careers. They also suggest that the ability (or inability) to reach large networks plays an important role in choosing crowdfunding as a financing source. Overall, this is consistent with the spirit of moral hazard and network benefits.

Tosatto et al. (2022) focus on means of communication and their influence on the success of crowdfunding campaigns in the cultural and creative industries. They suggest that a hierarchy exists of different communication methods with the e-mail method dominating others. In general, the topic of communication analysis is in line with the spirit of asymmetric information problems in crowdfunding and direct signalling with messages, etc.

Tosatto et al. (2019) argue that artistic freedom is an advantage of crowdfunding because under traditional financing strategies the firm's final product is usually known to investors, while crowdfunding offers creators the freedom to wait for input from the audience before deciding what they will produce, allowing for more creative freedom. They also mention legal freedoms where traditional financing options can involve legal obligations regarding intellectual property rights and restrictive contractual provisions, while crowdfunding projects are often less constrained by ongoing legal obligations.

In general, the learning market demand idea and its variations seem to be dominant in crowdfunding. Some of the advantages of crowdfunding as mentioned for example in Tosatto et al. (2019) are related to learning crowd wisdom, learning market demand, related marketing opportunities and audience proximity. The latter means that by involving the audience in a project's formative stage, crowdfunding allows creators to both adjust their final product to the tastes of their audience, as indicated in their feedback, and also to generate a sense of audience involvement in (and ownership of) the production process and the resulting final product.

So far, we have mainly discussed the usage of reward-based and donation-based crowdfunding. Galuszka and Bystrov (2014) focus on equity-based crowdfunding campaigns in the music industry by analysing the MegaTotal platform as an example. They suggest that equity participation encourages backers to contribute to a campaign's success by extending the artist's network. In general, this is consistent with the network benefits idea of crowdfunding as well as moral hazard issues.

Overall, creative art related industries are some of the most suitable for crowdfunding. Kickstarter statistics show that Films and videos is the #1 category, Music is #5[1] and their success rates are consistently among the highest on the platform.[2] Most theories and ideas of crowdfunding find confirmation in the crowdfunding of art including learning demand, marketing, network benefits, asymmetric information, moral hazard issues and behavioural biases. Artist and other creators want to learn the crowd wisdom about their ideas, their performances and their creations. This contributes enormously to the development of the creators. The risk of extreme fraud also seems to be mitigated to some extent (at least compared to other industries) because there is too much on the line for project creators, i.e., entire reputations and careers as actors and creators. For example, as follows from e.g., Cumming et al. (2023), the likelihood of fraud is positively correlated with the size of the campaign and art

[1] https://www.kickstarter.com/help/stats retrieved August 21st, 2025.

[2] See, e.g., https://ucladatares.medium.com/uncovering-what-traits-make-a-kickstarter-campaign-successful-dd4b62df9eb4.

campaigns are typically relatively smaller than other industries and negatively correlated with a campaign being done by a creator, which is usually the case in art projects.

10.2 Crowdfunding of Technology Firms

This section analyses crowdfunding campaigns of technology firms. We will start by discussing some papers analysing crowdfunding campaigns of technology firms and then we will discuss our own analysis of crowdfunding campaigns of technology firms in England. In general, the factors of success and motivations for crowdfunding are pretty similar to those of other industries. Many of the factors we discussed that work for art firms also work for technology firms. Note the following papers.

Yu and Fleming (2022) analyse the regional aspects of crowdfunding campaigns of high-tech firms. They find that a greater frequency of crowdfunding is observed in highly educated and urban regions, while the impact of crowdfunding campaigns is greater in poor regions. This is consistent with the network benefits idea of crowdfunding as well as behavioural/geographical biases.

Westerlund et al. (2021) find that successful technology-related crowdfunding campaigns put forward trendy topics, use wording that reflects novelty and focus on solving social problems. This is consistent with the spirit of asymmetric information and signalling theories of crowdfunding because it demonstrates that the quality of signalling (direct signalling in this case) plays an important role in crowdfunding.

Loewen et al. (2024) analyse crowdfunding campaigns of climate tech businesses. They suggest that equity-based crowdfunding is popular among these firms. In general, the tech sector and in particular climate tech, offers projects that are more technically challenging to understand as concepts and are more complicated in terms of providing their products and services as direct rewards to small investors. An example is POD point, a firm that that develops charging stations for electric vehicles. According to their managers they are very interested in long-term supporters who really like and understand their ideas, which is why their choice was equity-based crowdfunding.[3]

[3] https://www.crowdcube.com/companies/pod-point-1.
https://evobsession.com/pod-point-raised-267,750-via-recent-crowdfunding-campaign/.

Next, we focus on the analysis of crowdfunding campaigns among technology firms in England. We analyse what features of a city make it more or less efficient with regard to crowdfunding development. Previous research found that there is a local bias in crowdfunding which is consistent with the idea that large cities should have an advantage over smaller cities (see, e.g., Agrawal et al. (2015), Hornuf et al. (2022)). Mollick (2014) finds that the project mix of founders echoes the cultural products of the cities in which they are based (see also Mollick and Robb (2016)). We focus on other features including the economic development of a city, age structure, demographics and modes of commuting. For example, there exists some evidence that the number of bike commuters is generally growing even through tough economic periods.[4] Further, commuting by bike is related to better mental health.[5] Bike commuting may have a positive effect on the green aspects of communities (see, e.g., Testa et al. (2019)). Further, bike commuters are generally technically savvy, creative and energetic which is also associated with potential crowdfunding success. We also look at the population structure. Intuitively a larger fraction of young people should be positively associated with crowdfunding development as they would have more interest in internet-related innovations and should also positively affect the networking/exchanging ideas and theories of crowdfunding (see, e.g., Gerber and Hui (2013); see also Nayer et al. (2024) and Kumar et al. (2020)). The probability of crowdfunding success, however, may be negatively affected by a high fraction of young entrepreneurs as they have less practical experience, etc. We also look at such factors as the knowledge about business services, the level of education in the city, the employment level, the number of patent applications, the number of start-ups and the availability of bank loans. We focus on cities in the UK.[6] The UK is a country with a very

[4] See, e.g., https://cyclingindustry.news/commuting-bike-cycling-levels-uk/#:~:text=Fresh%20Sports%20Marketing%20Surveys%20data,work%20has%20held%20up%20strongly.

[5] https://www.ed.ac.uk/news/2024/cycling-to-work-linked-with-better-mental-health.

[6] Among other research on crowdfunding geography note Lin and Viswanathan (2016) that find the existence of a home bias in crowdfunding, i.e., funders prefer to invest in local projects; Kim and Hann (2019) that find that projects that were closer to banks attracted less funding from local investors; Josefy et al. (2017) find location effects also take shape through local altruism or by promoting projects that share similar values with local communities; Giudici et al. (2018).

high level of crowdfunding and other fintech developments (see, e.g., Dushnitsky et al. (2016)).[7]

We analyse 2388 campaigns by technology firms from the UK on Kickstarter between 2011–2020. We collect information about the number of backers, the target, the threshold and the percentage of funds raised. We compare the features used in crowdfunding campaigns across the major cities in the UK. We analyse the effect of such factors as city population, age, GDP per capita and education on the number of campaigns originated in the city and the probability of campaign success.[8]

We focus on the following hypothesis.

H1 The number of crowdfunding campaigns is positively correlated with ultrafast broadband access.

H2 The number of crowdfunding campaigns is positively correlated with the number of people with higher education.

H3 The number of crowdfunding campaigns is positively correlated with the number of entrepreneurial firms per capita.

H4 The number of crowdfunding campaigns is positively correlated with the number of patent applications per capita.

H5 The number of crowdfunding campaigns is positively correlated with GDP per capita.

H6 The number of crowdfunding campaigns is positively correlated with the fraction of commuters by bicycle.

We use data from Kickstarter, which is the most popular crowdfunding platform in the world. Over 18 million people from all the world belong to the Kickstart community. Kickstarter was launched in 2009 and has facilitated the successful funding of 255,292 projects.[9] There are also 22,932,900 people that have backed a Kickstarter project and 7,908,597 repeat backers. Kickstarter works on an "all or nothing" (AON) basis

[7] For other research on crowdfunding in the UK see, e.g., Langley (2016) that discusses cultural aspects of crowdfunding development in the UK.

[8] This data is collected from https://www.centreforcities.org/. https://www.ons.gov.uk/peoplepopulationandcommunity/housing/datasets/townsandcitiesanalysis/current.

[9] See, e.g., https://www.kickstarter.com/help/stats (retrieved 16/03/2024).

where collected funds are returned to investors and the project does not proceed when the amount of collected funds does not reach the established target. In this way the crowdfunding platform ensures the security of the supporters.

For our analysis we will be using an OLS regression. From the results of the regression analysis, it is possible to see the positive and negative correlation coefficient of the analysed factors and it shows relationships between dependent and independent variables. This allows us to either accept or reject the hypotheses. For example, to test H1, the formula for the regression is:

$$NC = \alpha + \beta * UB + c_1 * Pop + c_2 * GDP/capita + c_3 * ACT + c_4 * Edu + \varepsilon$$

where the dependent variable is the number of campaigns (NC) in a city. The independent variable is the number of households with ultrafast broadband internet at home (UB) and control variables include provincial population (Population), GDP per capita, average campaign target (ACT) in the city and the fraction of population with higher education (Edu), and ε is the estimation error. We normalize data using an approach similar to Beck et al. (2008). We also conduct multiple regression and robustness by using different variables.

Tables 10.1 and 10.2 provide descriptive statistics of our sample of projects and cities. Table 10.1 shows the number of campaigns, their average ($32,266) and median ($10,000) goals, the number of successful campaigns, the percentage of raised money, etc. As it can be seen, only 29.3% of campaigns were successful, which confirms that crowdfunding is a challenging way of raising funds.

Table 10.2 describes the cities used in the analysis.

Table 10.3 shows the numbers for some major cities. Table 10.3 presents the statistics of the crowdfunding data for England by major cities.

Table 10.1 Descriptive statistics of campaigns

Total number of campaigns	2388
Number of cities of origin	51
Average goal	$32,266
Median goal	$10,000
Average number of backers	178.74
Median number of backers	13
Average funds pledged	16,787.222
Median funds pledged	650.5
Average percent funded	122.626%
Median percent funded	7.58
Average pledged amount per backer	$84.50
Median pledged	$36.68
Max pledged amount	$3068.88

Table 10.2 Descriptive statistics for cities

Total number of cities	51
Number of cities with a positive number of campaigns	38
Average number of campaigns per city	31.84
Average GDP per capita (£)	33,377
Average Business Start-ups 2019 (per 10,000 population)	53,98
Average Commuting by Bicycle 2011 (%)	3,99
Average Commuting by Private Car 2011 (%)	62.48
Average Commuting by Foot 2011 (%)	11.60
Average Employment Rate 2018 (%)	74.70
Average Patent Applications 2018 (per 100,000 of population)	16.61
Average Population	624,311
Average Population Aged 18-29 2019 (%)	17.88
Average Population Aged 45-66 2019 (%)	26.12
Private Knowledge Intensive Business Services 2019 (%)	13.02
Ultrafast Broadband 2019 (%)	80.23
Working Age Population with a Qualification at NVQ4 or Above 2019 (%)	38.14
Working Age Population with No Formal Qualifications 2019 (%)	8.16

Sources https://www.kickstarter.com/discover/advanced?category_id=16&woe_id=23424975&sort=magic&seed=2693861&page={0}
https://www.centreforcities.org/
https://www.ons.gov.uk/peoplepopulationandcommunity/housing/datasets/townsandcitiesanalysis/current

Table 10.3 Some numbers for the major cities in the UK

City	*Number of campaigns*	*Population*	*Commuters by bike (%)*	*Population Aged 18–29 2019, % total*	*GDP per capita*	*Business Start-ups 2019 (per 10,000 population)*	*Ultrafast Broadband 2018 (%)*	*Working Age Population with a Qualification at NVQ4 or Above 2019 (%)*	*Patent Applications 2018 (per 100,000 of population)*
London	1035.00	10,151,260.00	3.62	16.43	53,126.00	107.33	81.46	53.30	13.64
Manchester	72.00	2,486,481.00	2.13	17.33	29,358.00	65.37	70.98	38.00	6.01
Birmingham	58.00	2,549,673.00	1.53	17.28	26,278.00	56.82	87.49	30.20	5.46
Nottingham	34.01	677,617.00	3.27	21.50	26,711.00	40.20	89.67	36.30	9.89
Bristol	49.00	746,049.00	6.07	21.12	38,603.00	55.91	87.25	46.70	20.06
Oxford	41.00	154,327.00	17.06	32.04	41,470.00	42.30	87.87	57.90	64.51
Cambridge	52.00	125,758.00	29.03	30.42	51,686.00	54.88	93.61	69.60	148.12
Leeds	31.00	789,194.00	1.75	21.40	36,492.00	52.63	78.48	40.10	6.46
Southampton	28.00	386,100.00	3.80	21.55	34,320.03	78.61	82.47	39.40	10.35
Liverpool	26.00	648,900.00	1.90	21.35	29,640.66	58.87	83.76	36.30	5.37
Coventry	14.00	371,520.00	2.61	24.70	28,354.8	43.60	82.64	36.40	95.53
Sheffield	23.00	850,260.00	1.46	19.83	23,489.77	41.16	53.32	41.30	5.96

The multiple regression results are reported in Table 10.4. Hypothesis H6 has the strongest confirmation, while H1–H5 are partly confirmed. The results show that the number of campaigns in a city is positively associated with GDP per capita, the city population, access to ultrafast internet, the number of patent applications and the fraction of people with a high level of working qualification. The number of commuters by bicycle has the strongest positive effect. As was previously mentioned, commuting by bike is related to better mental health, creativity and technical development, and may have positive effects for communities related to cleantech/green economy aspects, which may have positive impacts on crowdfunding. In general, the regression results are very strong. Ideally, raising funds via the internet should remove geographical barriers for firms (Agrawal et al., 2015); however, the analysis suggests that city characteristics are important for crowdfunding characteristics and success. This may be a result of cost and efficiency arguments. From a firm's point of view, the education level of a city provides an indication of the potential quality of products or services offered and can also be associated with the economies of scale for their business development. Further, the size of the population can reflect the potential quality of discussions ("between friends/communities") associated with campaigns, which may affect the amount of feedback and benefits funders can receive during crowdfunding (consistent with the learning idea—see, e.g., Chemla and Tinn (2019); see also Dushnitsky et al. (2016)).

These findings help entrepreneurs prepare their crowdfunding campaigns and also contribute to the growing literature that connects entrepreneurial problems in crowdfunding with public policy and development questions.

Table 10.4 Regression results when the dependent variable is the number of campaigns in a city

Variables	*(1)*	*(2)*	*(3)*
Intercept	−0.000082 [0.000274887401096106]	−0.00013363 [0.0001553]	−0.00010116 [0.00002729]***
Business Start-ups 2019 (per 10,000 population)	4.031233E−08 [0.00000036]		
Commuting by Bicycle 2011 (%)	6.777506E−06 [1.7130124E−06]***	6.6853748E−06 [1.5666817E−06]***	8.8329947E−06 [1.15513310E−06]***
Commuting by Private Vehicle 2011 (%)	−1.0236121E−06 [1.041743E−06]	−1.1229385E−06 [6.929991E−07]	
Commuting on Foot 2011 (%)	−5.5429897E−06 [2.340782E−06]*	−5.5991679E−06 [1.7725567E−06]**	−3.5522628E−06 [0.00000153]*
Employment Rate 2018 (%)	1.168226E−06 [1.479613E−06]	1.0463528E−06 [1. E−06]	
GDP per capita	9.368271E−10 [7.789199E−10]	9.9135726E−10 [7.18461628E−10]	
Patent Applications 2018 (per 100,000 of population)	4.870374E−07 [2.428118E−07]	5.01224028E−07 [2.1764235E−07]*	4.3288948E−07 [2.06749517E−07]*
People Born Outside the UK 2011 (%)	−1.388693E−07 [1.227918E−06]		
Population 2019	6.287361E−13 [4.042017E−12]		
Population Aged 18–29 2019 (%)	2.396772E−06 [3.145016E−06]	3.3783339E−06 [1.6382874E−06]*	2.75215509E−06 [1.2734324E−06]*
Population Aged 45–66 2019 (%)	−2.794153E−06 [6.231436E−06]		
Population Aged 67+ 2019 (%)	0.0000031 [3.2305480E−06]	2.0092932E−06 [2.17846301E−06]	
Private Knowledge Intensive Business Services 2019 (%)	−2.5978225E−06 [1.5390098E−06]	−2.3555959E−06 [1.33940638E−06]	

Variables	*(1)*	*(2)*	*(3)*
Ultrafast Broadband 2019 (%)	2.254724136E−07 [2.904338409E−07]	2.250689E−07 [2.723117E−07]	
Working Age Population with a Qualification at NVQ4 or Above 2019 (%)	1.7035288E−06 [9.92948164E−07]	1.4484328E−06 [7.9211636E−07]	1.7383485E−06 [4.97286501E−07]**
Working Age Population with No Formal Qualifications 2019 (%)	0.000003703 [0.000002348]	3.518344539E−06 [2.11560937E−06]	2.849823327E−06 [1.5068006E−06]
Adj. R^2	0.86850568201202	0.88107167414552	0.881217752545038
F-value	21.6402854345058	31.868440711915	62.8230537689823

***Indicates significance at the 1% level, **Indicates significance at the 5% level and *Indicates significance at the 10% level

Questions and Exercises

1. Reward-based and donation-based crowdfunding are the most popular types of crowdfunding among art-related projects.

2. Learning market demand, asymmetric information and signalling, network benefits, behavioural biases and moral hazard ideas usually find confirmation with art-related crowdfunding campaigns.

3. Equity-based crowdfunding is very popular among technology firms.

4. Reward-based crowdfunding is used by technology firms but in some cases long-term connections with backers are the key factor and firm may prefer equity-based crowdfunding instead.

References

Agrawal, A., Catalini, C., & Goldfarb, A. (2015). Crowdfunding: Geography, social networks, and the timing of investment decisions. *Journal of Economics & Management Strategy, 24*(2), 253–274.

Beck, T., Demirgüç-Kunt, A., & Maksimovic, V. (2008). Financing patterns around the world: Are small firms different?. *Journal of financial economics, 89*(3), 467–487.

Boeuf, B., Darveau, J., & Legoux, R. (2014). Financing creativity: Crowdfunding as a new approach for theatre projects. *International Journal of Arts Management, 16*(3), 33–48.

Cha, J. (2017). Crowdfunding for Video Games: Factors that influence the success of and capital pledged for campaigns. *International Journal on Media Management, 19*(3), 240–259.

Chemla, G., & Tinn, K. (2019). Learning through crowdfunding. *Management Science, 66*(5), 1783–1801.

Chiesa, C. D., & Dekker, E. (2021). Crowdfunding artists: beyond matchmaking on platforms. *Socio-Economic Review, 19*(4), 1265–1290.

Cumming, D., Hornuf, L., Karami, M., & Schweizer, D. (2023). Disentangling Crowdfunding from Fraudfunding. *Journal of Business Ethics, 182*(4), 1103–1128.

De Voldere, I., & Zeqo, K. (2017). *Crowdfunding: Reshaping the crowd's engagement in culture*. European Commission.

Dushnitsky, G., Guerini, M., Piva, E., & Rossi-Lamastra, C. (2016). Crowdfunding in Europe: Determinants of platform creation across countries. *California Management Review, 58*(2), 44–71.

Galuszka, P., & Bystrov, V. (2014). Crowdfunding: A case study of a new model of financing music production. *Journal of Internet Commerce, 13*(3-4), 233–252.

Garber, M. (2013). Kickstarters of Yore: Mozart, Lady Liberty, Alexander Pope. The Atlantic (June 29).

Gerber, E. M., & Hui, J. (2013). Crowdfunding: Motivations and deterrents for participation. *ACM Transactions on Computer-Human Interaction (TOCHI), 20*(6), 1–32.

Giudici, G., Guerini, M., & Rossi-Lamastra, C. (2018). Reward-based crowdfunding of entrepreneurial projects: The effect of local altruism and localized social capital on proponents' success. *Small Business Economics, 50*(2), 307–324.

Guimarães, A. D., & Maehle, N. (2025). More than raising money: The role of crowdfunding in the development of cultural projects. *Journal of Cultural Economy, 18*(4), 564–589.

Hornuf, L., Schmitt, M., & Stenzhorn, E. (2022). The local bias in equity crowdfunding: Behavioral anomaly or rational preference? *Journal of Economics & Management Strategy, 31*(3), 693–733.

Josefy, M., Dean, T. J., Albert, L. S., & Fitza, M. A. (2017). The role of community in crowdfunding success: Evidence on cultural attributes in funding campaigns to "save the local theater". *Entrepreneurship Theory and Practice, 41*(2), 161–182.

Keyhani, M., Neyshabouri, S. M., & Amereii, A. H. (2020). Crowdfunding Canadian theatre: An exploratory analysis of kickstarter data with US comparison. *Artivate: A Journal of Entrepreneurship in the Arts, 9*(1), 99–130.

Kim, K., & Hann, I. H. (2019). Crowdfunding and the democratization of access to capital—An illusion? Evidence from housing prices. *Information Systems Research, 30*(1), 276–290.

Kumar, S., Paray, Z. A., Sharma, N., & Dwivedi, A. K. (2020). Influence of entrepreneurship education and university ecosystem on individual's entrepreneurship readiness. In *Entrepreneurship and regional development: Analyzing growth models in emerging markets* (pp. 305–322). Springer.

Langley, P. (2016). Crowdfunding in the United Kingdom: A cultural economy. *Economic Geography, 92*(3), 301–321.

Lin, M., & Viswanathan, S. (2016). Home bias in online investments: An empirical study of an online crowdfunding market. *Management Science, 62*(5), 1393–1414.

Loewen, E., Li, W., Webster, C., & Lucena, P. C. (2024). *Crowdfunding for climate tech startups: A global analysis and the opportunity ahead. RMI.*. https://rmi.org/insight/crowdfundingfor-climate-tech-startups/

Mollick, E. (2014). The dynamics of crowdfunding: An exploratory study. *Journal of Business Venturing, 29*(1), 1–16.

Mollick, E., & Robb, A. (2016). Democratizing innovation and capital access: The role of crowdfunding. *California Management Review, 58*(2), 72–87.

Nayer, D., Rosenboim, M., & Malul, M. (2024). The two sides of crowdfunding success: Attributes and motivations of backers and entrepreneurs—Evidence from Israel. *The Journal of Entrepreneurship, 33*(1), 155–182.

Rykkja, A., Munim, Z. H., & Bonet, L. (2020). Varieties of cultural crowdfunding: The relationship between cultural production types and platform. *Baltic Journal of Management, 15*(2).

Testa, S., Nielsen, K. R., Bogers, M., & Cincotti, S. (2019). The role of crowdfunding in moving towards a sustainable society. *Technological Forecasting and Social Change, 141*, 66–73.

Tosatto, J., Cox, J., & Nguyen, T. (2019). An overview of crowdfunding in the creative and cultural industries. In H. Landström, A. Parhankangs, & C. Mason (Eds.), *Handbook of research on crowdfunding, research handbooks in business and management series*. Edgar Elgar Publishing.

Tosatto, J., Cox, J., & Nguyen, T. (2022). With a little help from my friends: The role of online creator-fan communication channels in the success of creative crowdfunding campaigns. *Computers in Human Behavior, 127*(107), 005.

Westerlund, M., Singh, I., Rajahonka, M., & Leminen, S. (2021). Technology project summaries as a predictor of crowdfunding success. *Technology Innovation Management Review, 11*(11-12), 33–44.

Yu, S., & Fleming, L. (2022). Regional crowdfunding and high tech entrepreneurship. *Research Policy, 51*(9), 104348.

Ending Thoughts

The first part of this book was focused on providing a general description of the terminology of crowdfunding and an overall introduction to crowdfunding and the different types of crowdfunding. It also covered the major ideas and theories of crowdfunding including learning market demand, asymmetric information and signalling, moral hazard including the cash-in-and-run problem, network benefits and behavioural biases. According to most empirical research, none of these theories are able to fully explain the real-life decisions made by entrepreneurs. Further, a significant gap exists between the theoretical and empirical papers on crowdfunding so not many theories have ultimate empirical confirmation. However, in most research related to crowdfunding, these basic ideas are used either as reference points or intermediate tools that help develop further ideas.

The second part discussed the different topics of crowdfunding. As was mentioned earlier, the objective of the book was not to cover as many topics of crowdfunding as possible but rather to review the major theoretical concepts and provide basic tools to understand the complicated area of crowdfunding and closely related areas, e.g., token issues. Many advanced theories of crowdfunding discussed in this book are still growing areas of research. We think that some areas are very promising including the choice between crowdfunding and other types of financing, the links between crowdfunding and corporate/national culture, dynamic versions of learning demand and asymmetric information-based theories including

© The Editor(s) (if applicable) and The Author(s), under exclusive license to Springer Nature Switzerland AG 2026

A. Miglo and V. Miglo, *The Theories and Developments of Crowdfunding*, https://doi.org/10.1007/978-3-032-10724-4

the new pecking order that includes traditional sources and reward-based crowdfunding, the connections between crowdfunding and bankruptcy including failure to deliver rewards, crowdfunding of large companies, the accounting of crowdfunding in particular the accounting of reward-based crowdfunding, the regulation of crowdfunding and the connections between crowdfunding and other areas of fintech including token issues.

Educators should spend more time teaching crowdfunding and fintech given that the topic has seen tremendous growth in recent years. Further we are personally big fans of further integration of universities and the financial sector. Practitioners should be given the opportunity to teach more courses and professors should allocate more time to practical work. Nobel Prize winner Josef Stiglitz (he is primarily known in our opinion for his expertise in the capital structure area including such topics as credit rationing and asymmetric information and capital structure is very closely related to crowdfunding) is a good example. Theories have become more and more complicated so if the gap between the theory and practice is not being constantly reduced, severe consequences will follow. The challenges of this approach are to find practitioners who have deep theoretical knowledge or to find professors who are able to work in managerial positions. Both combinations are pretty rare from our experience. Where we stand now, it is hard to imagine that in the near future a large volume of (constantly growing exponentially) complicated mathematical research will be able to seriously penetrate into the practical sector with satisfactory speed and intensity.

Our book is intended primarily to those who feel very excited about crowdfunding and more generally about entrepreneurial finance and start-up financing both theoretically and practically. We tried to make most of our points in a theoretically rigorous fashion and bridge the deep theoretical concepts with practical examples and cases. If you our dear reader feel this way, we will be very satisfied. And good luck with your exciting journey into the world of crowdfunding!

Index

© The Editor(s) (if applicable) and The Author(s), under exclusive license to Springer Nature Switzerland AG 2026
A. Miglo and V. Miglo, *The Theories and Developments of Crowdfunding*, https://doi.org/10.1007/978-3-032-10724-4

The manufacturer's authorised representative in the EU is Springer Nature Customer Service Centre GmbH, Europaplatz 3, 69115 Heidelberg, Germany. If you have any concerns regarding our products, please contact ProductSafety@springernature.com

Printed and bound by CPI Group (UK) Ltd, Croydon, CR0 4YY

21/09/2026

02219945-0006